The Age of Noise in Britain

The Age of Noise
in Britain

Hearing Modernity

JAMES G. MANSELL

University of Illinois Press

URBANA, CHICAGO, AND SPRINGFIELD

Printed and bound in Great Britain by
Marston Book Services Ltd, Oxfordshire

Library of Congress Cataloging-in-Publication Data
Names: Mansell, James G., author.
Title: The age of noise in Britain: hearing modernity /
James G. Mansell.
Description: Urbana : University of Illinois Press,
2016. | Series: Studies in sensory history | Includes
bibliographical references and index.
Identifiers: LCCN 2016023965 (print) | LCCN 2016047972
(ebook) | ISBN 9780252040672 (cloth : alk. paper) | ISBN
9780252082184 (pbk. : alk. paper) | ISBN 9780252099113
(ebook)
Subjects: LCSH: Noise—Great Britain—Social aspects—
History. | Industrial noise—Great Britain—History. |
City noise—Great Britain—History. | Noise control—
Great Britain—History. | Noise—Health aspects—
Great Britain—History. | Great Britain—Civilization.
Classification: LCC TD893.5.G7 M26 2016 (print) | LCC
TD893.5.G7 (ebook) | DDC 363.740941—dc23
LC record available at https://lccn.loc.gov/2016023965

Contents

Acknowledgments

I wish to thank my doctoral supervisors, particularly Bertrand Taithe, for their guidance and support, as well as those who broadened my outlook as a postdoctoral researcher, especially Maiken Umbach, whose mentorship was invaluable, and Scott Anthony, with whom I had great fun collaborating on the history of the GPO Film Unit. I am grateful to the University of Nottingham for affording me the time to write the book and to my colleagues in the Department of Culture, Film, and Media for their encouragement and friendship, especially Tracey Potts. My students on the module "Hearing Cultures" are also a constant source of inspiration. I might not have had the confidence to include Chapter 2 had it not been for the time I spent as part of the "Enchanted Modernities: Theosophy, Modernism, and the Arts" Leverhulme research network, and I'm thankful to all its members—Helena Čapková, Rachel Cowgill, Marco Pasi, Christopher Scheer, Sarah Victoria Turner, and Gauri Viswanathan—for the hugely enriching time we spent together talking about the importance of the modern occult. I'm also glad to have worked with Tim Boon and Aleks Kolkowski on a "Music, Noise and Silence" workshop series connected to the book's research, during which I benefited from conversations with some of the best sound studies thinkers around. I'm grateful to Mark M. Smith for his patience and encouragement in getting the book project off the ground and in bringing it to fruition, and to the staff at the University of Illinois Press for their kind assistance at every step. Thanks, also, to the many archivists and librarians who helped me access collections and approved materials for publication: quotation from the Mass-Observation Archive is by permission of Curtis Brown, London, on behalf of the Trustees of the Mass-Observation Archive. I couldn't have done any of it without the support of my friends and family. Writing this book has absorbed my energy for a long time, and I'm so grateful that when I've come up for air there have still been people around to talk to. The book is dedicated to my parents—Julia and Gilbert—whose quiet support was what I needed, and to Lucie, who has lived through every detail of it with me, and whose ideas and love are manifested on every page.

The Age of Noise in Britain

Introduction

> When the complete history of the present period comes to be written, it should surely be described as the age of noise.
> —W. S. Tucker, "The Age of Noise," a lecture to the Royal Aeronautical Society, quoted in the *Manchester Guardian* (January 20, 1928)

That historians should have left Tucker's prophecy unfulfilled is hardly surprising.[1] The early twentieth century is remembered for many things but not usually for its noise. It was an age of *modernity*, certainly, a term which historians have used as shorthand to describe ongoing upheavals in economy, society, and culture at this time. Yet for those who lived through it, who were caught up in what Marshall Berman has influentially described as the "maelstrom" of modernity, patterns were altogether more difficult to perceive.[2] Noise was sometimes evoked metaphorically in this context to ascribe meaninglessness to present-day developments. More often than not, however, those who chose to describe themselves as living in the "age of noise" referred directly to their acoustic surroundings. They took the clash and clatter of urban and industrial life as representative of topsy-turvy times. When it came to articulating their unease about living in a constantly changing world, they chose to point to what they could hear: "the rushing, banging, grinding, shrieking, hooting, rattling, and general thundering," as philosopher Adam Gowans Whyte described it in his 1932 "Reflections on the Age of Noise."[3] Noise was not just representative of the modern; it *was* modernity manifested in audible form. Discussing noise allowed commentators to express what it *felt* like to be living in modern times. Noise was clamorous, all-enveloping, and unpredictable. Discussions of the age of noise constituted a conscious engagement with the politics of modernity in which the modern was not primarily a set of ideas, institutions, or practices, but rather the sensed experience of an unnerving atmosphere.

The age-of-noise narrative circulated widely in early-twentieth-century Britain, as it did in other industrialized nations. Newspaper letter pages filled with complaints. "Every little while some sensitive soul whose nerves have been racked by the roar of traffic relieves his agony in a letter to his favourite newspaper," explained Gowans Whyte. "Other sufferers follow, each trying to improve upon the invective of his fellows."[4] A series of letters to the *Times* published in 1933 under the headline "The Age of Noise" formed one such exchange, focusing on the growth of motor traffic in urban Britain. "In this street," complained one letter writer, "the noise is becoming unbearable, owing to the pace of the traffic."[5] In his 1928 lecture, Tucker noted that it was not only the noise of motor traffic that troubled the sensitive hearer. "We have noise in the street, in the factory, in the office—and, through lack of satisfactory building material from the acoustical point of view, noise in the home."[6] Thanks to a whole host of new technologies—motor vehicles, airplanes, typewriters, gramophone loudspeakers, wireless sets, telephones, vacuum cleaners, even—noise was said to have penetrated every facet of daily life. Thanks also to the ongoing and ever-denser concentration of people in towns and cities, auditory respite was said to be increasingly difficult to find. Noise's rhythms and vibrations caught hold of the hearers day and night, refusing them let-up from the flux and pace of twentieth-century life. Noise imposed a modern state of being on its hearers, whether they liked it or not.

British newspapers reported on the major developments of the day from the perspective of the age of noise. To offer an instructive example, the practice of remembering the dead of the Great War with two minutes of silence on Armistice Day was greeted as recognition of the war's place in the age of noise:

> When everyone was wondering what would be the most striking way in which to commemorate the end of the war with all its tremendous burden of sorrowful memory, someone had an idea which the country at once seized on as an inspiration of genius. We should be quiet for two minutes! All our trams and 'buses, motor-cars, lorries and carts, all our gongs and bells and buzzers, our banging and hammering and thumping, even our chattering and shouting, should be hushed. The idea was that the magnitude of the moment should be emphasized by something as remote as the mind could conceive from our normal lives, and the universal enthusiasm with which we seized on the significance of silence proved—if proof were wanting—that everyone recognized Noise as the outstanding characteristic of our age.[7]

Not satisfied with two minutes of silence, the *Times* reported in 1927 that Londoners would be invited to participate "with finger on the lip," in a full week of silence, during which participants should "speak low" and walk "with soft and ginger tread."[8]

Newspaper reporting of noise revolved around the widely accepted claim that modern mechanical sounds caused a state of "nervousness" in those who are overexposed to them. A 1929 lecture on "How to Remain Sane" by the Sheffield physician Gilbert E. Mould offered a commonly repeated piece of advice: "Noise," he said, "is the most objectionable feature of modern life from the point of view of mental hygiene."[9] Newspapers sensationally reported cases of suicide committed by the noise-tormented, allowing them to convey an urgent sense of crisis about urban noise. The tragic suicide of a neurasthenic retired butler in 1933, for example, was accompanied by a quote from the Westminster coroner, who admitted with resignation that "intolerance of the noise, rush, and bustle of London life [is] a common symptom among highly strung people in these days."[10] Detailing a clergyman's suicide in 1929, the *Manchester Guardian* included a note—"I am over-sensitive. The noise has killed me. I cannot stand the world. I am not insane, but everything hurts me. There is no cure"—clearly intended to alarm its readers.[11]

Newspapers also reported on all manner of supposed cures for noise sensitivity. During the blitz of 1940, American scientists were reported to have proven that vitamin B1 could protect against nervous susceptibility to bomb noise. The *Manchester Guardian* ran a competition for the best response to this news. First prize went to Miss K. M. Fell of Swinton for a rhyme that encapsulates the simultaneous gravity and dark frivolity with which the noise question was treated in early-twentieth-century Britain:

> Two doctors from the burgh of Pitts,
> Seeking to counteract the Blitz
> (For noise, they think, results in fits).
> Declare that now we may cry "Quits"
> 'Gainst wars of nerves devised by Fritz.
> And so, when dining at the Ritz,
> 'Mid roar of bombs and Messerschmitts,
> The dauntless Briton calmly sits
> Munching B 1, the cream of Vits.[12]

Historians have pointed to the centrality of nervousness as a mode of narrating the early-twentieth-century experience of modernity.[13] Shell shock following the First World War was only its most extreme form. It was common, also, to identify the sensory overstimulation inherent in everyday urban environments as a source of mental strain. For example, social theorist of urban experience, Georg Simmel, influentially identified visual overstimulation in towns and cities as the primary cause of modern nervousness.[14] However, it was in fact more common in early-twentieth-century Britain for noise, rather than visual or other forms of sensory bombardment, to be identified as the primary cause of mental disorder in the populations of urban environments. A *Times* remark from 1922 sums up decades of commentary in this regard: "The world of our great towns, in which most of us now live, is one of disordered sounds even more than of disordered sights."[15] It was not just the chronically neurasthenic who were at risk. Cumulatively, the effect of its enveloping sonic bombardment was thought to drain energy and perpetually overstimulate the body's nerves. As government scientist A. H. Davis argued in 1937, "the city dweller adjusts himself in conversation, by raising his voice without knowing it. He takes cognizance, perhaps, of only the particular contribution of some excessively irritating motor horn or motorcycle, of the shattering clatter of a pneumatic drill, or of the obliterating crescendo of the tube train in which he is seated."[16] Over years, this kind of strain would lead, it was feared, to a waning of bodily vitality and ultimately, in some cases, to complete nervous breakdown. The Nazis's noisy aerial bombardment of British towns and cities during the Second World War was supposed, at the time, to be a deliberate attempt to accelerate this process.

Anxieties about noise, it should be noted, are far from unique to the early twentieth century. Through the nineteenth century, and before that, people complained about street sounds.[17] The post-1945 civil aviation boom brought with it a whole host of new noise complaints.[18] In contemporary Britain we are still frequently reminded of noise's threat to our peace of mind: in 2012, to offer one illustrative example, the London department store Selfridge's and Co. launched a "No Noise" initiative, installing a quiet room and proclaiming to shoppers that "as we become increasingly bombarded with information and stimulation, the world is becoming a noisier place."[19] Yet there is something peculiar about the early-twentieth-century obsession with noise. Selfridge's first installed a quiet room in 1909, and its 2012 "No Noise" initiative was as much about anchoring the brand in its Edwardian past as anything else. The age-of-noise narrative—which emerged in earnest in the first two decades of the twentieth century, intensified during and after the First World War, and circulated without let-up until the Second World War—was a specific response to the experience of living in the sensory environment of that period. Across early-twentieth-century Europe and North America, major towns and cities were said to be in the grip of a noise crisis unlike any known before.[20]

In Britain, the age-of-noise narrative was also the product of a no less historically specific anxiety about the progress of modernity at this time. The terrible sacrifices of the First World War prompted an acute crisis of faith in

Victorian ideals of progress, leading in turn to a significant reconfiguring of British attitudes to modernity after 1918. The crisis of noise was a warning, to those who heard it, that the progress of mechanical modernity should be held in check and redirected to more humane ends. Novelist Aldous Huxley put it most starkly of all when he argued, in 1930, that the plague of noise signified a tipping point for "modern civilization": progressively more technological development would now lead, he argued, only to less human happiness.[21] Noise thus encapsulated a paradox at the heart of early-twentieth-century modernity: the more it advanced, the more intolerable life would become. Hopes and fears for noise, such as Huxley's, were expressive, ultimately, of hopes and fears for the sensing human subject in an age of machines.

Taking the hopes and fears of Britain's age of noise as its starting point and case study, this book asks how we might come to reinterpret early-twentieth-century modernity by paying attention to its cultures of hearing. By rereading the available source material in search of insight into the heard experience, we may come to better understand how modern subjectivities were constituted, the book suggests. Subject formation depends upon external sensory referents. What people hear in their daily lives has a role to play in how they imagine themselves. It plays a part in connecting selves to others through, for example, the unifying cheers of a crowd or, conversely, the unwelcome sound of a neighbor's barking dog. It also plays a role in how people experience connection to place: to the quiet privacy of home, for instance; to the noisy rhythms of the workplace or to the sonic properties of specific locales. How one hears is also a marker of who one is. Hearing is not a passive experience; nor is it free from ideology. Choices about what to hear and how to hear it are part of the historical processes of self and social formation. Those who seek to wield authority and influence understand this only too well, even if historians and other analysts of power have been slow to catch up. To understand these processes in any given context requires historicization. How a society makes meaning out of its sounds is fundamental to how it constructs belonging, exclusion, order, disorder, and discipline. This book argues that, in early-twentieth-century Britain, hearing played a more than usually important role in these imaginative constructions, particularly in relation to the urgent, and contested, task of reimagining modernity. The age-of-noise narrative thrust hearing to center stage in the quest to define and reshape modern ways of being. Those who could convincingly make normative claims in relation to the modernity of sound and hearing—to define what constituted good and bad sounds and healthy or unhealthy ways of hearing—could in turn gain considerable authority as arbiters of both aurality and modernity.

Historical Studies in Sound

Until quite recently, attempting to unravel historical ways of hearing was an unlikely task for a historian to undertake. Many historians, still, would consider an age of noise to be a rather odd kind of periodization. However, in the last twenty years, appreciation has steadily grown of the value of analyzing sound and hearing in history. Historians have become far more sensitive to what and how people heard in the past. Peter Bailey, writing in 1996, was among the first to identify the need for auditory histories. He thought of noise—"an expressive and communicative resource that registers collective and individual identities"—as being of particular value for historical analysis.[22] His argument that historians should pay attention to "the changing function of hearing and sound within the combinations and hierarchies that pattern sensory perception" caught a prevailing mood, and found swift response in a range of pioneering histories of sound and hearing, from Alain Corbin's *Village Bells* (1998) to John M. Picker's *Victorian Soundscapes* (2003), Emily Thompson's *The Soundscape of Modernity* (2004) and Karin Bijsterveld's *Mechanical Sounds* (2008).[23] Mark M. Smith led the way in the incorporation of sound into social history and the history of war in *Listening to Nineteenth-Century America* (2001); Jonathan Sterne offered the first comprehensive cultural history of sound reproduction technologies in *The Audible Past* (2003); while Douglas Kahn made sound a concern in the history of the arts in *Noise, Water, Meat* (1999).[24] Interest in the history of sound and hearing has continued unabated, with Shelley Trower's cultural history of sound vibration, *Senses of Vibration* (2012), and Carolyn Birdsall's *Nazi Soundscapes* (2012), a history of listening cultures under National Socialism, accompanying edited collections and readers such as Daniel Morat's *Sounds of Modern History* (2014).[25] These sound histories form part of the emergence of a wider interdisciplinary field of sound studies, which incorporates work from scholars in media and communications studies, cultural studies, science and technology studies, music and sonic arts, film studies, and literary studies, among others. Jonathan Sterne's *Sound Studies Reader* (2012) and Karin Bijsterveld and Trevor Pinch's *Oxford Handbook of Sound Studies* (2012), accompanying earlier collections such as Michael Bull and Les Back's *Auditory Culture Reader* (2003), signal the maturation of a subject area fast becoming equivalent in scope to the interdisciplinary field of visual culture research.[26]

For the historians involved in the new sound studies, the guiding principle has been a simple one, even if the methodological and source work has been more complex. Sam Halliday describes it, in *Sonic Modernity* (2013), as the desire to show that "both sound and hearing are historical."[27] Hearing, like the other senses, is not a fixed and universal category.[28] It is constructed within political, economic, social, and cultural circumstances. Even the scientific understanding of hearing, as scholars including Alexandra Hui have shown, is dependent upon the cultural contexts which produce and sustain it.[29] In this respect, historical studies of sound have been engaged in extending the long-standing priority of social and cultural historians to locate as historical, and thus also as ideologically contingent, categories of human experience that might otherwise take a concretized form (such as class, gender, and race). However, sound and other new sensory histories have deliberately moved beyond social and cultural history's traditional dependence on linguistic and visual analysis (even if written and visual materials have remained important resources) in their attempt to recover more of the immediacy of past experience. We can never, as historians, hear as those in the past heard, but we can endeavor to understand some of the ways in which sound and hearing featured in the negotiation of everyday life in the past. My approach in this book is to locate sound and hearing within the wider experience and contestation of modernity in early-twentieth-century Britain.

Sound and Modernity

Before outlining some of the further contours of my argument in this respect, it is useful first to take stock of the conceptual role that modernity has played in recent sound histories. The concept of modernity has featured centrally in the analytical work of sound historians. One might even go so far as to say that modernity has been *the* organizing category in the historicization of sound and hearing. This is not in itself especially remarkable, since, as the editors of a recent *American Historical Review* (*AHR*) roundtable on the concept point out, "the ascription 'modern' is virtually ubiquitous in historical discourse. . . . It is difficult," they continue, "to imagine the very grammar of history without the vocabulary of modernity."[30] However, we should not forget, as the editors of this roundtable remind us, that analyzing the past according to the presence or absence of modernity is part of the interpretative process through which historians make history meaningful. Those who lived through the nineteenth and early twentieth centuries were aware of living through significant change, but historians, with hindsight, have applied greater analytical clarity to those changes than contemporaries ever could have. In doing so, historians impose an order on the past that reflects not only the realities of historical change but also their own interpretative inclinations. Making decisions about what kind of story to tell is, of course, in the nature of the writing of history, but given the conceptual centrality of modernity to so much of the recent historiography on sound and hearing, it is worth pausing to ask what kinds of interpretative patterns are imposed by the use of this term and whether sound history might benefit from renewed critical attention to the vocabulary of the modern.

Lynn M. Thomas, one of the contributors to the *AHR*'s roundtable, outlines the various historical transformations that historians have generally organized under the heading of modernity. She argues that these include

> divisions between the religious and the secular and the public and the private; the cultivation of scientific rationality and critical self-reflection; liberal political ideas that challenge social hierarchies rooted in kin, class, gender, or race; constitutional, representative, and bureaucratic forms of government; industrial production and expanded markets; mechanical reproduction and mass media; heightened urbanization, monetization, and consumption; accelerated transportation and communication; and a future-orientated conception of time that figures the present as a radical rupture from the past.[31]

Rarely do historical analyses attempt to unravel all of these transformations at once. Taken together, however, Thomas's list is a useful working definition of modernity as it has been used as an interpretative framework by historians, sociologists, and others.

Pioneers in the field of sound history consciously and emphatically located their stories about sound in relation to this interpretative framework, as many who have followed them in the writing of sound history have continued to do. In *The Audible Past*, for example, Jonathan Sterne analyzes new forms of expert listening in the nineteenth century (such as doctors' use of stethoscopes and the technical work of telegraphers) and argues that sound *matters* in modern history: "Through techniques of listening, people harnessed, modified, and shaped their powers of auditory perception in the service of rationality. In the modern age," he continues, "sound and hearing were reconceptualized, objectified, imitated, transformed, reproduced, commodified, mass-produced, and industrialized."[32] Enlightenment rationality and the drive for human mastery over nature, as well as the imprint of capitalist economic and social organization, are the hallmarks of the modernity of modern sound and hearing for Sterne. Sound and hearing, he adds, should be considered "central to the cultural life of modernity" because of the extent to which they feature in the modern impetus toward capitalism, rationalism, and science.[33]

Emily Thompson, in her book *The Soundscape of Modernity*, joins Sterne in placing this definition of modernity at the heart of her analysis of sound and hearing in urban America in the period 1900–1933. In charting "dramatic transformations in what people heard" and "equally significant changes in the ways that people listened to those sounds," she identifies "a fundamental compulsion to control the behavior of sound" as the key characteristic of sonic modernity.[34] Like Sterne, she traces the work of sound experts, in her case architectural acousticians, and argues that they were responsible for cultivating an ethos of efficiency in the drive to control reverberation in the urban soundscape. "From concert halls to corporate offices, from acoustical laboratories to the soundscapes of motion picture studios, the new sound rang out for all to hear," she explains. "Clear, direct, and nonreverberant, this modern sound was easy to understand."[35] The planned sound environments created by architectural acousticians were modern, Thompson argues because, on the one hand, they embodied the efficient values of early-twentieth-century American capitalism and, on the other, they could be packaged as products to be bought and sold. This was modern sound, she concludes "because it was perceived to demonstrate man's technical mastery over his physical environment."[36] Thompson, like Sterne, makes a claim for sound's historical relevance on the basis of its involvement in commercial and rationalist logics.

More recently, Sam Halliday has continued the analytical trend of explaining sound's historical relevance in relation to modernity, arguing that sonic modernity "can be delineated with a fair degree of specificity and detail."[37] With a greater emphasis than Sterne or Thompson on sounds themselves rather than on ways of hearing or listening, Halliday follows theorists Pierre Schaeffer, James Lastra, and Douglas Kahn in identifying *acousmatic sounds* (those that are heard separately from their visual source thanks to sound recording/reproducing technologies), *stored sounds* (again, made possible by sound recording), and the concept of *all sound* (the indiscriminate way in which sound recording technologies capture all sounds equally) as the tripartite constitution of sonic modernity.[38] Halliday uses these categories to examine modernist representation of sound in the arts, tying the ontological modernity of certain kinds of technologically reproduced sound to the evolution of modernist sonic imaginaries. Thus, there are not only identifiably modern ways to listen, hear, and intervene in sound, but also identifiably modern kinds of sound, those produced mechanically by phonographs or telephones, in Halliday's account, or those whose reverberation has been controlled by experts, in Thompson's.

These sound historians have felt compelled to explain the historical relevance of sound primarily in relation to the concept of modernity due to the predominance, as they have perceived it, of a visualist interpretation of the modern. From the visual metaphors that Enlightenment philosophers associated with the search for rational truths, to the argument of media theorists that modernity is encapsulated in the rise of print culture at the expense of oral-aural communication, to the claims made on behalf of cartography and surveillance as techniques of modern rule or, indeed, the definition of artistic modernism as a crisis of realistic visual representation, sound historians have perceived a powerful occularcentrism at work in scholarly discourses about modernity.[39] Occularcentrism not only threatens to sideline sound in the theorization of modernity but also to actively classify it as un- or premodern. Nostalgia for a lost world of face-to-face communication or of freedom from the insidious creep of scopic control lies implicit in discussions of modernity's visualism, sound historians imply. That is why they have been at pains to demonstrate that sound had a role of its own to play in the forward march of the modern. Sterne writes, for example, "Techniques of audition developed by doctors and telegraphers were constitutive of scientific medicine and early versions of modern bureaucracy. . . . These facts," he insists, "trouble the cliché that modern science and rationality were outgrowths of visual culture and visual thinking. . . . To take seriously the role of sound and hearing in modern life is to trouble the visualist definition of modernity."[40]

In their efforts to convince us that sound matters in modernity, sound historians were also mindful of a distinctly negative politics of modernity at work in the earliest sound studies theory produced in the 1970s. R. Murray Schafer's *The Soundscape: Our Sonic Environment and the Tuning of the World*, first published as *The Tuning of the World* in 1977, still provides much of the critical vocabulary of sound studies and is regularly cited as the foundational text in the field.[41] Schafer's work emerged from a concern with sonic ecology and draws a sharp distinction between valuable natural sounds, including music, and the polluting and disturbing character of industrial and mechanical sound. As a contribution to the debate about sonic value, Schafer's work fits squarely within the age-of-noise narrative outlined earlier. He categorized modernity as a damaging force that wrecks sonic pollution on the world. As a contribution to scholarly methodology in sound studies, however, Schafer's approach could be taken to imply the categorization of sound as ideally premodern. His approach certainly casts sonic modernity as a haphazard and meaninglessly noisy (and thus not properly sounding) by-product of industrialization and urbanization, deserving of analysis only as a means of ensuring its eradication. No wonder that Thompson, though admitting a debt to Schafer's use of the term *soundscape*, notes that she does not share his motivation for studying the modernity of sound.[42] To do so would have oriented the study of sound in opposition to modernity rather than as a contribution to our historical understanding of it.

In situating sound history as a vital component of the historical analysis of modernity, historians like Sterne and Thompson have been successful in convincing the mainstream historical profession to take sound seriously. Their work opened up new terrain, which has continued to bear fruit in the continuing and growing interest in the sounds of the past. Challenging the occularcentric analysis of modernity was a vital step in opening the way for new sensory histories of modernity. Sterne and Thompson took a widely accepted definition of modernity and demonstrated, beyond doubt, that sound should be taken into account when analyzing it. My approach, however, is to suggest that our understanding of the relationship between sound and modernity can be enlarged and enlivened by paying closer attention to how historical actors themselves understood the notion of modernity. I deploy the term *modernity* here not as an interpretative category by which to judge and explain history but rather as something that people in the past were themselves struggling to understand and come to terms with. In the early-twentieth-century context the term *noise* connoted both a hearer's distaste for certain kinds of sounds and a struggle to make sense of environmental change. The struggle to define modernity, I argue, did not produce a singular or definite sonic modernity or only one modern way of hearing. Modernity was, rather, a site of imaginative contestation through which various competing definitions of modern sound and hearing emerged.

In taking this approach, I follow a number of historians who, increasingly dissatisfied with a singular, abstract, and universally applicable model of modernity, have shifted their efforts toward a more historicist model. These historians argue that we should understand modernity less as an abstract category and more as a discursive resource that people in the past used to construct and contest self and social imaginings. Dipesh Chakrabarty suggests that we should pay attention to the multiple "claims to modernity" present in the periods we study, claims which, he argues, are "artefacts of both ideology and imagination." To be modern, he insists "is to judge one's experience of time and space and thus create new possibilities for oneself."[43] Lynn M. Thomas offers a similar argument, indicating that we should shift our analysis of modernity toward "how people have used the term 'modern' to make political claims and envision different futures." She adds, "Rather than historians engaging modernity as a static ideological formation or our own category of analysis, such an approach considers the modern as a 'native' category for claiming and denying political inclusion."[44]

We must, if we are to adopt this model, be open to the possibility that in any given period, multiple, potentially mutually exclusive, ways of imagining and claiming modernity operated alongside one another. Indeed, we must be open to the possibility that cultural phenomena that would register as distinctly unmodern according to a singular, abstract model, evolved in their own contexts as contributions to modernity. Taking this approach does not mean that anything claimed as modern should be admitted as such, but rather that the burden of historical work should shift toward mapping the various, potentially opposed, terrains of modern imagination at work in the past. Indeed, Thomas argues that this approach contributes to our understanding of modernity by "demonstrating just how diverse and dynamic definitions of the modern have been."[45] As the *AHR*'s editors put it, we should search not "for modernity in the sense of assuming what we are looking for, but to be prepared to 'discover' sources of modern development in very different guises."[46] Many of the historians who have made this move did so because of the problems inherent in applying a European model of modernity to other parts of the world. Their contestation and fragmentation of the concept has nevertheless influenced analyses of modernity in Europe, too. Writing about recent discussions of modernity in Britain, James Vernon and Simon Gunn note that historians are now more adept at recovering multiple and contested cultures of modernity and that they have become inclined to focus on "how a discourse of the modern is claimed and used to assert the interests of a specific subject, space, or politics."[47]

My argument in this book is that adopting such an approach can add to our understanding of sound in modernity. I do not wish to suggest a deficiency in Sterne, Thompson, or Halliday's approach, or indeed to replace their analysis of sonic modernity with my own. Rather, my proposition is that sound history can benefit by paying attention to the politics of modernity as it related to sound. Our historical understanding of sound in modernity can be enriched by paying closer attention to the multiple meanings of sonic modernity in the past. Antinoise discourse, which laid the foundation for an organized noise abatement campaign in the 1930s, followed a logic of modernity as crisis in which the modern was defined as a dangerously enervating force causing permanent decline in the mental health of those exposed to it. Although noise-controlling experts, such as architectural acousticians, sometimes found it useful to situate the value of their expertise in relation to this problem, they could not commit themselves fully to a modernity-as-crisis narrative because the possibility of their expert intervention necessitated an alternative logic of modernity as expert control. The professional psychologists who took up the problem of industrial noise in Britain were often highly critical of the antinoise campaign precisely because they found it to be unnecessarily pessimistic in its outlook for industrial and urban life. Indeed, industrial psychologists constructed their claim to modernity on the basis of its difference to antinoise discourse. One possible line of interpretation would be to see the positive construction of modernity, the one forwarded by psychological and architectural experts, as the more properly modern of the two, because it extended the principles of rational science and human mastery over nature to sound. However, in my account, the two stand as alternative and competing narrations of sonic modernity, each having its distinct contributions to make to the ways in which early-twentieth-century Britons heard their soundscape. They are discussed, in turn, in Chapters 1 and 3. Unraveling the distinctive features of these two modern imaginaries helps us begin to understand the multiplicity of modern hearing in early-twentieth-century Britain. Taken together, Chapters 1 and 3 suggest that a dialectic of hope and fear, of peril and possibility, structured much of the imaginative engagement with modernity during this period.

The negative and positive constructions of modernity discussed in these chapters were not, however, the only two ways of hearing modernity at work in early-twentieth-century Britain. Taking up Thomas's suggestion that, in addition to focusing on "native" modernities, historians should also unbundle the various transformations subsumed under the heading of modernity and deal with them afresh, I dwell, in Chapter 2, on the issue of spirituality as it figured in the response to the age of noise in order to question the relationship between modernity and secularization where sound and hearing were concerned.[48] Among the multiple ways of hearing modernity that I examine in this book, one took a distinctly spiritual form in its investigation of the occult properties of "magical sound." This way of hearing was constructed not only in response to the modern soundscape—indeed, as an enchanted response to the age of noise—but also, I argue, as a thoroughly and self-consciously modern way of hearing, albeit drawing upon an alternative set of imaginative parameters to those deployed by proponents of noise abatement and by expert controllers of noise.

In outlining divergent cultures of modernity at work in early-twentieth-century Britain, my aim is not to provide an exhaustive account of the varieties of sonic modernity at work in the early twentieth century. Rather, my aim is to show that the problem of noise, specifically, produced a number of different modern responses and that it became the target of competing claims to modernity. I deal with the modernity-as-human-mastery claim in Chapter 3 but my aim is not to situate it as the *most* modern way of hearing, but instead as one among multiple ideological claims to sonic modernity. As Chakrabarty points out, "If someone is 'modern,' then he or she is so with regard to somebody who is not."[49] The rationalizing experts discussed in Chapter 3 constructed their sonic modernity in opposition to competitors, including both the pessimists of the antinoise campaign and the re-enchanters discussed in Chapter 2. I argue in this chapter that if we are to fully understand the modern culture of rationalism, we must also understand its "constitutive outside," to borrow a phrase from Judith Butler.[50] In my account, the constitutive outside to secular-scientific ways of hearing are not *less* modern, but *part* of the fundamentally contested field of modern imagination. This book is intended, thus, as a contribution to the rethinking of modernity as well as a contribution to our historical understanding of sound and hearing. Like other sound historians before me, though, I suggest that the one can usefully facilitate the other.

Auditory Experts

My focus in discussing multiple and contested ways of hearing modernity in early-twentieth-century Britain is on the emergence of expert practices and discourses relating to noise. In this respect, my approach follows that of Sterne and Thompson, as well as Karin Bijsterveld, in identifying modern ways of hearing with the rise of expert hearers.[51] I situate the rise of modern expert hearing as altogether more fragmented and contested than these authors have done, but I follow them in arguing that understanding modern cultures of hearing requires analysis of the role of auditory experts. Why did noise become the target of expert problematization and intervention in the early twentieth century? There are two factors that help to answer this question and to explain why noise became such a prominent expert preoccupation in early-twentieth-century Britain. First, this was the period, according to Harold Perkin, of the rise of "professional society."[52] With its origins in the late nineteenth century but coming into its own during and after the First World War, Perkin describes the growth of professional society as the coming to prominence of a new class of experts and bureaucrats who exerted ever-greater social and political influence through professional bodies and through local and national government at the expense of the Victorian era's entrepreneurial class. This new professional elite instilled meritocracy and state intervention as the new social ideals of the age in contrast to the class-bound stratification and laissez-faire governance of the nineteenth century, according to Perkin. He argues that the "animating spirit" of the "collective self-interest" of the new professional class of early-twentieth-century Britain was the "service performed for society," the claim that professional experts could act objectively to improve the whole of society.[53] Nikolas Rose, too, identifies a significant shift in the early twentieth century toward the deployment of objective experts as agents of liberal state power. At one remove from the state, experts such as doctors, psychologists, and welfare officers produced knowledge of, as well as norms for, social organization. This allowed interventionism to be enacted in the name of objective rationality rather than under the banner of sectional political interest and as the initiative of experts on the ground rather than by actions of the state from above.[54]

In one sense, then, expert intervention in noise was part of the expert claiming of social problems as sites for power/knowledge, to borrow Michel Foucault's term.[55] Yet this does not quite explain why noise came to be such a hotly contested site of expert authority in the early twentieth century. In my discussion of expert discourses of noise in the chapters which follow, I build on John M. Picker's argument that discussions of, and struggles against, noise were formative to the very emergence of professional identity in the post-1850 period. Picker argues that in their campaign against street music and other street noises, the newly emergent urban professionals of Victorian Britain formed early strategies for "collective action and self-definition."[56] As "brain workers," urban professionals relied on the ability to separate them-selves from the sensory distractions of city life. Writer Thomas Carlyle was among the most famous contributors to the Victorian antinoise campaign and soundproofed his attic in order to have somewhere quiet to think. For Carlyle, Picker argues, "to rest, but more important, to *work*, depended upon denying outdoor commotion 'free access' to interior professional space."[57] The struggle for quiet and the struggle for "professional differentiation" went hand in hand for the Victorian middle class, according to Picker.[58] The desire to maintain sonic boundaries between public space and private space was in one sense middle class, since those who waged campaigns against street music and complained about noise were primarily from this social background, but, following Picker, I argue that late-nineteenth and early-twentieth century antinoise sentiment was, in fact, more specifically to do with professional and expert identity and agency as it emerged in opposition to Victorian industrialism and laissez-faire ideals. Picker argues that successfully bring-ing about a Street Music Abatement Act (passed into law in 1864) allowed urban professionals to "crystallize their own group identity and establish themselves as a formidable presence" in Britain.[59] Similar processes were at work after 1900.

The prominence of antinoise discourse and of antinoise action in the early formation of professional identity in Britain helps to explain why noise remained a preoccupation of expert professionals and a yardstick for profes-sional agency in the early twentieth century. During this period, according to Perkin, expert professionals had increasingly to compete with one another for prominence and for the right to speak objectively for society. According to Perkin, professional society took the form, after 1914, "of a competition for resources between rival interest groups. The doctors, the civil servants, the military, the social workers and administrators, the university and government scientific researchers [were] all manifestly in competition for public resources" in this period, he argues.[60] Perkin's theory helps to explain why dissonance rather than consonance characterized the expert response to noise in early-twentieth-century Britain. Expert professionals were in competition with one another for the right to speak objectively in relation to the noise problem and, sometimes, in direct rivalry for state recognition and funding. The multiple ways of hearing modernity that I discuss in this book were, thus, competing expert constructions of sonic modernity advanced in order to make a claim for expert agency and authority, for the right to speak objectively about noise. However, I wish to also propose a decoupling of the terms *professional* and *expert* in my broadening of the terrain of modernity. Those who advanced a program of sonic re-enchantment, discussed in Chapter 2, were not necessarily professional according to Perkin's analysis but were by their own definition experts in the occult workings of spiritual sound and hearing. They, too, situated their claim to expert authority in opposition to a Victorian status quo, in their case the materialism of Victorian science. They, too, were identifiably middle class and imagined their collective identity in opposition to noise. In my account, these experts had a no less legitimate claim to modernity or to expert knowledge than those whose expertise found employ in the service of the liberal state. Recovering the place of a spiritual imagination in middle-class constructions of modernity is part of my project to take account of the mixed economy of expertise and knowledge that came to be applied to noise.

One way or another, though, the age-of-noise narrative was produced and sustained by the rise of middle-class expert and professional authority, contested as it may have been. Defining noise as a problem allowed experts and professionals to define themselves as such, in contrast to manual workers and other "non-brain-working" people. It allowed them to construct norms for the industrial and urban soundscape, what Pierre Bourdieu might term an auditory "habitus," in which divisions between public and private sounds and between desirable sounds and undesirable noises, or indeed between celestial harmony and earthly dissonance, were imaginatively policed.[61] In making a claim for expert authority, professional groups often had to project norms of sound and hearing onto people of other classes, such as manual workers, or the spiritually uninitiated. They transformed middle-class aural proclivities into norms of the social body as a whole. They advanced techniques for the management of the "conduct of conduct," to borrow Nikolas Rose's Foucauldian turn of phrase, where sound and hearing were concerned.[62] In the discussion that follows, I do not intend to uncover experiences of sound so much as expert ideological constructions of those experiences. When expert professionals made claims about factory workers' experiences of noise, or of ways that people heard in the home, they were engaged in the production of a discourse of expert intervention and a claim to expert authority. One approach would be to attempt to determine the extent to which expert discourses of noise were shared by those who were targeted by investigation and upon whom claims to objectivity rested. This, however, would demand an alternative set of methodologies and sources to the ones I use and consider in this book. Here, I deliberately limit investigation to expert constructions of sound and hearing not only because these are an important place to start in understanding historical ways of hearing, but also because it is all too easy to assume singularity in elite power and authority. Access to the ability to make objective claims on behalf of society was a political process in and of itself. Rationalist scientists had to advance and defend their position. Those who attempted to find enchanting solutions to the age of noise had to work doubly hard in making their claim to expert agency. The politics of expertise is not only, in other words, to be found in the expert exercise of power but also in what counts as expert in the first place.

Sound and Selfhood

My approach to analyzing auditory expertise differs from that of scholars such as Thompson and Bijsterveld insofar as my interest relates primarily to expert claims about the hearing of noise rather than about noises themselves. In contrast to the dominance of a history of technology approach in the work of Sterne, Thompson, and Bijsterveld, this book is concerned less with the emergence of new sound technologies and more with the subjective experience of hearing noise as it related to the question of modernity. Discussions of the age of noise in Britain, I argue throughout this book, were fundamentally to do with anxieties about the self and its relationship to the social. In the post-Renaissance context, selfhood has been closely associated with the concept of individual thought. Descartes famously argued that in its capacity for conscious thought, the individual self exists separately from the world around it.[63] This culture of selfhood depended, however, upon an imagined barrier between the mental interior and the exterior world of sensation.[64] It was precisely this separation that was threatened by mechanical and urban noise. Because sound was associated with motion more closely than other sensations were, it was used as a scientific model to theorize what James Kennaway has described as "the porous boundaries of the self" in the modern age.[65] The potential for the porous self to be overwhelmed by the rapidity of vibrations passed to it from the outside was thought to be a considerable threat to mental well-being in the late nineteenth and early twentieth centuries. "To be penetrated by sound," as Greg Goodale puts it in his sound history of this period, is potentially "to lose one's sense of unity and be unable to differentiate one's self from the outside and from others."[66] Nervousness, neurasthenia, or full nervous breakdowns were said to be the results. Renewed ideals of selfhood came to be aligned, in response, more closely than before with silence. Carlyle's soundproofed attic was not just a place to work but also a place for the pursuance and preservation of quiet, intellectual, selfhood. It was an architectural metaphor for the quiet mind.

Early psychological theorists such as Gustave le Bon suggested that man's individual self, quietly rational, was lost to clamorously noisy collective instincts in the crowds of urban modernity.[67] Writing in the modernist periodical the *Little Review* in 1914, the divinity scholar George Burman Foster argued, similarly, that men erroneously celebrate noisy revolutionaries and political leaders because "Their words excite, move to tears, arouse boisterous and voluble antagonisms." But noise is not the true source of heroism for Foster. Faced with "moments in our lives when everything that we encounter disconcerts us; nay, when our whole being seems to be off the hinges, out of joint" only by heroically restoring our inner quiet will we survive:

> [T]he quiet hour must come in which a divine child of the spirit is conceived by the holy spirit; and the brightest light which we can kindle within will burn so quietly and clearly that no cloud of smoke shall ascend therefrom, and there shall be no flickering to bear witness of contact with the restless world. "There the true Silence is, self-conscious and alone."[68]

Foster hoped that "The day will yet come when we will estimate our life, not according to its noisiest, but according to its stillest hours."[69] As the spirits of machines made their presence felt through audible noisy vibrations, so the spiritual workings of the inner self were often said, as was the timeless acoustics of the countryside, to resonate beyond the range of hearing: "No sound is uttered,—but a deep / And solemn harmony pervades," as Foster put it, quoting Wordsworth.[70] Even those early-twentieth-century Britons who did not share Carlyle's obsession with quiet thought were conscious of the ever-present sonic demands of the modern world in which they lived. "Having filled our lives with incessant noise, huge shops, tall buildings, traffic, telephones, and wireless, we now desire to get away from it all—to have scope, however small, for our own individuality," explained one newspaper report in 1936.[71] The very possibility of maintaining quiet, individual self-hood over and above the communal din of modernity was the question at the heart of the age of noise.

My discussion of selfhood is intended to add a sonic dimension to the historicization of the twentieth-century self as it emerged in the discourse of medical and psychological experts. Historians of psychological expertise have tended to emphasize its visualizing and externalizing functions. Nikolas Rose, for example, argues that the purpose of psychology and psychiatry as expert disciplines is to "render subjectivity into thought as a calculable force."[72] Psychological examination, Rose argues, "makes human individuality visible, it locates it in a web of writing, transcribing attributes and their variations into codified forms, enabling them to be accumulated, summated, averaged and normalized."[73] In contrast, as Steven Connor has argued, "The self defined in terms of hearing rather than sight is a self imaged not as a point, but as a membrane; not as a picture, but as a channel through which voices, noises and musics travel."[74] I follow Connor in discussing sonically constituted selves, but point also toward the interest that early-twentieth-century psychologists themselves had in the hearing self. As a way of avoiding theorizations of the modern self which allow only for external visualization, Connor points in particular to the psychoanalytical theory of Didier Anzieu who, he reminds us, proposes that selves are formed within "sonic envelopes," which contain those sounds we hear as an extension or reflection of ourselves. In infancy, the mother's voice is the most important of these. "Noise," in this context, refers to sounds that are excluded from the sonic envelope of the self. As Connor explains, "the contrast between threatening and disorganized noise . . . and organized sound" is an important juncture of self formation in Anzieu's theory.[75] In the context of the early-twentieth-century's age of noise, Connor argues that "the opening of the self to and by the auditory was an experience both of rapturous expansion and of dangerous disintegration."[76]

The rapturous expansion to which Connor refers is often taken to be exemplified in the attitude of early-twentieth-century avant-garde composers such as Luigi Russolo and George Antheil who made music out of noise.[77] Goodale uses the work of these composers in his application of Anzieu's sonic envelope theory to the age of noise. He argues that before the First World War, modernist artists such as Russolo "embraced the shattering, transpiercing, and deterritorialization produced by noise" and that they represented a "penetrated, shattered, and multiplied" self in their works.[78] However, Goodale claims that by the middle of the century, composers such as John Cage had ceased to hear noise as a threat to the self and had instead incorporated it into their compositions as a friend rather than as a competitor to music. Noise "no longer destroys the self," in this context, according to Goodale, but "rather it envelops the self, protecting individuals against forces outside of the sound."[79] Goodale argues that "the dismemberment of the self" threatened before the First World War was prevented by composers like Cage. The sounds of modernity were incorporated into the sonic envelope of the twentieth-century self.[80] While this approach might serve us relatively well as a way of analyzing artistic practice, the danger of relying on Anzieu's theory is that it can impose a pattern on cultural historical processes, which were altogether more complex. Anzieu's theory certainly does not do justice to the historical specificities of sound and selfhood's entanglement in the varied expert psychological cultures of early-twentieth-century Britain. Debates about the nature of noise's impact on the human mind were right at the heart of the expert contestation of noise at this time. This contestation took the form of expert discussion of and debate about "nerves." Experts disagreed quite fundamentally about how, and indeed whether, noise caused nervous illness in those who heard it. Such disagreements played no small part in the direction that the various psychological cultures at work in early-twentieth-century Britain took in their approach to theorizing modern urban environments. It is not my intention to exhaustively account for the various ways in which sound and hearing featured in the early-twentieth-century's sciences of the self. Indeed, there are developments in the physiology and psychology of hearing that emerged in this period that I do not consider. My aim, rather, is to show that diverging conceptualizations of the hearing self had a central role to play in the claims to sonic modernity at work in early-twentieth-century Britain.

Ways of Hearing

Each of the following chapters deals in turn with a different way of hearing modernity in Britain in the age of noise. Their chronological focus is largely on the period between the outbreak of the First World War in 1914 and the conclusion of the Second World War in 1945, but in tracing the origins and influence of the age of noise, each chapter reaches back into the nineteenth century and onward into the twentieth. Each chapter details a different expert construction of the relationship between sound and selfhood. Since the age-of-noise narrative was associated first and foremost with accounts of mental illness, the first chapter, "Modernity as Crisis: Noise and 'Nerves,'" deals directly with its medical underpinnings. It charts the course of noise abatement discourse and noise abatement activity in Britain, paying particular attention to the activities of the Anti-Noise League founded in 1933 which, although it brought together all sorts of sound-sensitive activists, was led by medical men and drew primarily upon medical justifications for noise abatement. The chapter details the medical paradigm of neurasthenia within which noise was problematized in the antinoise campaign and argues that it was, from its origins in late-nineteenth-century neurology, entwined with a medicalized critique of modern civilization. Although their aim was to reduce the noise of everyday urban and industrial life in order to create a better sonic future, supporters of noise abatement were nonetheless united by a pessimistic outlook on the modern and by a yearning for the quieter conditions of the past. They sought to preserve quiet spaces in the urban environment so as to offer refuge to the vulnerable self but, following the trend set by Carlyle, emphasized that quiet conditions were necessary mainly for the protection of those involved in intellectual work. They thought of noise abatement as a cause principally of the "intelligent" classes in society in contrast to those "who cannot go for a picnic without taking a gramophone, the people who leave the wireless running all day like a dripping tap, and the people who ride motor-bicycles round and round the urban square and the village green."[81] The early-twentieth-century antinoise campaign was, I suggest, an extension of the aural politics of professional identity formation that Picker has identified as emerging in the mid–nineteenth century. The Anti-Noise League promoted a silent, individual model of selfhood, which it aligned with the intellectual cultivation necessary for professional work and against the noisy collective instincts of mass culture.

Chapter 1 also offers the first indication of why Anzieu's theory of the sonic envelope cannot neatly be applied to the early-twentieth-century context. This chapter argues that *nervousness*, a popular term for neurasthenia, was part of an emerging culture of psychological selfhood in early-twentieth-century Britain.[82] Although those who suffered from "nerves" were thought to have sustained physical injury to their nervous systems caused by the vibrations of noise, their weakened mental state was also put down to a lack of thought control. Theorizing noise's impact on the psyche was part of a phase in early psychology's development during which neither somatic nor psychosomatic explanations had come to dominate in the treatment of mental illness. Questions about whether noise's assault was primarily physical, or whether its threat signified a mental weakness, thus played their part in the early conceptualization of the psychological self and of the psyche's relationship with the sensory environment. Subsuming the peculiarities of psychology's historical development into Anzieu's psychoanalytical theory, however useful it may be in other respects, cannot help us to understand the historical specificities of the psychologized conceptualization of the hearing self as it emerged in relation to debates about noise in the early twentieth century.

Chapter 2, "Re-Enchanting Modernity: Techniques of Magical Sound," points to another peculiarity of the psychological self as it emerged at this time. Contrary to the usual assumption that modernization necessitated secularization, this chapter argues that spiritual conceptions of the self not only persisted but were, in fact, revived alongside early psychology and that they played a central role in popular understandings of nervousness. A nervous disposition was thought to indicate a soul out of tune with the musical harmony of the universe. Such ideas were popularized by the spiritualist and occultist movements that thrived in early-twentieth-century Britain—one of which, the Theosophical Society, forms the basis of the case study discussion in this chapter. Advocates of such movements proposed that modern mechanical sounds disrupt the spiritual harmony of the inner self. In contrast to supporters of noise abatement who thought that selfhood was best attained in absolute quiet, modern occult investigators claimed that, in an age of noise, true selfhood could be attained only by connecting the soul to the vibrations of restorative and divinely inspired sounds. Sometimes conventionally musical, other times less obviously so (in the case, for example, of Luigi Russolo's occult-inspired "art of noises"), these sounds were intended to set the soul vibrating to "the harmony of the spheres."[83] In the case of such occult practices, the self was conceptualized as a *product of*, rather than *in opposition to*, the vibrations of sound.

Attempts to re-enchant the modern soundscape by experimenting in magical sounds have, on the whole, been sidelined or overlooked by historians of sound because they do not comfortably fit within the narratives of rationalization, secularization, and disenchantment, which have come to structure the standard definition of modernity. Where the historiography on modern auditory culture has taken up the question of disenchantment, there has been a tendency to reinforce the chronology of modern secularization. Richard Cullen Rath, for example, discusses the extent to which the rise of modernity facilitated the exclusion of enchanted soundscapes in early America. He evokes a premodern world of enchantment in which moans, groans, and cries expressed religious deliverance but argues that the rise of modernity brought with it a "shift in the senses" in which these religious sounds were excluded by the visual structure of written language.[84] I argue in Chapter 2 that attempts to re-enchant the modern soundscape should be seen as one of the principal modes through which sonic modernity was experienced and articulated in early-twentieth-century Britain. In this chapter, I follow Wouter Hanegraaff in pointing to the ongoing presence and significance of magical traditions, specifically of the Western hermetic tradition of magic, in the early twentieth century, and build on the work of Alex Owen and Michael Saler in defining its place in the early-twentieth-century occult investigation of sound as part of the attempt to re-enchant modernity.[85]

The term modernity is usually associated with the steady onward march of science and rationality. While Chapter 2 is intended to disrupt and complicate such assumptions, the third chapter acknowledges that a rationalizing instinct was at the heart of another way of hearing modernity in early-twentieth-century Britain. Gowans Whyte's 1932 article, "Reflections on the Age of Noise," scoffed that modern civilization "prides itself upon its triumphs in science, in engineering, in social organisation, in multiplying the amenities of life; nevertheless it appears to stand helpless before one of the most elementary consequences of its activity—the distracting and destructive influence of ever-rising waves of sound."[86] Chapter 3 points to a significant group of sound experts at work in early-twentieth-century Britain who wished to prove that they were not so helpless. Distinct from noise abatement supporters' sonic nostalgia and from occultists' hopes for spiritual advancement through sound, the rationalizers discussed in this chapter believed that they could solve the problem of noise through rational scientific understanding of sound. They located the noisy present in a faulty Victorian modernity and sought to engineer a perfectly planned sonic future. These sound experts were, by and large, employed by the state or by state-affiliated agencies and subscribed to a new ethos of state intervention and planning that emerged in Britain after the First World War. The chapter focuses on their attempts to rationalize the soundscapes of the home and the workplace in particular and on their representation through propaganda of a nation united by the rational, rhythmical sounds of trade and industry. Sound was incorporated, this chapter argues, into the state-led technocratic management of the self and the social in early-twentieth-century Britain. This included the activities of newly professionalized psychologists who created norms for both the well-balanced psyche and for its relationship with the sensory environment.

The final chapter deals with the significant impact of the Second World War on Britain's everyday soundscape. It provides an extended case study in how the various expert ways of hearing modernity at work in early-twentieth-century Britain were mobilized to confront the crisis of total war. Here, the emphasis is on national identity as a source of selfhood. Certain kinds of sounds and ways of hearing were defined as characteristically national during the Second World War. Wartime heightens the politics of national belonging and intensifies, as Carolyn Birdsall has shown in the case of Germany during the Second World War, attempts to intervene in everyday sound and hearing.[87] In Britain, as in Germany, the war heightened the significance of both everyday sound (as a result of air-raid sirens, bomb noises, and radio broadcasts) and of national ways of hearing. The two came to be closely entwined in debates about good wartime citizenship, but this process took different paths in Britain than it did in Germany, not only because of the differing war experiences of these two countries, but also because of the specificities of national imaginaries at any given moment in time. While Chapters 1, 2, and 3 detail the specific forms that the transnational age-of-noise narrative took in Britain, Chapter 4 deals explicitly with the sonic politics of Britishness. During the war, the Anti-Noise League set itself the task of providing quiet rest breaks to air-raid protection workers and chastised those who did not understand the national importance of taking a sonic break from the blitz; government scientists attempted to measure the effects of noise on the psyche-at-war as part of wider efforts to protect national morale; even occultist theories of the vibrating self were put to use for the war effort through self-help manuals for the nervous. This chapter proposes that the "people's war" narrative, which has come to dominate the memory of the Second World War in Britain, requires scrutiny from an auditory perspective. Sound was used to project an image of wartime togetherness but also to construct the exclusionary norms of Britishness.

Taken together, the following chapters aim to disrupt visually orientated interpretations of modernity and point to the importance of sound in the imagination and negotiation of modern ways of being in early-twentieth-century Britain. As the final chapter shows, taking a sonic approach to modern British history can open up new ways of analyzing familiar topics, such as national belonging in the Second World War. The aim of Chapter 4, and indeed the aim of the book as a whole, is to point toward the importance of taking sound into account in our analysis of cultural and social history, and in doing so my hope is ultimately to prompt a new aural sensitivity in our engagement with the modern past.

1 Modernity as Crisis

Noise and "Nerves"

[T]he noise goes on, and it goes on getting louder and louder,
and more and more prolonged. And, by malignant fate, one
individual after another is, as it were, picked out from the crowd
for special attention by this modern fiend.
—Dan McKenzie, "The Crusade against Noise" (1928)

By the turn of the twentieth century, Britain had experienced over a century
of dizzying transformation. The beginning of the new century was marked
by widespread anxiety about the ongoing pace of change. This took the form,
among other cultural trends, of concern about modern life's impact on the
health of the human body.[1] Both within and beyond the medical profession,
commentators worried that "modern civilization" had overtaken the body's
innate capacity to adjust and predicted that the human mechanism would
buckle under the strain.[2] The shattered nerves of the soldiers who returned
from the trenches of the Great War epitomized the most extreme clash
between humanity and technologized modernity, but on the streets of all
towns and cities the exhausting influence of rush and sensation was increasingly apparent.[3] Being modern became increasingly synonymous with being
"nervous" in early-twentieth-century culture.[4] Modernity was overstimulat-
ing, energy-draining, concentration-sapping, an assault on the senses and
the nerves. It was cast as pathogenic, especially by those who wished to stifle
its momentum.

Georg Simmel, canonical sociologist of early-twentieth-century modernity, influentially identified *visual* overstimulation as the predominant characteristic of modernity's nerve-wracking influence. He argued that cities
bombard their inhabitants with optical information—adverts, buildings,
traffic, crowds of people—and that they become "blasé" as a result.[5] This
visual preoccupation has been maintained by philosophers of modernity
from Walter Benjamin to Michel Foucault.[6] However, it was, in fact, more

common in early-twentieth-century Britain for *sound* to be identified as the source of mental alteration in urban populations. Urban noise tended to be heard not as one among many pathological features of the modern age but as the preeminent manifestation of an unhealthy paradox at the heart of modernity: the more it progressed, the unhealthier it became. Noise was heard as an aural signifier of progress—industrial, technological, and social—but also as its potential undoing due to its nefarious influence on health. The constant hum and vibration of the sonic city was identified by medical experts as a key factor in the worsening mental state of its inhabitants. Often, as in McKenzie's description in the epigraph to this chapter, noise was described not just as a product of the modern age but, implicitly, as the vibrational embodiment of modernity itself.[7]

Towns and cities had long been thought of as noisy places, and people had long complained about street and neighbor noise.[8] As John M. Picker has shown, Victorian intellectuals, including the mathematician Charles Babbage and the writer Charles Dickens, campaigned against street noises in the mid–nineteenth century on the grounds that their "brain work" was being made impossible by urban cacophony.[9] Yet noise-sensitive Britons of the early twentieth century were adamant that their urban soundscape was more threatening to health than anything that had come before it. They identified new technologies, including, in particular, motor traffic and the loudspeakers of gramophone and wireless sets, as the source of this threat. Oxford University magazine, the *Isis*, insisted that nineteenth-century man had not been "reduced to a bundle of nerves by the incessant din of motor cars, barrel organs, electric trams, pianolas and gramophones, and all the hundred and one inventions of his Satanic Majesty which make our life a torment!"[10] Marking out early-twentieth-century noise critique from that which had come before it was the sustained expert medicalization of noise as a social problem—a crisis of "nerves"—and the deliberate attempt to pathologize modernity itself through this process.[11]

A firm consensus about noise as a public health crisis emerged at the end of the 1920s following a noticeable increase of motor traffic in urban centers. It was in this middle part of the interwar period that the noise problem was formalized in medical terms and a systematic response to it emerged in the shape of organized noise abatement campaigns. Following a report on noise and public health published by the British Medical Association in 1928, a national Anti-Noise League, led by prominent medical men, was established in London in 1933. Similar organizations sprung up in many of Europe and North America's major cities, often led, as in Britain, by medical experts.[12] These organizations lobbied national and local governments to take action against "unnecessary noise." While the solution to the problem of noise lay with engineers and architects whose expertise could be turned to creating quieter urban environments, doctors defined the nature of the problem itself in Britain and elsewhere. They dramatized it as a peculiarly modern problem and set the parameters within which other sound experts worked. This chapter deals, for that reason, with the role of medical experts in transforming the early-twentieth-century soundscape into a sociomedical problem.

Historians of noise Emily Thompson and Karin Bijsterveld have demonstrated the importance of understanding the interplay between cultural and scientific constructions of sound in the past. My aim in this chapter is to build on their investigations of early-twentieth-century noise abatement campaigns by focusing sustained critical attention on the medical foundations of these campaigns. While Thompson and Bijsterveld center their attention on the desire to control noise through scientific and technical mastery or through public education programs, this chapter focuses on the original medical basis, relating to claims about "nerves," through which noise was transformed into a public health crisis in the interwar period. This process, like the ones Thompson and Bijsterveld describe, depended on cultural as well as medical ideas about the sensate body in modernity.[13] My argument is that noise's medicalization in this period is deserving of attention in its own right. By analyzing this process, I argue, we can come to better understand why and how noise entered into the channels of public debate in the years after 1914, why the noise abatement campaign took the form that it did in the 1930s, and why it failed to achieve as much impact in legislative terms as its leaders would have liked in the period up to 1945.

Bijsterveld observes that "public problems need convincing drama" in order to be constituted as such. In the case of Britain's interwar noise abatement campaign it was the drama of "nerves" that played the pivotal role.[14] Medical supporters of noise abatement such as McKenzie argued that noise causes constant, arhythmical, vibration of the body's nervous system and that this physical onslaught leads to fatigue, exhaustion and, finally, to complete nervous breakdown.[15] At the intermediate stage, sufferers from overexposure to noise were likely to be distracted, jumpy, and incapable of sustained and productive work—key signs of nervousness, or neurasthenia as it was described in specialized medical texts. Supporters of noise abatement warned that neurasthenia would become an epidemic in Britain unless action was taken against noise. Although this drama of nerves may have been convincing to public audiences familiar with popular narratives of nervous illness circulating in literary, self-help, and news discourse at the time, in official circles it held less sway. This was because the theory of neurasthenia, dependent as it was on a late-nineteenth-century physiological explanation for nervous breakdown, was rapidly losing ground to a new psychological paradigm in the study and treatment of mental illness. Given that medical historians such as Marijke Gijswijt-Hofstra have argued that the First World War "marked the more or less final retreat of neurasthenia" as a credible diagnostic category, it is all the more surprising that it should have remained so prominent in the noise abatement campaign during the 1930s.[16] My argument in this chapter is that, despite its increasingly outdated status in scientific terms, the neurasthenic paradigm remained useful to supporters of noise abatement because it allowed them to categorize noise as a *physical* health hazard equal to smoke or dirty water in its damaging health effects. Psychologists, in contrast, were beginning to locate mental illness in the mind rather than in the body, and to replace the language of neurasthenia with the language of psychoneurosis. For supporters of noise abatement, it remained useful to draw upon older somatic rather than the newer psychosomatic explanations for noise's effects. As Chapter 3 points out, the new professional psychologists of the early twentieth century identified noise sensitivity as a symptom rather than as a cause of mental illness and, in doing so, reduced sound's significance as a concern in public health. The desire to develop medical justification for noise abatement was, this chapter argues, one of the reasons for the extension of the neurasthenic paradigm into the psychological age.

There were other, cultural, reasons for the noise abatement campaign's adoption of the neurasthenic model in their medicalization of city sounds. From its origins in the 1870s, neurasthenic theory had been intertwined with a critique of what writers on the topic referred to as "modern civilization." Supporters of noise abatement drew on this critique as much as they did the medical elements of neurasthenic theory. The interwar noise abatement campaign defined modernity as a crisis of human civilization, the solution to which, short of turning back the clock on technological revolution, was the preservation of quiet spaces of auditory refuge and sanctuary. These spaces were necessary because supporters of noise abatement equated self-hood with quietness and with the possibility of mental separation from the sensory conditions of urban mass society. Neurasthenia offered them a useful counter-model: the nervous patient was one who could not hold him/herself together, whose inner self was endlessly susceptible to the noises and sensations of the modern world. Nervousness, a term used interchangeably with neurasthenia, had come to be described as a paradigm of modern selfhood, as a modern state of being, in novels and in other forms of writing, including early examples of self-help publishing. Summed up by American self-help writer, Robert S. Carroll, as "a life of emotional intoxication and superficial judgments in the nerve-exhausting struggle" of the modern city, the nervous self was said to be addicted to "diversion and pleasure" due to the constant stimulation it received in the modern urban environment.[17] Self-help writers warned against this state of being and sought to find ways of returning people to calmer times. Rejecting this advice, avant-garde artists sometimes embraced neurasthenia as a state of selfhood allied to their embrace of the modern.[18] Most people were somewhere in between, neither fully embracing of modern flux nor entirely averse to its pleasures. Either way, cultures of nervousness encouraged processes of self-imagination in which the boundary between the inner self and the external sensory world was constructed as hazardously porous. The nervous self was situated in, and constituted by, the experience of living in the modern urban environment.

This was a model of selfhood that supporters of noise abatement vehemently sought to resist, for in some ways little had changed since Dickens's day. Noise abatement remained the cause of a particular class of people who believed, above all, that noise was a threat to the quiet thought and self-reflection necessary for intellectual leadership. While they attempted to cast noise as a threat to all kinds of people, the founders of the Anti-Noise League were particularly concerned about its effect on "the intelligent section" of society.[19] They tended to point to the professional classes whose day-to-day working life, they said, depended on peace and quiet. This chapter thus extends Picker's argument about the centrality of noise antipathy to Victorian professional identity.[20] The growth of modern urban noise represented, to supporters of noise abatement, a crisis of quiet intellectuality in the twentieth-century city in which the mental isolation necessary for thought to take place and for intellectual selfhood to form was destroyed by the intrusions of sound. This intrusive sound was the product of a mass modernity, typified by the motor car and the gramophone loudspeaker, which they saw as emanating from classes of people whose work and selfhood did not depend on quiet thought. "The world over there is an absence of quiet thought," wrote one prominent British noise abatement leader, paraphrasing Shakespeare, "and in its place much 'sound and fury' which often signifies nothing but sound and fury."[21]

This chapter examines the way in which supporters of noise abatement developed medical arguments in support of their fear that the urban soundscape was eroding the conditions for quiet, individual selfhood and examines the cultural politics inherent in this process of medicalization. It traces the evolution of neurasthenia, the medical theory from which the category of nervousness emerged, from its origins in late-nineteenth-century neurology to its structuring influence on interwar noise abatement discourse. Neurasthenia, it will be argued, was a theory in which medical and cultural critique intermingled. It was used not only to diagnose the effects of noise on health but also to characterize modernity, and the modern city in particular, as unhealthy and in terminal decline. The theory's pessimistic outlook on modernity led supporters of noise abatement to the conclusion that only reduction of noise and of the cultural forces that brought it into being could rescue humanity from itself.

Neurasthenia and the Origins of Medicalized Noise Critique

Neurasthenia, a condition of nervous exhaustion or lack of nerve force characteristic of those on the downward spiral into nervous breakdown, was popularized as a diagnosis in the 1880s and 1890s following the publication of three influential books by the American neurologist George M. Beard: *A Practical Treatise on Nervous Exhaustion* (1880), *American Nervousness: Its Causes and Consequences* (1881), and *Sexual Neurasthenia* (1889).[22] Despite having North American origins and the fact that Beard termed it a typically American disease, neurasthenia was quickly adopted by doctors in Britain and across Europe keen to explain the increasing prevalence of nervous disorders in their own countries.[23] The premise of Beard's theory of nervousness was that each individual has at his or her disposal a certain amount of nerve force, or energy, which can be augmented or diminished by lifestyle and by the influence of the environment. The body's nervous system was described by Beard as analogous to an electrical circuit: a current, produced at one end, was used up at the other. Indeed, Beard and his followers often treated neurasthenia with electrotherapy, believing that the nervous system's vitality could be rekindled by contact with an actual electrical current.[24] A healthy nervous system was thought, by Beard, to depend on an individual's maintenance of the right balance between "recharging the batteries" and expenditure of energy. Nerve force could, according to Beard, be "increased or diminished by good or evil influences."[25] Sleep was an example of a good influence. Overwork, on the other hand, was a common cause of neurasthenic breakdown. He also identified certain wasteful activities, such as masturbation and gambling, as depleting the nervous system's reserve of energy, providing a moral component to the neurasthenic diagnosis.[26] Another frequently used metaphor likened nervous vitality to economic capital or to the contents of one's wallet: expenditure that outstripped income was sure to lead to nervous breakdown. As Tom Lutz points out in his history of American nervousness,

"The links between medical thinking, economics, and the links to morality were constantly apparent to both doctors and patients."[27]

Among the very many symptoms of neurasthenia, Beard identified the following as telltale signs of the condition:

> Insomnia, flushing, drowsiness, bad dreams, cerebral irritation, dilated pupils, pain, pressure and heaviness in the head, changes in the expression of the eye … fear of lightning, or fear of responsibility, of open places or of closed places, fear of society, fear of being alone, fear of fears, fear of contamination, fear of everything, deficient mental control, lack of decision in trifling matters, hopelessness, deficient thirst and capacity for assimilating fluids, abnormalities of the secretions, salivation, tenderness of the spine, and of the whole body.[28]

Neurasthenics were also likely to show hypersensitivity to visual, auditory, and other sensory experiences as a result of the weakened state of their nervous systems. Such symptoms did not yet have any medical explanation and doctors were glad to be able to gather them under the new category of neurasthenia. Sufferers came to be easily recognizable not only by doctors, but also by the population at large, for whom neurasthenia was popularized through fictional accounts and through the advertising of various nerve tonics.[29] British physician and medical writer, Edwin Ash, argued in 1911 that "persons whose nervous systems are constitutionally weak form a definite type, and one which one can recognize easily amongst those around us." Outward signs of nervousness, according to Ash, included "nervous hands with tapered fingers and thin, active limbs."[30]

While particularly overworked or immoral people could induce neurasthenia by dint of their misguided behavior, for most sufferers of the condition the cause was nothing more or less than the overstimulation and strain inherent in modern life. "Civilization alone does not cause nervousness," Beard argued, since after all, "the Greeks were certainly civilized, but they were not nervous, and in the Greek language there is no word for that term."[31] Sped-up and sensation-laden modernity damaged the body's nervous system and drained its energy. "Modern nerve sensitiveness" was attributed, accordingly, to the peculiar strains of modern civilization.[32] As Ash, a prolific writer on nervousness, put it in 1919, "The pace grows and the brain reels under the stimulation of rapid transit, quick communication, and competitive stress. Only the fit can survive the turmoil."[33] Modernity's role in increasing the prevalence of nervous diseases had been widely propagated in late-nineteenth-century thought. In an 1880 lecture delivered to the Chicago Philosophical Society, for example, J. S. Jewell, a well-known American neurologist and president of the American Neurological Association, stated that he was, "firmly convinced" that modern civilization "carries with it the causes or conditions of decay, or even of its final destruction." Like Beard, he identified the nervous system as the "chief theatre" of this "ruin."[34] Among the stimulants that Beard identified as both characteristically modern and an especial drain on nervous energy were steam power, the periodical press, the telegraph, the sciences, and "the mental activity of women." These, he argued, were the hallmarks of "modern civilization."[35] The neurasthenic diagnosis thus explicitly contrasted the essentially healthy quality of preindustrial economies and cultural norms with the stress of late-nineteenth-century commerce, communication, and social upheaval. From the beginning, neurasthenia was a critique of modernity as much as it was a medical diagnosis.

Neurasthenia was welcomed into the diagnostic repertoire by late Victorian and Edwardian doctors because it offered them a means to explain cases of mental illness or breakdown that had no obviously physical, or "organic," cause. Such functional mental disorders had remained scientifically unexplainable throughout the nineteenth century.[36] By the middle of the twentieth century, these disorders were almost exclusively diagnosed as psychopathologies, that is, as having their origin in the mind rather than the body. But in the decades on either side of 1900, having a diagnosis at their disposal that identified somatic causes for a variety of mental illnesses was extremely attractive to medical practitioners. Coming just before the popularization of psychological theories and psychotherapeutic treatments, the neurasthenic diagnosis allowed doctors to offer advice about lifestyle and behavior while maintaining that nervous illness was a physical disorder of the nerves, a somatic illness, rather than a psychological disorder. As Barbara Sicherman argues, the neurasthenic diagnosis allowed doctors "to provide an essentially psychological therapy under a somatic label."[37] Neurasthenics were thought to be mentally deficient, but this deficiency was caused by physical disruption to the nervous system, including the brain, caused by the strain of living in modern times.

Because Beard's theory of neurasthenia identified the influence of modern civilization as the cause of functional disorder of the nervous system, it was attractive to those in search of medical explanations of noise's effect on the body. It stood to reason that if nervousness was caused by the conditions of modernity then noise, as a preeminent by-product of the mechanical age, might also be a significant cause of nervous illness. Ash, for one, promoted this conclusion in a raft of specialist medical texts and in books produced for the newly emerging self-help market over the course of the early twentieth century. His argument was based on the theory that noise causes the nervous system to vibrate irregularly. "Every vibration reaching the ear," he explained, "calls up a corresponding vibration in the brain. And so, also, the delicate brain cells in their turn have to bear the stress of an abnormal shaking, and consequently break down under the strain. In this way a disharmony is set up which spreads until the whole nervous system is jangled and out of tune."[38] Writings on the nervous system often likened its operation to that of a musical instrument, which, if working properly, was said to be in tune, but if broken, was discordant and out of harmony with nature.[39] Self-help books for the nervous, such as Ash's, made use of this analogy to assist readers in their understanding of the nervous system, but it also allowed them to make a stronger case against noise.

Although Beard himself had not identified noise as a major contributor to nervous illness, he did consider it to be a factor worthy of consideration. This may help to explain why noise and neurasthenia remained so closely conjoined in early-twentieth-century medical thought and in medical self-help literature. Beard wrote in *American Nervousness*, that, despite being a topic "which seems to have been but incidentally studied . . . the relation of noise to nervousness and nervous diseases is a subject of not a little interest."[40] His initial discussion of the topic relied heavily on claims about the unnatural vibrational and rhythmic qualities of noise. He argued that man-made noise is inharmonious and unrhythmic in comparison to the regularity and structure of the natural soundscape:

> The noises that nature is constantly producing—the moans and roar of the wind, the rustling and trembling of the leaves and swaying of the branches, the roar of the sea and of waterfalls, the singing of birds, and even the cries of some wild animals—are mostly rhythmical to a greater or less degree, and always varying if not intermittent; to a savage or to a refined ear, on cultured or uncultured brains, they are rarely distressing, often pleasing, sometimes delightful and inspiring.[41]

On the other hand, "appliances and accompaniments of civilization" cause "noises that are unrhythmical, unmelodious and therefore annoying, if not injurious." These include, "manufactures, locomotion, travel, housekeeping even."[42]

The medical justification for noise abatement was indeed suggested by Beard in *American Nervousness*, a book that explicitly identified the physical damage caused by the irregular sound waves of modern noises as a potential contributory factor in neurasthenic illness:

> [W]hen all these elements are concentrated, as in great cities, they maintain through all the waking and some of the sleeping hours, an unintermittent vibration in the air that is more or less disagreeable to all, and in the case of an idiosyncrasy or severe illness may be unbearable and harmful.[43]

Noise causes "severe molecular disturbance," according to Beard, and for this reason is an exhausting influence on the nervous system.[44] Because the operation of the body's nervous system is essentially rhythmic and regular, according to Beard, the unrhythmical noises of modernity had the potential to undermine bodily order. In contrast, "rhythmical, melodious, musical sounds are not only agreeable, but when not too long maintained are beneficial, and may be ranked among our therapeutical agencies."[45] For Beard and those who followed him in the study of nervous illness, harmony and rhythm were important concepts for explaining the health or otherwise of the body's nervous system in the conditions of industrial and urban modernity.

The First World War was an important turning point in medical discussions of noise and nervousness. It was widely acknowledged during and immediately after the war that shell shock, the functional nervous disorder affecting those who fought in the trenches and often categorized as a neurasthenic condition, was caused at least as much by the sensory experience of shelling as it was by fear of death, and that among the most harmful of these sensory attributes of the war was the noise associated with shelling.[46] Ash's book on *The Problem of Nervous Breakdown* explained, in relation to shelling, that "the noise alone is sufficient to cause such vibrations in the brain and special sense organs as not infrequently to overwhelm them; shells and bombs, mines and aerial torpedoes, bursting with ceaseless din, have combined in such an assault of sound as the human nervous system has never before been asked to explain."[47] He added in his book *Nerve in Wartime* that, "it is not surprising that soldiers go raving mad on the field of battle, where the continual noise of bombardment is a most powerful factor in shattering nerves."[48] In addition, the mental fortitude required of the British population at home under the strain of wartime conditions made the threat of neurasthenia not only a question of individual wellbeing, or of economic productivity, but also a question of national defense, as Ash noted: "With nations as with individuals, it is nerve which determines success or failure in any undertaking."[49] The preservation of nervous energy increasingly came to be seen as a patriotic duty during and after the First World War.

The first major medical text on noise appeared in Britain during the war, in 1916, and drew heavily on Beard's original formulation of neurasthenia. *City of Din: A Tirade against Noise* by Dan McKenzie, stuck closely to Beard in its statement that "Civilization is noise. At least modern civilization is. And the more it progresses the noisier it becomes."[50] McKenzie, who practiced at the Central London Throat and Ear Hospital and edited the *Journal of Laryngology and Otology*, was among the first in Britain to systematically make the connection between modern civilization, noise, and nervousness.

"We have to pay for our comforts in racket," he wrote. "What tinnitus is to a deaf patient, the noises of civilization are to the city-dweller. The modern city is suffering from tinnitus, as incessant, as persistent, as distracting, as that symptom can be at its worst."[51] In contrast to the countryside, whose "pleasant sounds" bring "joy, health, and quiet breathing," the London of the early twentieth century was filled with noises, "of a deeper, more thunderous, and more overpowering nature than in former days," which amounted to a "continual battering of the nerve-centres."[52] McKenzie thus explicitly adopted Beard's explanation of noise's effect on health. Like Beard, McKenzie defined noise in relation to the rhythmic structure of music. He suggested that music should be regarded by the "philosopher of Quiet," as "the provision of a sanctuary of refuge in the heart of the City of Din." In music, "not only the bruised spirit but also the aching ear may find rest and healing."[53] Music was an example, for McKenzie, as for Beard, of a "good" and restorative influence on the nervous system's reserve of energy.

Given the ancient belief in the therapeutic health benefits of music, it was a logical step to attribute damaging health affects to noise and to define noise as a chaotic other to music.[54] The relationship between music and noise in the writings of Beard and McKenzie should also be understood in relation to Jon Agar's claim that an order-disorder dualism was at the heart of twentieth-century noise abatement. Bodies and machines, Agar argues, are both potential sites of disorder.[55] The disorderly noise made by machines caused bodily disorder in those who were subjected to it day and night in the modern city. Although Agar makes no mention of it, music played an important role in defining what sonic order should sound like. Doctors such as Beard and McKenzie therefore played a role not only in problematizing noise in medical terms, but also in defining noise as a sonic category distinct from natural sounds or certain kinds of music, with rhythm or its absence being the key determinant in this differentiation.

For McKenzie, whereas rhythmic sound "carries us forward as on wings, the sound stimulus passing direct from ear to muscle in such a way as to render our movements automatic" as in dancing or marching, "arrhythmic" sound, on the other hand, takes us to a "strange" and "unfriendly" world of "chaos" in which our muscles are caused to move irregularly.[56] A state of nervousness is brought about precisely by the unpredictable temporal character of arrhythmic sound. Because we never know when we will be startled by a loud and unexpected noise in the modern city, we become nervous in expectation of the shock, whose arrival may come in a minute, or this evening, or indeed not for a week or a month. Thus, the term *nervousness* signified not only sensory overstimulation but also fearful anticipation of temporally unpredictable auditory shocks. McKenzie evoked this experience in a later article: "You are lying awake at night listening in the darkness," he wrote, "with that expectant intentness that constitutes its torture, to the tram surfacemen cutting through a steel rail with the cold chisel, the sharp, shrieking ring of each blow echoing through your brain like a recurrent pang of physical pain."[57]

Music remained a common reference point for those wishing to define noise throughout the early twentieth century. A 1940 article in the noise abatement magazine *Quiet* by the famous conductor, Sir Henry Wood, for example, argued that "music of the great masters played by a fine orchestra is not 'silence' but it brings to us a quiet, and calm, in these senseless and unhappy days, like unto a silence following a great noise."[58] Wood's reference to "music of the great masters" is suggestive of the cultural politics of this discourse: only the right kinds of music would bring about the restoration of nervous energy. New kinds of music, including both jazz and certain kinds of modernist experimental music, were held to be as damaging and wasteful of the body's nervous energy as noise due to their unnatural rhythmical and vibrational structure.[59] It should also be noted, however, that the kind of nerve sensitiveness identified by Beard and Jewell as a product of modern civilization was considered to have arisen partly as a result of the high cultivation of the senses demanded by the arts. "The more a part of the nervous system is used the more extended its development," wrote Jewell. For this reason, nervous disorders were thought to be most common in those who devoted themselves more than others to "the study and practice of art in its various forms."[60] Thus, while it may have provided a refuge for men such as McKenzie and Wood, cultivation of heightened musical sensitivity led, according to Jewell and others, to a concomitant sensitivity to noise. While music offered respite from the age of noise, it was also partly to blame for the highly strung state of what might be termed the "sensitive classes."

This reveals another important aspect of the neurasthenic diagnosis. Neurasthenia, in contrast to hysteria, for example, was often reserved for middle- and upper-class patients, and often also for men, at least in the pre–First World War period.[61] Neurasthenia, like noise, was an especial threat to those occupied in intellectual work, because they were most likely to overstrain their nerves through long hours of mental activity and through overexposure to aesthetic pleasures. Ash indicated the class and gender specificity inherent in the neurasthenic diagnosis. "The average person," he wrote, "probably never realises the ceaseless loss which is incurred to the nation by the premature breakdown of men who would unquestionably do lasting work of the greatest public importance as lawyers, social reformers, preachers, journalists, physicians or surgeons, were they able to recover their lost health."[62] This is a further reason why neurasthenia and noise abatement came to be such closely intertwined discourses in early-twentieth-century Britain. Those who typically led interwar noise abatement campaigns, as this chapter goes on to point out, were men of the professional classes who, like Dickens and Babbage before them, objected to urban din on the basis that it distracted them from their brain work.

Twentieth-Century Nervousness: Narrating the Age of Noise

It is clear enough from texts such as *City of Din* that the diagnostic category of neurasthenia underpinned the medicalization of noise in the period up to and including the First World War. The question remains, however, why neurasthenia remained so prevalent in the interwar campaign against noise, which gathered pace in the late 1920s, leading to the establishment of organizations such as the Anti-Noise League in the early 1930s. Historians of medicine have argued more or less unequivocally that, following the popularization of Freudian psychoanalysis in the early years of the twentieth century, neurasthenia was replaced by a psychological paradigm in the explanation of neurosis that had no recourse to claims about physical damage to the nervous system. *Neur*asthenia was replaced by *psych*asthenia, they point out. Sicherman, for example, argues that the uptake of the pioneering work of psychpathologists such as Freud and Pierre Janet caused Beard's theory of neurasthenia to be "effectively demolished by 1920."[63]

Yet when, in the late 1920s, the British medical profession took it upon itself to lobby government ministers about the damaging effects of noise on health, their main frame of reference was neurasthenia. In 1905, the Betterment of London Association had written to the government's Street Noise Abatement Committee, a hangover from mid-Victorian street noise campaigns, stating that "the medical profession testifies very sympathetically to the great increase in nervous diseases caused by the increased volume of irritating and disturbing noise which so continually assails the ear, injuring nerves and brain."[64] It was not until the late 1920s, however, that medical organizations, including the British Medical Association (BMA) and the People's League of Health, began to seriously urge government ministers and officials to consider noise as a threat to public health. The medical profession's unity on the question of noise was ensured by a resolution passed at the BMA's annual meeting in Cardiff in October 1928. Shortly afterward, the Association sent a "Memorandum of Evidence on Noise and Public

Health" to the Minister of Health, Neville Chamberlain, stating that "in the interest of the public health the British Medical Association support any measures which may be taken so to alter or amend existing legislation as to give greater power to local authorities to suppress unnecessary noise" and suggesting that "any noise from 11pm to 6am which is capable of being prevented or mitigated and which is dangerous or injurious to health, shall be a nuisance within the meaning of the Public Health Acts."[65]

Neurasthenia was at the forefront of the BMA's justification for this legislative change. Its memorandum claimed that noise was a concern to "the neurasthenic, the sufferer from functional nervous disorder, whose condition, if not actually caused by such noises, is aggravated by them."[66] Yet more starkly, it noted that "much neurosis of the inhabitants of big cities may be regarded as analogous to the shell shock that followed deafening bombardments during the war."[67] The People's League of Health sent a joint deputation with the BMA to the Ministry of Health in December 1928; it was introduced by the eminent physician, Sir Thomas Horder, who had made his name at St. Bartholomew's Hospital in London and regularly treated members of the Royal Family. The members of his deputation made frequent reference in their evidence to the link between noise and neurasthenia. Professor George Robertson, for example, explained that "the effect of noise, especially prolonged noise, on the nervous system may be in the nature of a constant strain and drain on nervous energy and this may lead ultimately to exhaustion. It is this action of noise, causing nervous and mental exhaustion, that leads to neurasthenia."[68] He added that neurasthenia was "a condition commoner now than formerly" and that this was due in no small part to the effects of modern urban noise. Robertson added for good measure that "the consequence of neurasthenia, apart from the misery it entails, is a loss of national efficiency, which is an important matter in these days of struggle and competition."[69]

The physician and psychiatrist, Sir Robert Armstrong-Jones, who was at the time the Lord Chancellor's Visitor in Lunacy and had previously been Consulting Physician in Mental Diseases at St. Bartholomew's Hospital, made the all-important claim that neurasthenia, once a condition affecting mainly educated men, was now manifesting itself across the class spectrum. He drew attention in particular to noise as a cause of sleeplessness in working-class men:

> He goes to bed tired and exhausted, but he is repeatedly roused, and his sleep disturbed by loud and most disturbing noises. He rises in the morning shaky, confused, and unrefreshed after his so-called "night's rest." His health suffers,

his work deteriorates and he eventually joins the highly sensitive neurasthenic, who jumps even when the clock strikes."[70]

There could, doctors hoped, be little doubt in the minds of the government ministers who received this advice. The growing noisiness of cities threatened to bring about mass neurasthenia in urban populations.

It remained common right through the 1920s, '30s, and '40s for discussions of noise to take place in the context of concern about neurasthenia and the nervous energy of the nation. National newspapers eagerly reported this advice in the same way that they now report on expert medical advice about the damage to health done by alcohol and fatty food. In its report of a lecture by engineer and physicist, A. M. Low, to the Manchester Publicity Association in 1936, the *Manchester Guardian*, for example, noted that "the man who thought he had got so used to the noises of a works or a city that they had no effect on him, and that he would be really uncomfortable in the country without noise, was wrong. When people said that they had got rid of the effects of noise it simply meant that their bodies were putting out energy to counteract its effects."[71] This displacement could end only in neurasthenic breakdown, it was argued. The same article continued its paraphrasing of Low by warning that it was not enough to protect only the ears from noise, since "our whole bodies [are] sensitive to sound … it was useless to think that by stopping our ears we could escape it; it would enter through the bones of the head."[72] Modern noise was described as a residual and perhaps unnoticed environmental force causing a gradual and imperceptible decline in the mental health of urbanites, no matter what their class. The fact is that even if psychological paradigms were gaining ground in the explanation of mental illness, the somatic paradigm of neurasthenia remained useful as a means by which to transform cultural antipathy to noise into a medical theory that was not only scientifically credible, at least in the short term, but also easily explainable to nonspecialist audiences, who would have been familiar with ideas about nerves and nervousness. The language of nerves gave discussions of noise an immediate narrative coherence in relation to the dangers of modern life that translated easily onto the pages of the daily newspapers.

However, we should not be too quick to assume that the prominence of neurasthenia in medical explanations for noise's effect was purely for rhetorical effect. The case of interwar noise abatement requires an alteration to the medical historical consensus that neurasthenia was more or less entirely discarded as a serious diagnostic category after 1920. Medical writings on noise demonstrate that the new psychological paradigm of the early twentieth century did not mark as sharp a break with pre–First World War somatic explanations of mental illness as medical historians have often been inclined to think. The case of Edwin Ash usefully illustrates this point. Although he practiced as a conventional physician at St. Mary's Hospital in London, Ash enthusiastically adopted the principles of psychotherapeutic treatment, and his popular self-help books written between 1910 and 1928 were based on psychological principles.[73] He was a keen advocate of suggestion and autosuggestion in the cure of nervous illness, indicating that such illnesses *could* be overcome through the power of the mind. But at the same time, he maintained that those who experienced nervous breakdown were indeed suffering from *physical* deterioration of the nerves. Ash had proposed psychotherapeutic cures for neurasthenia as early as 1910 in his book, *Mind and Health: The Mental Factor and Suggestion in Treatment with Special Reference to Neurasthenia and other Common Nervous Disorders.*[74] Here and elsewhere, Ash explicitly combined somatic and psychological models in his explanation of neurasthenic breakdown. While neurasthenia, argued Ash, is "a disease of disordered function; an exhaustion of nerve-centres," it is also brought about by "a weakening of thought-control opening the way to a breakdown."[75] It was precisely this duality of physical illness and psychological vulnerability that led to neurasthenia. One without the other was unlikely to have much effect. "As a matter of practical experience," wrote Ash, "one usually finds causes both mental and physical in any particular case [of nervous breakdown], and it is difficult to disentangle the separate causative ailments, but an entirely wrong conception of nervous conditions will be obtained by those who over-estimate the influence of either cause."[76]

In the case of noise, Ash's theory of a two-pronged cause of mental breakdown meant that although neurasthenic symptoms could be brought on by noise's vibration in the nervous system, their effect could be mitigated by proper training of the mind. This was an approach explicitly advocated by other popular psychological self-help writers, including H. Ernest Hunt, whose 1918 book *Self-Training: The Lines of Mental Progress* argued that "successful living" is "largely a matter of building correct dominant ideas into the subconscious." The result of this mind training, Hunt argued, "is ease and absence of friction; wrong dominants ensure the opposites, disease and friction."[77] Influencing the operation of one's subconscious mind also entailed, according to Hunt, "training the senses."[78] Hunt argued that sense data from the exterior world passes through the nervous system directly into the subconscious, and that it falls to "the intricate machinery of the inner self" to transform these signals into "sight, sound or some other form of sensation."[79] If the mind has this powerful role to play in distinguishing sensations, then it stands to reason, according to Hunt, that we can train our subconscious mind, through the technique of autosuggestion, to resist the potentially disruptive influence of certain forms of sense experience, including noise. Like Ash, Hunt thought that mental breakdown could be observed in the physical deterioration of the nerves, but he believed that such deterioration could be prevented by harnessing the power of the conscious mind.[80] This argument was also put forward by American medical self-help writer Carroll, who explained that nervous patients show a "high capacity for response to external and internal stimuli" but argued, like Hunt, that this was a result, in part, of their mental "lack of selective and inhibitory control."[81]

Ash, for his part, was actually quite pessimistic about the possibility of using mind-training to resist the damaging effects of noise on the nervous system. He thought that noise was one of the principal factors responsible for what he termed "Londonitis," the particular form of neurasthenia brought about by living in the sensory conditions of early-twentieth-century London. Even with the rightly trained mind's power to resist neurasthenic breakdown, noise remained a pathogen of the utmost severity. Writing in 1928 at the time of the deputation on noise to the Ministry of Health, Ash concluded that "unless something is done to lessen the persistent noise and vibration to which the nerves of Londoners are so continually subjected breakdowns from this cause will eventually become an important factor in their lives. To-day it is not only the very sensitive who suffer; many who had always thought their nerves to be strong enough have been complaining bitterly of the noise and stress of London life."[82] The only way to mitigate noise's effects, thought Ash, was a program of noise abatement and regular excursion to the quiet of the countryside or the seaside.

The compatibility of somatic and psychological models in the early-twentieth-century medicalization of noise suggests that there was a good deal of continuity between Beard's original formulation of neurasthenia in the 1880s and the BMA's evidence about noise and nervousness of the late 1920s. Although such continuity runs counter to most histories of neurasthenia in the early twentieth century, it confirms Mathew Thomson's argument that we should remain sensitive to the continuities between late-nineteenth-century physiology of the nerves on the one hand and the early-twentieth-century's psychological explanation of nervous breakdown on the other.[83] It is precisely in the realms of this continuity, evident in the writings of self-help writers like Ash and Hunt, that urban noise was successfully transformed into an interwar public health crisis. Thomson points out that early-twentieth-century psychology emerged gradually out of several preexisting paradigms of ill health, of which neurasthenia was one very important reference point.

"Through the physiological screen of the nerves," explains Thomson, "a realm had already been opened up that was separate from the gloom of insanity, where a mix of physical and psychotherapeutic explanation and cure, rather inconsistently but in a cultural sense successfully, operated."[84] Petteri Pieti-kainen has, furthermore, pointed out that neurasthenia was not removed from the *Diagnostic and Statistical Manual of Mental Disorders* (DSM) until 1980, and claims, in support of Thomson, that during the twentieth century, despite a sharper separation between neurology and psychiatry than had been the case in the nineteenth century, "it was often anything but clear" to doctors whether the source of mental illness was in the body or in the mind.[85]

What *had* changed between Beard's initial formulation of neurasthenia and the BMA's use of it in relation to noise in the late 1920s was the class profile of the neurasthenic sufferer. While in the 1880s and 1890s the diag-nosis had been reserved mainly for middle- and upper-class patients (Carroll even described it as an "aristocratic disorder"[86]), by the interwar period it had become common to claim, as the BMA did in its 1928 memorandum on noise, that nervousness was now an epidemic affecting all classes of people. However, despite making such claims to government ministers, it is clear that, internally, the BMA and the People's League of Health were still more interested in the effects of noise on professional people than on manual workers and others. The BMA circulated an American report, upon which it drew for its first 1928 memorandum, which claimed that noise was especially threatening to the productivity of professional men. "Men of affairs, principals and executives," explained this report, "are perceptibly weakened by the incessant if unconscious strain upon their nervous systems caused by the din of typewriters and adding machines, and by the Babel of noise penetrating their offices from outside."[87] Their "capacity for clear thinking, hard work, and energetic action" is destroyed by noise, the report claimed. It was for this reason that the BMA's memorandum, while stating that the question of noise should be taken up "in the interests of public health," added that noise was particularly damaging to the productivity of "those occupied in brain work."[88] The interwar campaign against noise was launched, thus, in the interests of an alliance of self-identified professional "brain workers" who, despite making claims about the effects of noise on all classes of people in order to strengthen their case for legal change, were concerned first and foremost with protecting their own peace and quiet.

This alliance of brain workers foregrounded neurasthenia in their interwar campaign against noise in part because medical writers had successfully adapted it to the psychological age, but also, no less significantly, because it had remained current in broader, cultural, discourse. Neurasthenia had begun its life in Beard's formulation as *both* a medical diagnosis *and* a cultural critique of modernity, and it remained so in the interwar period. This depended not just on the willingness of doctors to update and make use of the neurasthenic diagnosis, but also on the continuing cultural and literary life of neurasthenia, which had itself begun at the end of the nineteenth century. Fiction writers of the 1890s, particularly those involved with the decadent movement associated with fin-de-siècle cultural pessimism, had been keen to incorporate neurasthenic and noise-sensitive characters into their literary narratives.[89] Decadent, ill, and overstimulated, fin-de-siècle writers often inhabited the neurasthenic persona in addition to depicting it on the pages of their books. Marcel Proust was the neurasthenic writer par excellence. So afflicted by neurasthenia was Proust that, finding city noise unbearable, he sealed himself in a cork-lined room.[90]

Gradually, as a consequence of this literary tradition, the figure of the noise-tortured neurasthenic became emblematic of the modern condition in cultural as well as in medical discourse. By the interwar period, decadent fiction and its authors had passed into the mythology of modernity. In Paris, the epicenter of Proustian decadence, the doctors who led the campaign against noise were particularly keen to illustrate their work with examples drawn from decadent fiction or from the lives of decadent writers.[91] When they did so, they drew deliberate parallels between the cultural crisis of the fin de siècle and the renewed cultural crisis of the interwar period.[92] This was a feature, too, of the British interwar noise abatement campaign. The late 1920s and 1930s were seen by the leaders of this campaign as caught up in a similar malaise to that which had affected the 1890s. Economic crisis and worsening international tensions along with more and more distracting and distressing technological innovation was at the root of this new cultural crisis. Narratives about neurasthenia were deliberately revitalized in the interwar period by those who remained pessimistic, or who were pessimistic anew, about the future of modern civilization. Neurasthenia remained useful not only as a way of medically explaining the effects of noise on the human mind and body, but also as a way of lending narrative coherence and cultural significance to the campaign against noise. British antinoise campaigners were aided in this process by fiction writers themselves. Since Dickens's day, writers had formed an important and vocal component of the brainworking alliance of antinoise campaigners. Science fiction writer, H. G. Wells, was the most prominent of these in interwar Britain. He was directly involved in the Anti-Noise League. In addition to being, as an intellectual brain-working man, the quintessential sufferer from noise, Wells's fiction also provided an imaginative bridge in the British noise abatement movement between the cultural pessimism of the 1890s and that of the 1930s. It was an important conduit through which the relevance of neurasthenia as a cultural category was maintained.[93]

Wells had produced his best-known work, including *The Time Machine* (1895) and *The War of the Worlds* (1898) in the 1890s.[94] *The Time Machine*, in particular, in which the ruling class of the future is revealed to have been weakened by the influences of mechanical civilization, was indebted to the theory of neurasthenia.[95] It was not until the early 1930s, however, that Wells began to explicitly link technological modernity with neurasthenia. His 1933 book, *The Shape of Things to Come*, published in the same year as the Anti-Noise League's formation (and remade as a film in 1936), is a pivotal text. Like *The Time Machine*, this book was a prediction of a dystopian future for civilization in its current state. Rather than situating this as a distant future, though, *The Shape of Things to Come* is based on an imagined history textbook from the year 2106 that recalls the entirety of the twentieth century. The notable chapter is entitled "1933: 'Progress' Comes to a Halt." In it, Wells wrote, imagining himself as a historian of the future, that "the year 1933 closed in a phase of dismayed apprehension."[96] Wells described the ailing economy, the unemployment, and the social unrest of 1933, adding that "everywhere, in everything, there was an ebb of vitality. A decline in the public health was becoming perceptible."[97] To this he added, "in the face of its financial and political perplexities mankind was becoming neurasthenic."[98]

The Shape of Things to Come is narrated from the perspective of the utopian world state of 2106 in which centralized control had been taken of commerce and employment. This is presented by Wells as the ultimate solution to neurasthenia, implying that nervousness and the free market are irreversibly bound up. "A struggle for sanity had to take place in the racial brain," explained Wells, "a great casting out of false assumptions, conventional distortions, hitherto uncriticised maxims and impossible 'rights,' a great clearing up of ideas about moral, material and biological relationships."[99] In his earlier novel, *The Secret Places of the Heart* (1922), Wells had made explicit reference to the *longue durée* of neurasthenia between the 1890s and the interwar period. The novel begins with a consultation between an overworked and nervous businessman, Sir Richmond Hardy, and his physician, Dr Martineau. Sir Richmond is the archetypal neurasthenic man. He is a senior figure in "The Fuel Commission," and Dr Martineau acknowledges that "we certainly can't afford to have you ill." Sir Richmond protests that, "I'm jangling damnably ... overwork." He also explains that he lies awake at night worrying about an economic and social "smash up." Dr Martineau's reply makes the all-important bridge between the 1890s and the interwar period:

> "This sense of a coming smash is epidemic," said the doctor. "It's at the back of all sorts of mental trouble. It is a new state of mind. Before the war it was abnormal—a phase of neurasthenia. Now it is almost the normal state with whole classes of intelligent people. Intelligent, I say. The others always have been casual and adventurous and always will be. A loss of confidence in the general background of life. So that we seem to float over abysses."[100]

Beard's linking of neurasthenia with national economic efficiency is present in this quote in the direct link made between Sir Richmond's nervousness, the fate of the imaginary Fuel Commission and the prospect of a national economic "smash up." Wells emphasized the potential disaster that would occur if educated, professional men were no longer able to lend society their expertise and leadership.

Wells was not the only interwar British novelist to take an interest in the cause of noise abatement. Aldous Huxley, another whose fiction was based on pessimistic visions of the future, heard noise as the preeminent symbol of an unhealthy civilization. His most famous novel, *Brave New World* (1932), tells of a dystopian future in which a total state has come to control the thoughts and actions of its populace. Unlike the benevolent future state of Wells's *The Shape of Things to Come*, Huxley's vision is deeply sinister. On the face of it, Huxley's future might be considered a utopia in which pain, suffering, unhappiness, and sexual frustration have been abolished through the means of genetic engineering and the mysterious "soma" drug that induces an immediate state of happiness. The class system has also been genetically fixed so as to render the social position of the elite secure and the menial work of the underclass enjoyable. Yet Huxley did not intend *Brave New World* to be read as utopian. He subtly undercut the apparent bliss of his future state in, for example, his explanation of the conditioning of lower-class babies, for whom the appeal of books and flowers is removed.

Given books to look at, the babies in the state nursery are simultaneously subjected to "a violent explosion. Shriller and ever shriller, a siren shrieked. Alarm bells maddeningly sounded. The children started, screamed; their faces were distorted with terror."[101] When given flowers, furthermore, the babies are subjected to electric shocks. "Books and loud noises, flowers and electric shocks—already in the infant mind these couples were compromisingly linked. . . . They'll grow up with what psychologists used to call 'instinctive' hatred of books and flowers. Reflexes unalterably conditioned. They'll be safe from books and botany all their lives."[102] The reason for this social conditioning is to render menial work fulfilling: "A love of nature keeps no factories busy," explains the doctor in charge of the program.[103] That Huxley chose to make a particular connection between the end of reading and the pain caused by violent noise in this section of *Brave New World* is indicative of the intellectual critique of noise shared by writers and doctors in 1930s Britain.

Huxley's nonfiction account of noise appeared in the preface he wrote in 1930 for M. Alderton Pink's book *A Realist Looks at Democracy*.[104] Pink's book was an elitist critique of liberal democracy's weaknesses. Pink claimed that the book was written in support of "the view widely held by the younger thinkers to-day [including by Huxley himself] that the germs of decay can already be observed in the mechanical society built up in our scientific age."[105] Pink argued that civilization could not go on progressing in the age of the machine and that increasing education and democracy would in fact bring only "diminishing returns." In his preface, Huxley cited noise as the foremost evidence of this law of diminishing returns. The increased mechanization of production, supposed Huxley, will bring ever-increasing amounts of leisure time to the working classes. This would lead to the "noisiest age in all history" precisely because of this increased leisure time. "The aim and end of all amusement is to kill thought; therefore, noise is an essential part of amusement," wrote Huxley. "And the more leisure men have and, consequently, the greater their need of thought-preventing amusement, the more noise will have to be made."[106] Although they only rarely admitted it, it is clear that most members of Britain's noise abatement movement shared Huxley's conclusion that the modern noise problem was caused by the leisure activities of "the masses." The *British Medical Journal*, for example, identified the source of noise as the thoughtless majority who, "in the stillness of the evening, if such an anachronistic term may still be permitted ... switch on the 'loud speaker' or grind noisy tunes from the gramophone." Identifying jazz as the music of choice for such people, the article complained that "it is as though the stresses of life were so unendurable that they must make a great noise to keep their spirits up."[107]

In support of his theory that this increase in noise would have a negative impact on society, Huxley continued by deploying an argument that would have been very familiar to readers of the *British Medical Journal*:

> The wireless and the gramophone have introduced the sonorous equivalent of a boiler factory into every home. But however willing the jazz-loving spirit, the flesh is weak. A point is reached, after which noise gives diminishing returns in thought-killing pleasure and produces instead disturbing pathological symptoms. Alienists attribute a considerable percentage of the recent increase in

the incidence of nervous disease to the unremitting noisiness of contemporary business and leisure.[108]

This was a warning to his educated readers that they should not join the noisy masses in their love of sonic distraction.

However, Huxley was more pessimistic than Wells about the problem of noise. He did not think that noise abatement would succeed in fighting the tide of noisy entertainment and predicted a future not dissimilar to that depicted in *Brave New World*. Huxley argued that noise was an inevitable, unavoidable, and irreversible feature of technological progress. Whereas Wells saw a solution to noise suffering in the end of the capitalist free market, Huxley thought that there would come a time when only the altering of human biology would suffice: "Increase in the amount and intensity of (for example) education and noise will bring correspondingly increasing returns (the one in virtue, knowledge, etc., and the other in thought-preventing pleasure) only on one condition—that individuals shall become, with each generation, progressively more educable and more tolerant of noise," explained Huxley.[109] "But this is possible only if we select and breed from the most highly educable and noise-tolerant of existing strains," he continued. "No form of social progress is possible beyond a certain point . . . unless there is a continuous heritable improvement of individuals. Which brings us back to our old and yet, alas, not very satisfactory friend, Eugenics."[110] Huxley, thus, cast the noise problem as a site of class conflict but, reversing his *Brave New World* prediction, thought that educated people would have to be genetically engineered so as to free them of their sensitivity to the mass population's noise. The relationship between the elite and the mass was, therefore, at the forefront of Huxley's hostility to the urban soundscape. His writings were intended to link the question of sound with the question of humanity's evolution and future leadership. This he certainly did share with supporters of noise abatement.

Treating the Neurasthenic City

Doctors and writers built a consensus among themselves about the dangers of noise, especially to educated people. However, gaining the support of government authorities was altogether more difficult. This required noise abatement advocates to make a convincing case that noise was objectionable not only to intellectual elites but also to the population at large. Here, supporters of noise abatement were on shakier ground. The government ministers and officials who received the 1928 deputations on noise and health from the BMA and the People's League of Health were not convinced that the mass population was as affected by noise as doctors made out. A Ministry of Health minute sheet reads, "I fear that I cannot consider that the public health grounds adduced in the memorandum are very strong," but added, tellingly, "though doubtless the BMA are on the side of the angels."[111] This draft note was subsequently passed to the Minister:

> It may be questioned whether the total of street noises, or even the sudden street noise, is worse in these days than it was in Victorian London. . . . Are modern noises, in fact, producing neurotics? Noise—including the unexpected sudden discordant noise—is certainly agreeable to a large section of the population. Some will even tolerate it, and pay for it, in the form of jazz music. Others seek it at Hampstead on Bank holiday, or make it, with any agency, whenever they feel like it and happy. It is not unknown even at the older Universities.[112]

The Ministry of Health had, in other words, identified the class politics inherent in the antinoise campaign in 1928. Noise was the bête noire of professional men, but those whose job it was to maintain a neutral view were not always convinced, even if they felt sympathetic to the cause of noise abatement, that noise was as great a public health crisis as the BMA made out.

It was not only lawmakers who expressed doubt about the medical justification for noise abatement. In his article, "Reflections on the Age of Noise," Adam Gowans Whyte noted that much of the medical discussion of noise seemed to be based on conjecture rather than hard-and-fast evidence. "Assuming that intense noise is a definite cause of nervous disorders, we ought to find marked differences between residents in the main and in the side streets of towns, and between town-dwellers and country-dwellers," he mused. And yet, he went on, "Setting aside the individuals who share Thomas Carlyle's acute sensitiveness to noise, it seems as if the majority of people who live in noisy thoroughfares reconcile themselves in time to the cataract of sound."[113] The raising of such doubts, including by the Minister of Health, frustrated the BMA. Its *Journal* admitted in 1929 that "the concrete evidence demanded by Mr Chamberlain is extremely hard to come by. It cannot be shown on the stage of a microscope or in a jar of spirit, nor can the effects of noise on the nervous system be satisfactorily separated from the many other nocuous results of modern life."[114] Disappointed by its failure to convince the Ministry of Health about the public health dangers of noise, the BMA chose not to undertake any further lobbying of its own.

Nevertheless, there remained a strong consensus among leading medical men, and among their supporters in the literary world, that noise *was* a threat to health. Their task now was to build wider support for this consensus. They chose to do this through a single-issue pressure group, the Anti-Noise

League, which set about lobbying government ministers and educating the public about the dangers of disordered sound. At the forefront of their activities was a concerted campaign to build understanding of and sympathy for the argument that noise causes neurasthenia. Prior to the formation of the Anti-Noise League there had been two earlier attempts to form national noise abatement organizations in Britain. An effort was made in 1930 to set up a Noise Abatement Society following the publication of a short book, *England, Ugliness and Noise*, by "two young bank clerks," Ainslie Derby and C. C. Hamilton, who felt strongly about city noise.[115] Their book was proudly introduced by a quote, "The human body cannot become used to noise without a loss of energy," from A. M. Low.[116] The book was sold as a source of fund-raising for the new society, but despite the efforts of supporter Sir Arthur Wilson, a diplomat, insufficient funds could be raised, probably due to the straightened economic circumstances of 1929–1930. Two years later, in November 1932, the *Times* announced the launching of a Noise Abatement Association led by Captain John Stevenson with the backing of prominent physician Sir Thomas Horder along with A. M. Low and the Bishop of Norwich, Bertram Pollock.[117] This Association seems to have fared little better than the earlier Society.

It was Horder himself, by this time sitting in the House of Lords as the first Baron Horder of Ashford in the County of Southampton, who established the first successful noise abatement organization, the Anti-Noise League, in 1933. The first annual conference of the League was held in July 1934 at the University of Oxford, a symbolically important center of quiet learning, where a local Noise Abatement and Pedestrians Association had been operating for some time. A promotional flyer for the League proclaimed, "The object of the Anti-Noise League is to promote the cause of quiet and to prevent interference with the amenities of life by avoidable noise."[118] The League sought to do this though the circulation of antinoise literature, such as leaflets and educational pamphlets as well as its own dedicated journal, *Quiet*; by lobbying for new legislation on noise control; by financially supporting research on soundproofing and quieter technology; and by acting as a source of information and support to those suffering from the effects of noise.[119] Its first year of work included lobbying the Ministry of Transport during the drafting of the 1934 Road Traffic Act, the result of which was the insertion of a clause outlawing the use of motor car horns during night time. "Zones of Silence" were created in London in which it was illegal to sound a horn between 11.30 P.M. and 7 A.M. This early triumph indicates that the Anti-Noise League was proving more successful than the BMA had before it in the task of influencing government ministers. Yet this accomplishment was based on an unchanged medical argument with neurasthenia at its heart.

Lord Horder, as well as being president of the Anti-Noise League, was also its public face. He used his political connections and public recognition to generate momentum for the movement and to build consensus around the public health justification, relating to neurasthenia, for noise abatement. In January 1935, he made a radio broadcast appeal to the public for donations to the Anti-Noise League, which emphasized noise's hidden costs to health as a reason to support the movement. "Your resistance to noise, a great deal of which is endless and preventable, costs you something that you cannot afford to pay, and a lot of you are 'overdrawn' already," explained Horder.[120] Here, he made explicit reference to Beard's theory of nervous energy, making use, too, of the economic metaphors that also had been common in Beard's day. He promised his audience, if they chose to donate to the Anti-Noise League, "a good return for your investment. I can promise you a gain in health, in security and in the enjoyment of life, which will amaze you when the nervous energy which you now spend on this endurance of unnecessary noise is released for the purposes of unhampered work and equally unhampered play."[121]

Horder was a passionate campaigner on sociomedical affairs, involving himself in a number of campaigns, along with noise abatement, which had to do with the intersection of medicine and society, including eugenics, and even suggested the idea of establishing a government Ministry of Happiness. "Research into, and observation of, the nature of disease, have shown us that the social causes of illness are just as important as the physical ones," wrote Horder.[122] This interest in the social face of medicine led him to noise abatement and the associated critique of modern civilization that had come to support it. Justifying the involvement of the medical profession in noise abatement, Horder wrote that "one of the amenities for which some of us have for the past three years been pleading is QUIET. Noise has increased tremendously of late years, whereas our capacity to absorb it without prejudice to our health and happiness has probably diminished. As with the case with the amenities in general, therefore, it becomes a doctor's duty to try and do something about it."[123]

The continuing prevalence of the familiar critique of modern civilization was a mainstay of Horder's antinoise work in the 1930s. He explicitly linked his crusade against noise with the need to control new technologies: "It has become a trite remark that this is the age of the machine. It is also trite that instead of the machine relieving us of toil and trouble it has tended to increase both of these."[124] Henry Richards added that "Noise is the child of the age of machinery and of the internal combustion engine. . . . It is a modern danger which has increased, is increasing, and must be diminished."[125] Horder likened this need to control technology with the struggle against infectious diseases in the nineteenth-century city:

> In much the same way as there have arisen conglomerations of human dwell-ings, huddled together without design or plan, starving people of light and air and spreading disease, so there has come upon us, as the result of increased motor-traffic, increased transport, aeroplanes and louder forms of amusement, a spate of uncontrolled noise for the suppression of which we must organise ourselves. It is necessary that we be saved from the nerve-racking effects of noise as it is that we secure air and light and freedom from infectious diseases.[126]

Using nineteenth-century analogies allowed Horder to explain his struggle against noise in terms that would, he hoped, make it both urgent and intel-ligible in the public mind and to the government ministers he wished to influence.

Horder also made frequent reference to the specific danger that noise posed to the body's nervous system. In an address entitled "The Strain of Modern Civilization," he explicitly discussed the neurasthenia caused by modern urban life: "In the street the trained eye detects in the physiognomy of the people the early stages of that concern which, in the consulting room and in the hospital ward, shows itself so frequently as the more established picture of 'Anxiety neurosis'—unloading itself upon the digestion, the cir-culation, and other bodily functions."[127] This neurosis is the result, accord-ing to Horder, of "the anxiety connected with the competition of living," and "of the precariousness of life itself in the streets." This link between nervousness and modern life was indebted to Beard's theories, but unlike his nineteenth-century predecessor, Horder reserved his greatest criticism for, "noise—needless, provocative, ill-mannered, selfish noise."[128] Horder described the antinoise movement as, "in its essence, a constructive and a protective movement, for it aims at the conservation of nervous energy. It economises human effort."[129] The threat of noise was clear enough for him. It "doesn't kill us as foul air and typhoid and diphtheria do," he explained, "but it does wear down the nervous system, which is the master stuff of our bodies."[130]

Despite attempting to reach a wide audience through its radio broadcasts and pamphlets, Horder's League aimed to retain an especial appeal to pro-fessional people and often emphasized that educated people's neurasthenic breakdown—because it deprived the nation of much-needed expertise—was an urgent concern. Horder was open about the fact that members of his League were more likely to be drawn from educated and professional society than not. "Have I not said, more than once," Horder pointed out in 1935, "that it is to the intelligent section of the community that the League appeals."[131] Claims about the damage done by noise to the health of the mass population were necessary in order to build support for noise abatement in government, but it is clear that this was never the motivating factor behind the work of the League. Instead, Horder and his followers, as the BMA had been before them, were primarily concerned with the effect of noise on the brain workers who provided leadership in society. In order to ensure the ongoing ability of this class of people to lead, it was necessary, Horder argued, to protect the possibility of quiet thought and of a selfhood constructed beyond the reach of noise. "Ladies and gentlemen," he explained in a 1935 speech, "our aim is equanimity: *we want to explore the hygienic value of a quiet mind*, if only because we ourselves have little hope that we can save civilization without it."[132]

The link between noise and nervousness as well as the class distinctions at work in noise abatement was underscored by the visual rhetoric of the Anti-Noise League's campaign. The logo in Figure 1.1 was attached to all the League's official publications. As a visual summation of the League's identity, it is a useful source for identifying the main themes of noise abatement in Britain during the 1930s. Central to the image is the professional man, identified by shirt, tie and jacket. With his head bowed and his fingers in his ears, this man is evidently trying to think, but any intellectual activity is made impossible by the cacophony that surrounds him. The chaotic geometry of the cityscape background identifies motor vehicles as the principal disturbance, while the pressure point and its surrounding concentric circles suggest the physical pain and interference to thought caused by the urban soundscape. When the logo was used on a poster (as was often the case; the Anti-Noise League inherited many of the Empire Marketing Board's former billboard sites), a lightning strike was placed diagonally at the top right and bottom left to enhance the sense of shock caused by noise.

The League's event with the highest profile was the Noise Abatement Exhibition held at the Science Museum in London in June 1935. Opened by the Prime Minister, the exhibition had, from the start, involved close collaboration with government ministries that were involved at the planning stages in each of the exhibition's four distinct sections: health and noise, research and development, transport and machinery, and buildings.[133] "The object of the Exhibition," wrote R. F. Millard, General Secretary of the Anti-Noise League, "besides displaying noise absorption appliances, etc., is to present a general and practical survey of the noise problem in its many aspects and to

FIGURE I.I Logo of the Anti-Noise League as featured in *Noise Abatement Exhibition: Science Museum, South Kensington, 31st May–30th June 1935* (London: Anti-Noise League, 1935), 91.

indicate ways and means of mitigation."[134] The building section, for example, presented a replica house, with some rooms soundproofed using the latest materials and others built using traditional materials. In each, structural-borne and airborne noises, such as gramophone loudspeakers, typewriters, and ordinary conversation, could be compared.[135] Convincing visitors of the health impact of noise was a vital aspect of the 1935 exhibition. Figure 1.2 shows one of the exhibition stands. Emphasizing the health dangers of noise, it contained, in the center, a mock thermometer used as a metaphor to map the medical dangers of various types of noise. Normal sounds, such as a quiet garden, were at the bottom of the thermometer, showing them to be medically normal, while pathological sounds such as pneumatic drills were toward the top, in the area that indicates the onset of serious illness. Placed on either side of the thermometer were book displays and large posters of the Anti-Noise League's logo, as well as posters that read "Help to Banish Unnecessary Noise" and "Quiet Brings Comfort, Health and Efficiency." These were intended to support Horder's argument, published in the exhibition handbook, *Silencing a Noisy World*, that the Anti-Noise League aimed to help people "escape from what are, literally, the hammer-blows of needless

FIGURE I.2 Photograph of the Anti-Noise League stand at the 1935 Noise Abatement Exhibition held at the Science Museum, London featured in *Quiet* (March 1936): 22.

noise upon this vital tissue we call our nerves."[136] They were also intended to illustrate arguments made by McKenzie in his book *City of Din* which, still in print, was sold to exhibition visitors.

Among those who delivered public lectures attached to the 1935 Science Museum exhibition was H. G. Wells, whose connection to the Anti-Noise League was a personal one, since he had taught Horder at college and was now treated by the physician.[137] Despite indicating his support for the cause of the Anti-Noise League by speaking at the exhibition, Wells said he was in fact reluctant to call for absolute quiet. He warned that the campaign against noise should not be pressed too far. A report of his speech noted, "Mr Wells declared, he could not work in absolute silence; he liked the undercurrent of noise, and if he could not hear a distant piano or the subdued sounds from the street he was under-stimulated."[138] Nevertheless, Wells went on to acknowledge to the attentive crowd of noise abatement supporters that intrusive urban sound was indeed becoming a problem: "Just as people were able to detach themselves from each other visually, so they ought to be able to achieve auditory isolation," Wells was reported to have said.[139] He continued, "It had not dawned upon him until recently that he wanted to hear himself think. One was always at an audible level, saying things over to oneself, and the invasion of unnecessary extraneous noise was thus becoming a more and more serious interference with the privacy of individual life."[140] Wells's speech emphasized the sanctity of the private individual and the quiet interior self-hood that made this individuality possible. Noise represented a transgression of the exterior world of urban and mass culture into the inner sanctuary of the mind. Delighted with this, Horder admitted, "Despite your earlier remarks today . . . I was never personally in doubt that you were with us."[141] Horder explained that this was because of the appeal of his League to "intelligent," thinking people, including writers. Wells's presence at the opening of the exhibition was symbolically important for this reason; it demonstrated that noise abatement was a cause shared by members of the "intelligent section" of the community, rather than just medical experts. Wells was also, as this chapter has already pointed out, an important dramatist of the neurasthenic age and useful to the Anti-Noise League's campaign for this reason.

Wells's testimony against noise at the 1935 exhibition highlighted an important theme in interwar noise abatement discourse. While Horder worked tirelessly to build understanding of neurasthenia, Wells and others emphasized noise's ability to dissolve the barriers between public and private space in the city and in turn to transgress the boundary between the interior self and the exterior sensory world. For those members and associates of the Anti-Noise League, such as Wells, who were not primarily preoccupied with medical matters, preservation of quiet spaces in the city was the main concern.[142] Antinoise campaigners and their supporters hoped, above all, to reestablish the spatial order of public and private. The Anti-Noise League strongly objected, for example, to shopkeepers placing loudspeakers outside their shops in order to entice customers. The League obtained evidence from the British Broadcasting Corporation, with the cooperation of the Home Office, that complaints about "loudspeaker abuse" had gone up from 298 in 1932 to 508 in 1933 with such letters coming in faster during the summer months when neighbors were more likely to have their windows open.[143] While medicine may have been the channel through which attacks on noise were built, the need to wrestle back control over the auditory spaces of London and other towns and cities was an important additional goal of the movement.

Neurasthenia had a role to play here, too. Neurasthenic theory, as earlier parts of this chapter have argued, was based on the assumption that biological systems, including the body's nervous system, work to natural temporal rhythms that, if interrupted, lead to disease and decay. It was no less dependent on an implied natural order of spatial separation. The human body depended for its health on the ability to remain connected to, but not be overwhelmed by, its surrounding environment. The damage done to the body's nervous system by modern civilization was partly a result of unnaturally strong, mechanically produced, sense experiences intruding into the body's interior from the outside world, upsetting the natural biological order of inside and outside. This biological logic of insides and outsides was extended to the city. If it was to be returned to health, the city had to adhere to the biologically determined order of space and time. In this sense, the medicalization of noise in early-twentieth-century Britain was also a medicalization of urban space. Machines such as motorcars and gramophone and wireless loudspeakers threatened to upset this natural order as a result of the arrhythmic and spatially transgressive sounds that they caused. *Quiet* often employed visual codes to highlight the incompatibility of biological order and urban machines through images accompanying its articles. One photograph from 1937, for example, showed a queue of trams in the center of Liverpool with people scattered on either side, the implication being that man and machine could not coexist in urban harmony without prejudice to the mental health of the sensitive. The caption reads, "No one can estimate the terrific effect the incessant thunder of tramcars has on the nerves and lives of thousands of city workers."[144]

Among those in the Anti-Noise League who, like Wells, came from a professional background other than medicine, and whose focus was trained on the noisy city rather than the afflicted body, was Sir Henry Richards, a retired Chief Inspector of Schools. He was responsible for the Anti-Noise League's extensive work in school building acoustics, but in his public-facing work for the League, Richards directed his criticism of noise at the chaotic auditory characteristics of the modern urban environment. In his contribution to the League's *Silencing a Noisy World* exhibition book, Richards added a starkly political dimension to the attempt to control urban noise. He argued that the political revolutions of communism and fascism that had characterized the topsy-turvy world of early-twentieth-century Europe were in fact connected to the increasingly sound-filled environment of the modern city. "The excitement, the restless, hungry emotions which make the world so dangerous," argued Richards, "are not perhaps unconnected with the unending din of ordinary life organised skillfully for political purposes."[145] During a lecture to the Royal Society of Arts, Richards asked, "Is there no connection between the material and the mental and the moral unquiet which shakes the whole world—that universal restlessness which seems literally afraid of quietude and reflection?"[146] Underlining his theory that noise and "political movement" were intrinsically linked, Richards commented:

> Sound and movement do appear to play an extraordinarily important part in political developments, and great European convulsions are accompanied by ceaseless bands, processions and dramatic salutations. Whether noise is the cause or effect of this world-wide abandonment of the tranquilities of life it is hard to say, but of this I feel convinced, a campaign for peace and quiet in our streets and roads is not without its political and social significance.[147]

Here, Richards was consciously attempting to define British rationality and middle opinion in contrast to the noisy upheavals of fascism and communism and, in turn, was making a claim for the importance of peace and quiet in sustaining the British status quo.

Richards may well have had in mind the controversy over the use of loudspeakers in political campaigning, a flashpoint of conflict in the policing of noise in mid-1930s London. The Metropolitan Police and the Home Office were unsure of how to deal with the use of loudspeakers during political campaigning in the build-up to the 1935 general election. This became an issue of conflict between supporters of noise abatement and those who wished to make full use of new sound technologies in political campaigning.[148] Richards's broader point, however, was that noise, with its ability to kill thought, could have disastrous political consequences. Noise's ability to move was multifaceted: it moved through the city without respect for private spaces, it moved the base emotional instincts of those who came into contact with it, and it caused political movement through its ability to rouse crowds into action, as in Nazi Germany. For Richards, the campaign against city noise could hardly have been more urgent in political terms.

Others who contributed to the Anti-Noise League's critique of the modern urban soundscape included senior members of the Church of England. This is not surprising given the premium placed by Christianity on quiet reflection through prayer. The Archbishop of Canterbury, Cosmo Lang, had spoken at the Anti-Noise League's Oxford conference in 1934 and was considered among its principal public supporters. The League later published a letter from Lang in *Quiet* in which the Archbishop offered his support for the campaign to control city noises. He argued that this campaign had a spiritual, as well as a medical, justification:

> To a degree which we scarcely realise the ever increasing hurry of physical movement is infecting the soul of the nation, disturbing the nerves, and distracting the mind. Its effects are aggravated by the incessant and surely needless noise which accompanies it. You are only too well aware of the bodily

and mental results of this evil combination of rush and noise. I am naturally specially concerned with its spiritual results. These cannot but be serious and far-reaching. ... As you know, I have recently ventured to make an appeal to the nation to recover its hold on religion. But in the midst of all this rush and noise it is difficult for any man to possess his own soul; and without stillness it is impossible to know God.[149]

Lang, thus, made an explicit connection between the noise and the Godless-ness of the modern city, connecting two major urban anxieties of the early twentieth century. His reference to the inability of modern man to "possess his own soul" was a religious version of the Anti-Noise League's assertion that individual selfhood depended upon spaces of quiet retreat.

The Anti-Noise League also received support in its crusade to control modern city sounds from the Campaign for the Protection of Rural Eng-land (CPRE) who were concerned about the spatial transgression of urban noise into the countryside. The Anti-Noise League was preoccupied on the whole with questions of urban sonority and tended in their rhetoric to contrast the unhealthy city with the restorative peace and quiet of the countryside, but it was supportive of fears expressed by other organizations, including in particular the CPRE, that the sounds of modern urban civiliza-tion might eventually, if unchecked, engulf all of England. Such fears were trained particularly on new modes of transport whose noisy intrusion into the countryside was felt to disturb the timelessness of the rural soundscape. The CPRE, set up in 1926 to safeguard the countryside from the intrusion of industry and suburbanization, maintained an interest in noise abatement from 1930 onward, the year in which Darby and Hamilton's book *England, Ugliness and Noise* was circulated with interest among its members.[150] The CPRE regularly corresponded with the Anti-Noise League, and the two organizations cooperated on a number of projects during the 1930s, including sharing information and expertise about the negative impact of airplane noise on the countryside. Because of the existence of an organized noise abate-ment movement, the CPRE chose not to undertake any extensive antinoise work of its own before the Second World War, seeing it as somebody else's business, and actively emphasized that its primary aim was to preserve the "visual amenities" of the countryside.[151] Yet its members sometimes urged a more proactive approach, pointing out that the quietness of the country-side was no less important than its visual beauty. One member wrote to the Secretary of the CPRE in 1935 to point out that government ministers were considering passing legislation on the use of wireless sets in cars (thanks to the lobbying of the Anti-Noise League), and that it was to be hoped that the Council had played some role in encouraging such measures, since "It is of little use to save 'beauty spots' and restore buildings, if anyone can roll up in a car and turn on jazz bands and shrieking sopranos to destroy all the peace of a moorland road or a riverside."[152]

It was important for the Anti-Noise League to gather the support of organizations such as the Church of England and the CPRE, as well as the endorsement of prominent public figures such as Richards and Lang. Given the doubts that existed within government about the medical justification for noise abatement, arguments such as Richards's about the role of noise in urban unrest and Lang's about the incompatibility of urban noise and spirituality—as well as the CPRE's about the role of mechanical noise in destroying the peace and timelessness of the English countryside—were undoubtedly useful in garnering sympathy for the antinoise cause. For even though they remained skeptical about the medical case against noise, government ministers were increasingly willing, by the late 1930s, to introduce the kind of legislation that the Anti-Noise League wished to see. In 1939, the government issued a model bylaw for the use of local authorities that made it an offence to create noise in public places or within earshot of public buildings such as schools and hospitals. A whole section of the bylaw was given over to wireless and gramophone loudspeakers, proposing to make it illegal to use them in public places or in such a way as to cause disturbance to neighbors.[153] Prosecutions could be brought, in the boroughs that adopted the bylaw, under the terms of the 1936 Public Health Act.[154] Yet the Anti-Noise League managed to push through this bylaw despite never having fully convinced government authorities of the link between noise and nervous illness. Following an Anti-Noise League deputation to the Ministry of Health in 1938, for example, the Ministry noted that little had been done "by way of collecting new evidence on the medical side, for instance that certain preventable modern noises are specific causes of deafness or some neurasthenia in a way in which other and different noises in the past were not."[155] What this suggests is that, convincing medical evidence or otherwise, government officials were willing to accept the need for a certain amount of noise abatement. They did so because, the Anti-Noise League being "on the side of the angels," they were more-or-less sympathetic to Horder and his supporters' antipathy to noise. The organized and persistent campaigning of the Anti-Noise League was difficult to ignore, especially given the high-profile nature of leaders and supporters such as Horder, Richards, Wells, and Lang. As Chapter 3 points out, however, the lack of convincing medical evidence about the effects of noise meant that the Anti-Noise League remained frustrated about the pace of legislative change, their campaign remaining only a partial success prior to the outbreak of the Second World War.

Conclusion

Noise abatement was a campaign concerned, at root, with the survival of the quiet individual self in the noisy age of mass modernity. In noise abatement discourse, noise represented collective flux and the prison-house of bodily immanence, while silence stood for the detached, rational, transcendent mind so highly prized in the Western philosophical tradition. "Each one of us knows," explained the psychologist Eugène Minkowski in 1926, "the need of isolation from environment and to have a *tête-à-tête* with one's self . . . we let environment act upon us, but afterwards we again melt the elements that thus come to us from the outside in the crucible of our interior life, to make of them the material of our reflections, and of our personal activity. We wish neither to be blended with, nor to be separated from, our surroundings."[156] Minkowski's definition of a self delicately poised between contact with the external environment and total "blending" with it neatly encapsulates the anxiety of those who supported noise abatement campaigns in the 1930s. H. G. Wells had said more or less the same thing at the 1935 noise abatement exhibition. Minkowski, like Wells and Horder, thought that machines were primarily responsible for sensory disequilibrium in modern life. "Technology seeks to master time and space through its discoveries," Minkowski wrote, and "since we are only too happy to reap the benefits from the progress which technology is constantly achieving, we cannot but be obliged to it. Yet, this feeling of gratitude does not fully characterise our true situation. Quite often we feel overcome by a profound weariness, as if the rhythm of life which technology has produced does violence to us. This is because technological progress is achieved to the detriment of other essential values."[157] Horder put it thus in 1951: "To a large extent this business of noise is one more example of the conflict between man and the machines that he has made. The question here, as in other and more vital directions, is whether he is going to be 'done in' by the machine or is he going to control it?"[158]

Despite their reservations about technology, most supporters of noise abatement thought of ever-increasing mechanization as inescapable and did not seek to reverse this process. Aldous Huxley, for example, thought that the human race would regrettably but inevitably have to evolve in order to adapt to the new technological soundscape. In her history of twentieth-century noise abatement campaigns, Karin Bijsterveld describes this outlook as "antimodern, yet not antitechnology."[159] While they may have been resigned to a technological future, British noise abatement supporters did, nevertheless, view technology as part of a new, modern world, which they could tolerate only if the conditions necessary for mental, and auditory, isolation were preserved. Rather than characterize such a view as antimodern, however, this chapter suggests that we should read the culture of nerves and its accompanying critique of modern civilization as a constitutive part of the discursive construction of modernity at this time. Modernity came to be meaningful as a concept, in other words, through the work of movements such as the noise abatement campaign. In this campaign, modernity was constructed as a problem to be overcome and as a force to take refuge from. This negative construction was *part* of the response to living in a rapidly changing world, one important mode of experiencing and defining the modern through sound. It overlapped with and informed—but also sometimes stood in opposition to—other ways of hearing modernity in the early twentieth century.

2 Re-Enchanting Modernity

Techniques of Magical Sound

Stir the senses and you will also stir the brain! Stir the senses with
the unexpected, the mysterious, the unknown, and you will truly
move the soul, intensely and profoundly!
—Luigi Russolo, *The Art of Noises* (1916)

The Anti-Noise League's campaign spurred a range of scientific endeavors
to quiet the world and to soundproof its spaces of auditory refuge. Chapter 3
argues that this rationalizing response was another way of hearing modernity
in the age of noise. However, it should not be assumed too hastily that the
kind of dissatisfaction outlined in Chapter 1 led only to a reinvigoration of
conventional scientific rationality in the pursuit of a better-sounding Britain.
Nor, for that matter, did all sound experts of the period equate selfhood with
quiet separation. Among those who took up the problem of noise there were
some who deliberately rejected the secular-scientific outlook that we have
come to associate so closely with the project of the modern. This chapter
insists on pausing to take stock of an alternative modernity that, although
it fits less comfortably into our usual understandings of the modern past,
flourished in the first half of the twentieth century. In contrast to supporters of noise abatement, the experts of this alternative modernity thought
that true selfhood was to be attained not in auditory isolation but rather
by connecting the body to the vibrations of magical sound. Taking part in
what Alex Owen has described as an occult revival in modern Britain, these
experts sought renewed knowledge of sound's spiritual dimensions in order
to counteract the negative effects of noise.[1] They heard modernity not in the
clang of factories or in the screech of motorcars but rather in the mysterious
sounds that promised, they thought, to re-enchant the world.

The link between sound and spiritual experience has deep historical roots.
Richard Cullen Rath and Leigh Eric Schmidt argue that it was the rise of
print culture and of Enlightenment rationality that eroded what had once

been a lively culture of religious aurality in the West.[2] In early America, according to Rath, "the true voicing of one's heart in a heavenward groan, moan, or cry was the same as deliverance."[3] But, as Schmidt explains, Enlightenment philosophers of the seventeenth and eighteenth centuries identified hearing as a "superstitious sense" that posed "a potential danger to the clearsightedness of reason." They insisted upon "a markedly new acoustics" that sought to "tame the endless effusions of religious enthusiasm" associated with sound.[4] My argument in this chapter is that a renewed interest in the spirituality of sound coincided with the age of noise and that this revival, in turn, provided its own set of solutions to the problems of urban and industrial noise. Rath concludes that the "shift in the senses" enacted by the print revolution, during which the visuality of written language gradually excluded the possibility of extra-linguistic religious experience, trapped modern man in Max Weber's "iron cage" of disenchantment, a state in which, to cite Weber, "there are no mysterious incalculable forces."[5] Yet, by 1914, a concerted attempt to re-enchant modernity, and its sound worlds, was already well underway.

The case of avant-gardist Luigi Russolo, the Italian futurist who infamously conceived of and experimented with an "art of noises" in the 1910s and 1920s, highlights the necessity of accounting for this project of re-enchantment in the history of modern aurality.[6] Russolo's much commented upon, but also much misunderstood, art of noises has been used by historians to elucidate early-twentieth-century cultures of noise. Emily Thompson concludes that Russolo's desire to make music out of noise was an inevitable product of his "acoustically conscious" age.[7] Karin Bijsterveld argues that we should liken Russolo's work to noise abatement, since "both noise abaters and noise artists strived to attain a genuinely elitist control of sound."[8] There is nothing wrong in either of these claims, but what of Russolo's own insistence that his art of noises was, in the first instance, a magical experiment in the raising of the spirits of the dead?[9] Music historian Luciano Chessa points out that Russolo's noise concerts, which took place in Paris and London as well as in Italy, assumed the form of religious ceremonies, and that they were inspired not so much by a wish to represent city noise than by an esoteric theory of sound vibration, which conceived of the art of noises as a means of connecting the hearer to occult spiritual realities.[10] Indeed, as Chessa argues, "the futurist future was by and large a spiritual one."[11] It is no wonder that historians have overlooked the spiritual elements of Russolo's contribution to modern sound culture: Chessa argues convincingly that futurism's occult foundations were systematically excluded from the historical record by art critics who viewed them as unmodern and thus as irrelevant to the movement's place in the history of artistic modernism.[12]

Such an obvious pattern of exclusion should alert us to the need for greater historical sensitivity to the project of re-enchantment as well as to the possibility of nonsecular modernities. Where sound historians have made useful headway, in this respect, is in their recovery of the close entanglement between the evolution of new sound technologies and the growth of the nineteenth- and early-twentieth-century spiritualist movement. Not only did spiritualists believe that the voices of ethereal spirits could be heard in the crackle of telephone, wireless, and gramophone sets, but, as Anthony Enns and others have argued, the invention and design of these very technologies was often itself based on the idea that, as the science of sound progressed, it would eventually uncover auditory traces of the spirits of the dead.[13] Inventor of the phonograph, Thomas Edison, was among those who welcomed the idea that sound technologies might lead to new knowledge and understanding of the spirit world. "I have been at work for some time," he wrote, "building an apparatus to see if it is possible for personalities which have left this earth to communicate with us."[14] The wireless was evoked as a model to explain why telepathy would eventually enter the realm of scientific truth: just as sound vibrations could be communicated through the air, it stood to reason to spiritualists that thoughts could also.[15] As Jonathan Sterne puts it, then, "the spirit world was alive and well in telephony and radio."[16] The work of Enns, Sterne, and others indicates that a revival of interest in esoteric spirituality was very much bound up with the technological revolution in sound. As Shelley Trower has demonstrated in her history of vibratory cultures, the dividing line between spiritualist and mainstream sciences was indeed a permeable one, especially where sound was concerned.[17]

Placed in this context, Russolo's desire to spiritualize noise and to use it as a means of rekindling religious experience starts to look more like the norm than the exception. Yet within historical sound studies there has not yet been a systematic attempt to account for the significance of spirituality in the twentieth-century experience of sound. This chapter makes a contribution in this direction by extending the insights of scholars such as Enns and Trower about spiritualism to the related but distinct campaign to re-enchant modernity. The occult revival outlined by Owen, which emerged in the 1870s and 1880s and which had become, by the 1890s, "one of the most remarked trends of the decade," gave greater institutional and ideological shape to the spiritual revival begun by spiritualism.[18] Although spiritualism fulfilled some of the functions of religion, namely by accounting for the spirit's life after death, leaders of the occult revival committed themselves more squarely to the project of recovering divine knowledge and experience through occult investigation.[19] Operating through newly founded organizations such as the

Hermetic Order of the Golden Dawn and the Theosophical Society, this new movement consisted, according to Owen, of "an upsurge of interest in medieval and Renaissance Christian mysticism, heterodox inspirational neo-Christianity, and, most notably, a nondenominational—sometimes non-Christian—interest in 'esoteric philosophy.'"[20] While spiritualism emerged from popular origins and found a widespread following among working-class people, the new occultism was, as Owen notes, an "elite counterpoint" to spiritualism insofar as it circulated, for the most part, among educated and middle-class followers. Indeed, it could be argued that the occult revival provided an alternative expert discourse for those who felt unable to support, or who were directly excluded from, the dominant modes of professional and middle-class authority at this time. Historians have noted the extent to which spiritualism and occult movements such as Theosophy allowed women to exercise expert power at a time when there were precious few opportunities for them to do so through more conventional avenues.[21] It is no coincidence that in contrast to Chapter 1, many of the sound experts discussed in this chapter are women.

In their revival of mystical traditions and in their investigation of the occult forces of nature, Theosophists, upon whom this chapter focuses as a case study, constructed their alternative mode of expert authority in opposition particularly to that of mainstream science. They attacked it as "materialist," that is, as a paradigm which excluded, a priori, the possibility of finding evidence of man's spiritual life. One way to interpret this move, as did the art critics who carefully circumnavigated Russolo's occult interests, would be as an antimodern throwback to a pre-Enlightenment age of superstition, or at the very least as an irrelevance in relation to the broader cultural logic of modernity. However, my argument in this chapter is that, as with the cultural pessimism discussed in Chapter 1, the project of re-enchantment was in fact a constitutive element of early-twentieth-century cultural modernity's multitudinous character. The occult revival was a re-enchantment of modernity, rather than a return to enchantment, because, as a wide range of commentators have pointed out, it did not reject the drive to discover, classify, and calculate, but rather sought to integrate the study of spirituality and the divine into these most modern of instincts.[22] Owen characterizes the occult revival as modern precisely because it sought evidence for mystical forces *through*, rather than in opposition to, the Enlightenment paradigms of rationality, objectivity, and universalism. When Theosophists attempted to achieve direct contact with God by cultivating knowledge of, and expertise in, the occult forces at work in divinely ordained nature, they were searching for scientific proof of the magical and spiritual forces at work in the world.

Gordon Graham argues that modern occult movements "can be thought of as attempting, in their different ways, to rescue religion by giving some of its varieties a 'scientific' credibility that Christianity was held to lack, or to have lost."[23]

Wouter J. Hanegraaff goes further, describing movements such as Theosophy as "the mirror of secular thought" because, in order to prove the existence and value of spiritual phenomena, they adopted the rationalizing and empiricist instincts of modern science.[24] Owen and Hanegraaff have, in their writings on modern occultism, done a good deal to dispel the secularization myth that has so powerfully structured the writing of modern history. "Far from involving anything like a disappearance of religion," Hanegraaff argues, "secularization can be understood as referring to a profound *transformation* of religion." He points to the occult revival as an important element of this transformation process.[25] Owen, similarly, rejects the secularization narrative on the basis of her research on Britain's occult revival and argues instead that "what is recognisably modern about the post-1880 period is not so much its disenchantment as the evident unresolved tension between the spiritual and the secular."[26]

Therefore, rather than view re-enchantment as antithetical to the modern, this chapter insists, following Owen and others, that the project of re-enchantment was produced by, played an active role in shaping, and was in every respect *within* rather than outside the trajectory of early-twentieth-century cultural modernity. Although it drew some of its inspiration from the past, it also had a hand in some of the most radical cultural developments of the age. Corinna Treitel has classified the occult revival as modern precisely because of the role that it played in generating other distinctly modern cultural trends, such as artistic modernism.[27] Art historians, including Linda Dalrymple Henderson, have now done a good deal to recover the extent to which a variety of modernisms, from cubism to surrealism and futurism, drew inspiration from occult movements, particularly Theosophy.[28] The experimentation fundamental to modernism undoubtedly owed much to the influence of the Theosophical Society. Theosophists openly encouraged modernist innovation in the arts as a way of investigating the occult properties of color and of sound. Russolo was among those avant-garde artists whose experimentalism was inspired directly by texts associated with the Theosophical movement.[29]

A second unquestionably modern cultural category that owed a debt to occult investigation was that of the psychological self. In its preoccupation with self-transformation as the path to spirituality, Theosophy and other occult movements made a contribution to emerging psychological cultures of selfhood in the late nineteenth and early twentieth centuries. Owen argues that although modern occultism "refused a purely secularized formulation of human consciousness," its investigation and conceptualization of the psyche followed a path similar to that of mainstream psychology in its theorization of the multiplicity of selfhood and in the "elision of self and consciousness."[30] Indeed, the "extreme modernity of the magical enterprise" is, for Owen, encapsulated in the extent to which it "sought the infinite in a newly psychologized but potentially divine self."[31] Modern occultists sought a "science for the soul," to borrow Treitel's phrase, in which the inner self would be rendered knowable and explainable, and thus admissible into the canon of scientific truth but not ultimately reducible to the material world.[32] Historians of psychology have pointed to a close relationship, at least at first, between occult and mainstream scientific investigation of the psyche. Drawing attention to the interaction between new psychological ideas and occult revivals in nineteenth-century Britain, Rhodri Hayward has argued, "Both mysticism and the new psychology were techniques for transforming hidden, introspective knowledge into public language."[33] In his survey of psychological cultures in twentieth-century Britain, Mathew Thomson adds, furthermore, that the subsequent popularization of psychology owed a good deal to the groundwork laid by the occult revival.[34]

It was in the context of occult investigation of spiritual self-realization that Theosophy came to take up the problem of noise. English Theosophist and composer, Cyril Scott, stated in 1933, "We are much troubled by the nerve-shattering noise to which in all large towns we are subjected, . . . The jarring sounds of motor-horns, whistles, grinding brakes and so forth," he continued, "exercise a cumulative and deleterious effect upon the entire organism." In contrast to the Anti-Noise League's call for quiet, however, Scott suggested instead that "certain composers will be used to evolve a type of music calculated to heal where those discordant noises have destroyed. Such men, consciously aware of their responsibility towards humanity, will indeed be as faithful custodians of the sacred two-edged sword of Sound."[35] While adherents of noise abatement believed that noise brought about nervousness as a result of the irregular vibration it caused in the body's nervous system, Theosophists thought that the right kind of sonic vibrations could inspire mankind to knowledge of true, spiritual selfhood. The one-time concert violinist turned musical mystic, Maud MacCarthy, a follower of Theosophy, devoted herself to furthering this magical agenda in early-twentieth-century London, describing her attempts to harness the healing and inspiring power of sound as "musical futurist development" because, through the power of sound alone, she thought, could the intellectual, spiritual, and social evolution of mankind be achieved.[36] Such arguments were not limited to individual composers or Theosophical devotees. The final section of this chapter returns to the self-help writers discussed in Chapter 1 in order to demonstrate the close relationship not only between occult philosophy and popular psychology but also between cultures of nervousness and cultures of re-enchantment in early-twentieth-century Britain.

Selfhood through Vibration: Theosophical Theories of Sound

The potential for magical sound vibrations to undo the damage done by noise was a recurring theme in nineteenth- and early-twentieth-century Theosophical thought. Because the age-of-noise narrative had become so central to narrating the experience of modernity, Theosophical occultists took it up as a challenge in their quest for twentieth-century re-enchantment. Situating Theosophy's solution to the problem of noise requires some outlining of the basic principles of Theosophy as they developed after 1875, the year in which the Theosophical Society was founded in New York by Helena Petrovna Blavatsky and Henry Olcott Steel. Aiming to be at once a religion, a philosophy, and a science, the Theosophical Society set itself the task of uncovering the universal truth behind all world religions. "Nearly all religious systems," wrote Steel, "have preferred their specific and distinctive tenets to their true universal basis and inherent tendency, and have thus become the most discordant of influences in the world they would regenerate."[37] Despite aiming to foster "a kindly reciprocity and mutual tolerance between men and races," the Society nonetheless privileged and promoted in particular "the study of Aryan and other Eastern literature, religions and sciences."[38] This was because Theosophists believed there to be an "ancient wisdom" about the divine workings of the universe, known especially to the ancient Greeks, which had been preserved in certain practices of the Hindu and Buddhist faiths in the East.[39] "The Pythagorean, Platonic and Neo-Platonic schools have so many points of contact with Hindu and Buddhist thought that their issue from one fountain is obvious," argued Annie Besant, who became president of the Theosophical Society in 1908.[40] Having been founded in the United States, the Society operated under Besant from Madras, India, underscoring the Oriental source of Theosophical wisdom. The West's regeneration, Besant thought, could take place only through closer contact with the East, and indeed she regularly returned home to speak at the English Theosophical headquarters in London where her knowledge of Hindu and Buddhist traditions reached a wide and devoted British audience.

A central component of the ancient wisdom preserved in the East was the ability to prove the existence not only of the physical world, but also of no less than six other "planes of existence." Materialist scientists shortsightedly investigate only physical matter. But, according to Theosophists, the universe consists of seven types of matter in total, of which physical is only the densest. Finer and finer gradations of matter work alongside it, their existence remaining occult by the standards of mainstream "materialist" science because the undeveloped human senses cannot immediately perceive it. Above the physical in the hierarchy of matter are the emotional, mental, intuitional, spiritual, monadic, and divine planes of existence, the seven "kingdoms of nature" as the British Theosophical writer C. W. Leadbeater described them.[41] Man's essence emanates from the divine plane; within every man is a "spark of the divine fire" of God, in Leadbeater's words.[42] The cycle of life is such, however, that from their divine beginnings men and women must descend to the lower physical plane before being reunited once again with the higher spiritual worlds. This downward and upward arc is part of the constant dynamism of God's universe. "Though man descends from on high," explained Leadbeater, "it is only through that descent that a full cognizance of the higher worlds is developed in him."[43]

The physical body exists, according to Besant, "to receive contacts from the physical world, and send the report of them inwards."[44] This is the day-to-day life of sense experience which, although it would appear to most people to be the be-all and end-all of their life, is in fact only one small part of it. Ether, the mysterious matter investigated by spiritualists, was, although invisible to the eye, part of the physical plane in Theosophical theory. Spiritualists had thus, Theosophists argued, made only the smallest of advances on materialist science. The finer gradations of matter beyond the physical that make up man's higher existence are no less materially real than the physical world, but man, at the early stages of his physical evolution, is unaware of them because he has not yet learned how to perceive or control them. Alongside our physical life, emotions take material form in the finer gradations of matter operating on this plane. Although most people, including spiritualists, do not realize it, feelings are materialized in the "astral" matter of the emotional plane, creating vibrant flashes of color as "thought-forms," which leave the thinker and impact upon the astral matter of those around them. In their influential book, *Thought-Forms* (1905), Besant and Leadbeater explained that thoughts produced by the spiritually untrained mind create indistinct clouds of color and affect, while the thoughts of spiritual initiates in the act of meditation create beautiful geometric forms and fully formed emotions.[45]

Our higher intellectual life, quite separate from the physical operation of the brain, is no less real in this sense, made up as it is of yet finer matter from the mental plane of existence. The mental plane, equivalent to the psyche in mainstream psychology, is the pivotal level in Theosophy's scheme, because it is at this tipping point that man, if he had received proper spiritual training, could transcend the earthly realm of physical and emotional matter and be united with "the Great Mind in the Kosmos" and proceed onward from there to knowledge of the higher planes of intuitional, spiritual, monadic, and finally divine existence.[46] Where Theosophists differed from regular psychologists, therefore, was in their claim that the category of "mind" transcends the body and unites man with much wider cosmological forces.

Theosophists believed that the original spark of God within man was his true self, or his soul. "It is customary to speak of man as having a soul," wrote Leadbeater. "Theosophy, as the result of direct investigation, reverses that dictum, and states that man *is* a soul, and *has* a body."[47] Made up of the finer divisions of matter on the third plane of existence, the mental plane, the self was described by Besant as the "tiny germ in the seed" of man. This seed is nourished by its contact with physical, astral, and lower forms of mental matter. "This seed is dropped," explained Besant, "into the soil of human life that its latent forces may be quickened into activity by the sun of joy and the rain of tears, and be fed by the juices of the life-soil that we call experience, until the germ grows into a mighty tree, the image of its generating Sire."[48] The soul of man is the seed of God planted on earth, but realization of this fact depends upon our ability to properly harness and control the influences of the lower forms of matter that nurture our soul. Not until we have recognized and cultivated the useful properties of physical, astral, and mental matter can we be reunited with our spiritual selves. Most people remain ignorant of their true divine selves since for the most part, explained Besant, "the 'I' is the physical body." Man draws from the physical body sensory enjoyments, "and he thinks of these as himself, for his life is in them." To the scholar, continued Besant, "the 'I' is in the mind, for in its exercise lies his joy and therein his life is concentrated."[49] Yet, she argued, "Few can rise to the abstract heights of spiritual philosophy" necessary to realize true selfhood.[50] Besant's books, including *The Ancient Wisdom* (1897) and *Man and His Bodies* (1917) were nonetheless intended to be practical handbooks offering instruction to those who wished to attempt it, and in this respect occupied a similar place in the publishing landscape as early psychological self-help manuals.

Besant explained in these books that sensory pleasure and intellectual endeavor are not ends in themselves, but steps toward the realization of true spiritual selfhood. The purpose of the denser forms of matter, experienced, for example, through sensory enjoyment, is to nourish the finer forms and allow men and women, eventually, to realize the truth of their inner, transcendent selves. This process operates, crucially, through the resonance of vibration. Dense matter rouses the finer forms into being through its slower vibrations. All matter vibrates, but the finer forms, once roused into being, vibrate at much faster rates than the denser forms. Leadbeater described the vibration rates of the different planes of existence as being the equivalent of the octaves of musical scales. The seven planes of existence "may be considered as a vast gamut of undulations consisting of many octaves," he explained. "The physical matter uses a certain number of the lowest of these octaves, the astral matter another group of octaves just above that, the mental matter a still further group, and so on."[51] Ascending to knowledge of true selfhood, then, was a case of ascending the octaves of our inner vibratory existence, each higher part dependent upon the tone set up by the lower ones.

It was up to each individual, though, to ascend the octaves of his or her inner musical being by cultivating the right kind of vibratory influences in daily life. "Nature provides materials vibrating in all possible ways," explained Besant, and it is incumbent upon each one of us to choose the right kinds. The more developed we become on the mental plane the better able we are to make those choices. "By his thoughts," explained Besant, man "strikes the keynote of his music, and sets up the rhythms that are the most powerful factors in the continual changes in his physical and other bodies."[52] The journey to self-realization is a process, according to Besant, of training the mind, step-by-step, to harmonize the finer matter of the body into a divine sonic resonance. This musicalized conception of the body and soul was inherited from Pythagorean and Platonic writings. The Theosophical theory of vibration drew directly upon the Pythagorean concept of the "harmony of the spheres," which proposed that earthly musical scales and harmonies have their equivalence in planetary spacing and motion, signaling a divine order of sound at work in the universe.[53] Plato, too, suggested that the constantly moving universe causes a cosmic sound inaudible to the physical ear but which resonates with man's inner being. Causing our inner self to vibrate in harmony with this divine order of sound was the key to unlocking our latent spirituality in Besant's version of Theosophy.

Once our inner self has been set vibrating to the harmony of the spheres, our bodies also become resistant to potentially damaging vibrations that would otherwise cause us harm and hold back our spiritual development. "A pure body repels coarse particles because they vibrate at rates discordant with its own; a coarse body attracts them because their vibrations accord with its own," explained Besant.[54] Urban and industrial noise, significantly, was included among the coarse vibrations that, Theosophists thought, could be repelled by those who had purified their bodies. Besant explained that once our body has been set vibrating harmoniously, it will be "impervious to the jangling noises of earth."[55] Yet precisely because Theosophists conceived of selfhood as a matter of divine resonance and of vibrational cultivation, modern, mechanical noise was said to pose an acute threat to spiritual self-realization. According to Leadbeater, sound, like thought, takes material form on the astral and mental as well as the physical plane of existence. Mechanical noises, such as the "strident screech of a railway engine" or the "scream of the steam siren which is sometimes used to call together the hands at a factory" produce "sharp pointed projectiles," which have "the disintegrating power of a serious electrical shock."[56] In his book, *The Hidden Side of Things* (1913), Leadbeater complained, "An enormous number of artificial noises (most of them transcendently hideous) are constantly being produced all about us, for our so-called civilization is surely the noisiest with which earth has ever yet been cursed." For those who have not ascended to full spiritual selfhood, noise's effect on the astral body is not unlike "that of a sword-thrust upon the physical body."[57] Leadbeater went on to warn that "the perpetual roar" and "the ceaseless beating of disintegrating vibrations" in modern cities not only inhibits self-realization but will lead to increasing cases of "nervous breakdown and insanity" if left unchecked. Living next to a noisy street, he explained, was like living beside "an open sewer."[58] Spiritual harmony and mental health thus went hand-in-hand for Theosophists. They agreed with proponents of noise abatement that noise causes nervousness, but argued, in contrast to those such as Lord Horder, that spiritual self-realization, achieved through bodily contact with spiritual vibrations, was the only remedy to this problem.

Those who attain true spiritual selfhood and who are aware of the higher part of the mental plane may hear the spiritual thought-forms of other initiates, or indeed the messages of Devas (the term used by Theosophists to refer to angels). This process, and the extent to which it simultaneously allows the perceiver operating on higher planes of existence to remain unharmed by the vibrations of noise, is depicted in the 1929 drawing *Silence* by the American artist Emil Bisttram, a follower of Theosophy (Figure 2.1).[59] This image mirrors, in interesting ways, the logo of Britain's Anti-Noise League discussed in Chapter 1. In place of the professional man attempting to think is a figure closed off from the physical sense impressions of the world. In place of the chaotic street soundscape are the thought-forms of initiates or Devas that reach the mental plane of the thinker, setting up, in turn, finer

FIGURE 2.1 Emil Bisttram, *Silence* (1929).

and finer vibrations of matter within the innermost self. Although this is a physically silent scene, it is replete with references to occult vibrations that, although inaudible to the ear, may by perceived by the higher self attuned to the harmony of the spheres.

The ability to receive spiritual thought-forms was a relatively rare quality, however. For most people, harmonizing the vibrations of the subtler matter of the body and soul was a case of putting themselves in contact with forces in the natural world that were already, unlike the coarse vibrations of artificial noises, vibrating at the rate of the subtler spiritual matter. Music, especially that composed by Theosophical initiates, was one such agent. Just like any other natural phenomena, music operates through both the denser and finer forms of matter, according to Theosophists. "While the physical ear is responding to the vibrations in the coarser matter of the gases which form the air," explained Besant, music also impacts directly upon the finer matter of our emotional and mental bodies. Gradually, as the composer learns how to write music vibrating in finer and finer matter, he may learn how to elevate the hearer to knowledge of the higher planes. "As the music is made to express finer and finer emotions," explained Besant, "responsive, sympathetic thrillings may be set up" in the hearer.[60] The hearer is "lifted on the wings of the vibrations that are music" and may thus "reach the threshold of the spiritual world."[61] Composer Cyril Scott, like Besant, argued that in addition to the sounds we physically hear, there are "unheard strains" in music that "possess hidden powers of a 'telepathic' nature" and that "affect our subtler bodies directly or through the 'emotional atmosphere,' and so educate the soul."[62] In *Thought-Forms*, Besant and Leadbeater offered visual illustrations of religious music's astral forms as perceived by those who have developed their "finer senses."[63] In contrast to the sharp projectiles of noise that Leadbeater chose not to illustrate, these beautiful vibrational forms bring evolutionary benefit to the subtler bodies of their hearers and "persist and continue in vigorous action long after the sound itself has died away," according to Leadbeater.[64]

Because Theosophists conceived of the body's vibrations as an earthly echo of the harmony of the spheres, the art of music came to be thought of as one of the most powerful and direct stimulants of the higher emotional and mental planes of man. Scott's book on this topic, *The Influence of Music on History and Morals* (1928) was subtitled *A Vindication of Plato*, a reference to Plato's theory that "Mousikē" provides "the soul with motion."[65] Scott explained that "throughout the ages, philosophers, religionists and savants" have realized this "supreme importance of sound."[66] Unlike sculpture, which operates on the physical plane, and painting, which impacts upon the astral matter of man through color, music's finer vibrations were said by Theosophical leaders to appeal to the mental plane, the level at which the soul resides.[67] The more divinely inspired music the body comes into contact with, Theosophists argued, the more the body itself begins to resonate to the harmony of the spheres, taking on an inherent musicality of its own. Besant wrote that at the early stages of our existence, our denser bodies give out a jangling noise, in keeping with the noisy world around us. As we become more spiritually attuned to higher worlds, however, our bodies become more and more musical: "As we grow into spiritual reality," Besant wrote, "transcending the dissonance of the world in which we live, we are playing the true music, creating the true melody, and are summing up our being in one pure note with countless harmonious overtones."[68] A writer to the *Theosophical Review* described this moment of self-realization, drawing attention to the mysterious combination of physical silence and spiritual sound alluded to in Bisttram's drawing:

> Faint nature-sounds rise from the depths. Entering Me, the struggling notes gain strength in harmony; attuned in Me, they burst forth, triumphant—all sounds contained in One.
>   Oh that harmony! Unutterable, never-to-be-forgotten! The hushed eternal Mass-bell; the Lord speaking—the Silent Voice![69]

Music was thus elevated to the highest status among the arts by Theosophists, an agent capable of aiding the spiritual evolution of mankind. This philosophical elevation had a far-reaching cultural and intellectual influence on artists and composers, providing a central reference point for aesthetic modernism as it developed in the decades on either side of the First World War. Theosophical ideas were taken up by a number of well-known avant-garde composers, including Alexander Scriabin, Henry Cowell, and Dane Rudhyar, as well as Luigi Russolo, all of whom believed that formal experimentation was required in order to produce the finer, spiritual vibrations of a fully magical music. They sometimes did so, as in Scott's case, specifically to counter the damaging effects of mechanical noises. Russolo's art of noises may be interpreted in this way, too: not only did he create what he thought were spiritually powerful sounds, but at the same time, through his artistic intervention, he hoped to transform the coarse, earthly, vibrations of noise into the finer, spiritual, vibrations of mystical music. The spiritual evolution of mankind depended upon ever more spiritually elevated music, and it was precisely this motivating factor that inspired the avant-gardism of figures like Russolo.

In addition to composers who based their compositional aesthetic on Theosophical teachings, high-profile visual artists and filmmakers attempted to replicate the vibrational qualities of music in their work. Wassily Kandinsky, for example, described his abstract paintings as musical compositions as part of his own version of Theosophy, which he set out in the influential book *Concerning the Spiritual in Art* (1911).[70] For modernist aestheticians such as Ricciotto Canudo, who published one of the earliest and most influential theories of abstract cinema in 1911 as well as being involved in the French Theosophical Society, music was a "religion of the future" because, by worshipping it, mankind would eventually ascend to divine harmony.[71] Canudo argued that "by answering to our contemporary religious impulses which as yet remain unsatisfied," music can "become all-powerful. Its action already is beginning to be felt, and the great symphonic séances that rapidly increase in number show how the public is becoming more and more faithful to music."[72]

Rejecting the idea of institutional religion, Canudo believed that spiritual elevation was best achieved by bringing the body and the soul into contact with the beautiful, mystical, abstract forms upon which music is based because the shape of music comes closest to revealing to us the shape of God's universe. The abstract forms of music should be replicated not only in the sonic but also in the visual arts, including cinema, according to Canudo. Avant-garde "visual music" filmmakers such as Oskar Fischinger were among those who took up this project while maintaining a keen interest in the occult.[73] Music, most magical of nature's forces, thus became a religion in its own right for those modernist artists and art theorists influenced by Theosophy.

Magical Sounds in the Modern City

Far from remaining in the realms of theory and aesthetics only, Theosophical ideas inspired a series of practical social experiments in the techniques of magic sound in early-twentieth-century Britain. These experiments were intended to bring vibratory benefit to the widest possible number of people by offering them an alternative to noise. While composers such as Cyril Scott tried to build Theosophical principles of vibration into their music, others concentrated on the ways in which sound could be put to use as an agent of mass social renovation, equivalent in scale to the Anti-Noise League's campaign against "unnecessary noise." Theosophy was by no means a jealously guarded secret, and many of its devotees saw their role as being essentially practical in nature, a matter of making Theosophical techniques of spiritual self-realization known to the ordinary man and woman. One such devotee was Maud MacCarthy. Though little-remembered today, MacCarthy's work—as a celebrated concert violinist, as a pioneer of ethnomusicology and of the study of Indian music, as an early practitioner of music therapy, and also as a practical occultist—deserves more attention than it has hitherto received.[74] Believing that the influence of magical sound vibrations alone had the power to lift mankind out of its base materialism and barbarous warmongering, MacCarthy's life's work was to undertake ever more ambitious social experiments in the art of magical sound. Through her work, and that of others like her, Theosophical influence extended far beyond the confines of pamphlets, lecture halls, and individual pieces of art or music. Indeed, MacCarthy was interested less in the aesthetic application of Theosophical ideas than she was in their practical social use. "Theosophy," she exclaimed in 1914, "is needed 'at the street corners!'"[75]

   Born in Ireland in 1882 but brought up in Australia where her father Charles practiced as a physician, MacCarthy came to London as a child prodigy violinist in the 1890s. Having built up quite a reputation as a concert soloist, MacCarthy had to retire in 1905 due to the onset of neuritis. She was dogged by painful physical illness throughout her life, and it was often in relation to these episodes that MacCarthy developed her theories about the restorative and healing effects of musical sound. Her contact with the Theosophical Society began at around the turn of the twentieth century; in 1900, at the age of eighteen, she signed up as a member and had evidently become familiar with the writings of Annie Besant by this time. MacCarthy's interest in the magical properties of sound was drawn directly from her early experiences as a concert performer. "I would ponder and try to understand why one note or chord of music produces one psycho-physiological effect, and another, a different one," she explained. "My mind was a seething *why* about music." One day, at the age of twenty-five, "a new stream of life came to me," she remembered, "and with it a mystic outpouring of sound, so that I heard much of 'the music of the spheres.'"[76]

MacCarthy had been admitted by Besant into the "Esoteric Section" of the Theosophical Society, the group for the most advanced initiates in the organization, in 1905. Two years later, having given up her life as a concert violinist, MacCarthy moved to India to continue her Theosophical studies in sound with Besant, with whom she developed a close working relation-ship, remaining at the Society's complex in Adyar, Madras, for several years. This was a formative period in her life, the point at which she developed her distinctive interest in the social, as opposed to the narrowly individualistic, applications of magical sound. Whereas in the writings of Besant and other Theosophical leaders, the emphasis was on the way in which individuals, by dint of their own mental undertaking, might cultivate spiritual elevation through vibration, MacCarthy's work focused instead on the need to create harmonious vibrations within and across nations. In a 1909 lecture, Mac-Carthy explained, "All the laws of individual, and municipal, and national life are founded on the basic law of vibrations," by which she meant that not only individual health, but also collective, social health, was dependent upon harmonious vibration. She went on to explain, "The nation in which there are the greater number of minds thinking in harmony" is a successful nation, and "it succeeds because for every man whose nature vibrates in accord with the life in another man, there is added to the working energy of that man and that nation."[77]

Evolution, not only of individual people or of particular nations, but of the whole of humanity, depended, she thought, upon the development of harmonious vibrations. It was no good for only a handful of initiates to achieve spiritual realization, for in order to ascend to the heavenly realm, mankind must resonate as one unit, she believed. "Evolution is the repetition of homogeneous principles in varying keys and widening octaves, onward and outward, until each octave in the universal gamut has given forth its tones," she wrote.[78] This was MacCarthy's version of internationalism, a world order of harmonious resonance in which nations, one by one, would be brought into vibratory compatibility. It was also the true natural path, thought Mac-Carthy, because the higher self within each one of us emanates from the same source—that is, from God. The pursuit of evolution toward divinity depends on our ability to realize the collective "oneness" of our inner selves. "We say that harmony is happiness," she wrote. "Now the word 'harmony,' however you apply it, connotes the having of relation with others. That is how, in manifestation, the One Self is realized in the many."[79] These relations can be brought about only by establishing simultaneity of spiritual vibration, man's inner music, in every member of the human race, and this shared selfhood, MacCarthy added, could only be brought about by "modifying bodies."[80]

Such body modification could best be brought about through magical sound, according to her. In order to bring about the evolution of mankind it was necessary to develop music that not only vibrated in finer and finer spiritual matter but also with an increasingly universal, transnational appeal. Because the techniques of magical sound had been preserved most accurately in the traditions of Indian Hindu music, it was necessary, MacCarthy believed, to gradually extend the principles of this musical tradition to the music of other peoples of the world. Besant, too, was convinced that Hindu music offered a model for future musical development. "I have not found in Western music," she wrote, "strong and ennobling as it is, that peculiar and elusive power which Hindu music predisposes to the higher forms of meditation."[81] Part of MacCarthy's work while in India, therefore, was to undertake investigation of traditional Indian music, learning to perform on classical Indian instruments and to sing in the microtonality of traditional Indian scales. Learning to accurately produce musical notes in smaller gradations than the semitones of Western music was especially important. Besant explained that "A chromatic scale in the West gives the limits on a Western piano," but "in the East, many notes are interposed, and the gradations are so fine as to be indistinguishable to a Western ear until it is trained to hear them."[82] It is these magical notes, quarter tones and still smaller subdivisions, which cause the "subtlest vibrations in the higher bodies" and "thrill" the body "to spiritual ecstasy."[83] The idea that the spiritual body vibrated in finer matter than the physical body had its equivalent, therefore, in musical tonality. The finer the subdivisions of tone produced, the greater the spiritual effects would be. Chessa argues that the glissando effects in Russolo's art of noises, and Russolo's wider fascination with "enharmony," were inspired by this same Theosophical theory of microtonality.[84]

MacCarthy returned to London in 1911 as one of the foremost Western experts on Indian music and was invited to give a performance-lecture on the topic to the Musical Association (forerunner of today's Royal Musical Association) that same year.[85] However, once back in the hustle and bustle of the metropolis, MacCarthy realized, if she had not realized it before, that modern Britain was very far from existing in vibratory harmony, cursed as it was by the sensory "plagues" of materialistic civilization, as she put it.[86] Modern men and women "are born into the morass of competitive existence," complained MacCarthy. They "choke, splutter and struggle in it."[87] Selfhood, Theosophically defined, was almost impossible to obtain in the sensory conditions of early-twentieth-century London. "How can one be 'individual' when one's entire life is mechanized?" MacCarthy asked indignantly.[88] Evoking in detail all of the sensory impairments to selfhood, she later recalled what her life was like in London during the 1910s and 1920s, a period during which she returned to work as a rank-and-file orchestral violinist:

> In the morning I often awoke to an atmosphere which was impregnated with ozone produced by a machine, to counteract the effect of devitalised air! My clothes were artificial. I felt, every time I put them on, as if part of myself had been killed. I lived—under continual protest—in the character of that artificial self. I used cosmetics to hide the ravages of late hours (my job took me into the stifling atmosphere of theatres). I rushed about in taxis. At one time I had seven telephones in my house. My nerves were outraged. My soul and my senses were tortured, day after day, year after year, by noise, smoke, dirt, city sights and squalor. I had to take endless medicines to assist my deadened body. I had to live and work late hours in the glare of electric light, and often had to sleep in the hours of daylight. I was merely one among millions who purvey re-creation to the public; yet I neither recreated myself, nor the public![89]

Among the sensory tortures that plague modern civilization, noise was among the worst, according to MacCarthy. Precisely because magical sound vibrations have the potential to so powerfully transform the soul, the coarse vibrations of noise are doubly damaging to the Theosophical initiate in his or her struggle for spiritual harmony. "If a man is capable of being thrown into extasy by harmonies of sound," explained MacCarthy, "the same life that answers thus to their lofty suggestions will perceive greater discord in the harsh jangle of common noises. The pain of these to him will consist in his having the power to vibrate to the other, and in feeling cramped and frustrated by noises which less developed people would not notice at all."[90]

The solution, however, was not to seek a quieter world, for the soul thrives on the vibration of sound, but to replace noise with the vibrations of magical music. "As in every other sickness," she explained, "the sufferings of a sensitive personality may evoke their own cure."[91] Upon her return to London from India, MacCarthy set to work on designing this magical cure.

She began by establishing a series of Sunday morning concerts at the headquarters of the English Theosophical Society in London, using these occasions to experiment with different musical techniques, instruments, and composers. Competing with conventional Christian services across the capital, MacCarthy's devotional concerts went some way to establishing what Canudo had called for in his book *Music as a Religion of the Future*. "The Theosophical School of Music," as MacCarthy described it, "has been formed," she explained, "to provide a nucleus through which the finer forces of music may again flow out to the world. In order to provide this nucleus," she continued, "music must again be studied in the light of occult tradition."[92] She added, rather grandly, that "we must endeavour to restore the ancient musical priesthood to the world, regarding the production of music as a sacrament, and ourselves as the vessels through which the Masters and the other great Beings Who help on evolution may manifest Themselves through sound to mankind."[93] The Masters to whom MacCarthy referred here were the most powerful and mysterious group of spiritual beings living on earth. The Masters are capable of hearing the harmony of the spheres, according to MacCarthy, and they transmit this sound through their mental vibrations, but it is only heard by those who had dedicated themselves to the art of spiritual hearing. Such people were few in number, but MacCarthy considered herself to be among them. She used the Sunday morning concerts to identify others with the power to hear, and re-create, the harmony of the spheres.

One of the composers with whom MacCarthy collaborated at these concerts was John Foulds, a cellist with Manchester's Hallé orchestra who had himself pioneered Theosophical sound experiments at the Manchester University Settlement in Ancoats.[94] MacCarthy identified Foulds as the finest composer of Theosophically inspired music in the country and sought out ongoing collaboration with him at the Sunday morning concerts. With the Hallé struggling financially, Foulds had been making ends meet by working as a cinema organist in Manchester and gladly took up the opportunity to move to London and further his career as a full-time composer under the sponsorship of the Theosophical Society.[95] In addition to identifying composers such as Foulds, MacCarthy's intention at the Sunday morning concerts was to bring the widest possible range of concert performers into contact with Theosophical ideas by inviting them to participate in the performances. Members of the London Symphony Orchestra, the Queen's Hall Orchestra, and the Philharmonic Society participated, and MacCarthy hoped that, given time, Theosophical principles would spread throughout the musical world in Britain. "I have employed the best orchestral players," she explained, "with a view to establishing the T.S. [Theosophical Society] in a firm reputation with the musical world."[96] The point of this, of course, was that from humble beginnings as a Sunday morning concert series, Theosophical techniques would spread to all the major concert halls in Britain, turning them into temples of healing and self-realization, and establishing music as a religion of the future.

Among the most important musical principles which MacCarthy developed at the Sunday morning concerts was the need to work in "natural intonation." She explained that sound based on natural intonation was "sound proceeding without impediment, that is, harmoniously, through a body or bodies, producing the effects of joy, life, health, wisdom, godliness, and other like qualities of universal splendour."[97] Its opposite was "sound proceeding discordantly, that is, irregularly, through these bodies, and producing the opposite effects."[98] Unnatural intonation included mechanical and urban noise but also music that had been written without knowledge of the spiritual self and without understanding of the need to cultivate vibratory harmony in the hearer. The instruments and scales used in Western music do not work in natural intonation because they divide the sounds of nature into artificial divisions of tones and semitones and cannot easily, therefore, incorporate the microtones which Besant and MacCarthy had identified as being the key to re-creating the harmony of the spheres. Those who can hear the harmonic working of the cosmos realize that it is made up of "infinite shades of tone, quality, and meaning." "Nature, divine nature," MacCarthy explained, "is All-Sound—one vast perfect and unbroken gradation—unbroken into scales."[99] "Our instruments on the physical plane," however, "fall short of the perfection" of this sound, she argued.[100] It was for this reason that she would not use instruments with a tempered pitch such as pianos and organs. "Tempered pitch, being an artificial contrivance which was not used until some five centuries ago," explained MacCarthy, "is useless for occult purposes."[101]

MacCarthy's own performance specialty was singing in microtonality. She used this technique in the sound healing for which she became well known in London in the 1930s. She described this work as "phono-therapy," the ability to cure "by means of pure sound-waves alone."[102] MacCarthy claimed that "every organ, each nerve centre of the body, has a note. My sensitivity is so acute that when I begin a treatment I can almost invariably hear the note or notes in the patient's anatomy which require to be dealt with."[103] A *Daily Mail* journalist who visited MacCarthy's clinic described the phono-therapy process:

> From her deep-set eyes, aglow with fire, the soul of a mystic shines forth. Putting her palms on my spine, a low musical note which is outside the normal range of a woman's voice broke from her lips; a single sound, starting as a hum, growing in volume and power, making my ears ring, and resounding in my body with the sensation of gently lapping waves.[104]

One of MacCarthy's patients wrote to confirm:

> The Treatment sets up such harmony in all ways—at least it feels like that when one's nerves are not merely soothed and rested but set in happy vibration. I sleep so quietly now. With nerves thus harmonious my hearing is helped.[105]

MacCarthy probably undertook such work mainly in order to pay the bills, for after she began a romantic relationship with Foulds during the First World War, prompting the scandal which resulted in their banishment from the Theosophical Society (she was already married to the Theosophist William Mann), the couple struggled financially. MacCarthy's real calling was for much more elaborate social work and for sound healing on a far wider scale. Alongside the Sunday morning concerts, she set up the Brotherhood of Arts, Crafts and Industries, an organization that sought to restore the religious principles of work, as she saw them. Later describing this as the "Temple of Labour," MacCarthy believed that in place of the "inhumanity of our industrial system," the world should return to medieval-style labor guilds in which workers would learn a craft and work in cooperation with one another.[106] "If we are once more to produce those things which are necessary to life, and are therefore beautiful, we must return to handcrafts," explained MacCarthy. "There can be no craftweal without handcraft, because the Spirit of man is the real Worker, and the mechanism of that Spirit is flesh—the brain and heart and hands of man—not machinery."[107] She established a test workers guild in Notting Hill at which, she explained, "we proved that a London street may be made neighbourly."[108] The workers' communities that MacCarthy encouraged would also be centers of spiritual devotion. "There should be rooms," she wrote, "where the tired workers are healed and renewed by sound used therapeutically, and by colour and form used in the same way."[109] Although sympathetic to the argument of social reformers that urban workers needed better housing conditions and increased wages, she believed that, without cultivating harmonious inner vibrations through the application of divinely inspired music, mankind was doomed to continue along a ruinous path. "It is no use talking to people about cooperating with the Government for the improving of their sanitary conditions," she explained, "if we allow their minds to be hourly polluted by the most potent force in nature—sound."[110] MacCarthy thus considered noise to be the most urgent of public health hazards. Temples of Labour would also, therefore, be temples of magical sound.

MacCarthy's most spectacular sonic experiment was to organize an annual commemorative event for the war dead of the First World War. At this event, an especially composed requiem by Foulds was performed. Based on the Theosophical principles of music that MacCarthy had established at the Sunday morning concerts, Foulds's *A World Requiem* was also openly internationalist in its libretto, a text that MacCarthy had written based on excerpts from the Bible, Bunyan's *Pilgrim's Progress*, and the works of the Hindu poet Kabir.[111] As with Foulds's many other works, *A World Requiem* was intended, first and foremost, to cause sympathetic spiritual vibrations in its hearers. This aim took precedence over the need to draw upon the formal conventions of Western harmony and melody. It was for this reason that Foulds's works, including his *Requiem*, were sometimes described as modern in style by critics.[112] A remarkable feature of *A World Requiem*, apart from the fact that it called for an enormous orchestra and a chorus of a thousand voices, is that by virtue of their persistence and thanks in part to the support of the British Music Society's Theosophically inclined member, Arthur Eaglefield Hull, Foulds and MacCarthy managed to convince the British Legion (now the Royal British Legion), the charitable organization for the support of ex-servicemen, to back the work as the official musical commemoration of the Great War. Under the terms of the agreement with the Legion, *A World Requiem* was to be staged in an official national ceremony—the Festival of Remembrance—at the Royal Albert Hall in South Kensington each year on Armistice Day, November 11th. Beginning in 1923, audiences, including royalty, packed into the Albert Hall, an iconic symbol of British national culture, to hear Foulds's Theosophical war requiem.

What the British Legion did not at first realize was that *A World Requiem* had been conceived by Foulds and MacCarthy as an experiment in hearing, and re-creating, the harmony of the spheres. Subtitled "A Cenotaph in Sound" and advertised as such on promotional flyers (as in Figure 2.2), the work was intended to embody MacCarthy's definition of natural intonation; it contains several uses of quarter tone notes produced by the string section of the orchestra. The work was also conceived "clairaudiently," that is, as telepathic vibrations received from the Deva with whom MacCarthy had cultivated a communicational bond. MacCarthy wrote in 1924 that "The inner

FIGURE 2.2 Front
cover of the 1923 Festival
of Remembrance concert
program.

history of the 'World Requiem' is a very beautiful thing . . . the second part
of the work was actually outlined in a definite and masterly way, from the
other side."[113] The sounds that Foulds and MacCarthy heard clairaudiently
were so beautiful that they could not easily be re-created on conventional
Western instruments, so Foulds was forced to design a new instrument, the
Sistrum, a harplike object strung with a multitude of tiny cymbals, to re-
create the sound.

The idea was that *A World Requiem* would receive an annual performance
in the Royal Albert Hall and that it would eventually be adopted throughout
Britain and the British Empire as the official musical commemoration of
the war. Performances were indeed set up in Birmingham and Bristol, and
a BBC radio broadcast was arranged from a studio in Glasgow. The amateur
choristers who sung the work, drawn in London from choirs such as the
People's Palace Choir, the Central London YMCA Musical Society (which
Foulds had directed for some years), the Dulwich Philharmonic Society, and
the Islington Choral Society among many others, were deeply attached to
the work. Writing collectively to the British Legion in 1925, they said, "We
have come to look upon that work and its annual performance as an expression of our deepest feelings about those who gave their lives in the war."[114]

Audiences, too, responded positively to the *Requiem*. One audience member, probably influenced by Foulds's program notes outlining the spiritual meaning of the work, wrote to confirm:

> To me, it seemed like music of another sphere—and one bit especially made me think and WONDER IF THAT WILL BE THE MUSIC WE SHALL HEAR WHEN WE PASS FROM THIS PLANE TO ANOTHER. It sounded like thousands and thousands of murmurs welcoming someone towards them and then a hush as if one's breath had been taken away with the sheer joy and beauty of it all . . . I . . . feel that it is the music of another world.[115]

The positive reaction of audiences to the obviously mystical character of *A World Requiem* supports Jay Winter's argument that spiritualism and Theosophy played an important role in the immediate cultural aftermath of the First World War, providing a point of spiritual reference for mourning and memorialization in Britain as elsewhere.[116]

Despite popularity with choristers and audiences, the case of *A World Requiem* also demonstrates the potential incompatibility of Foulds and Mac-Carthy's Theosophical ideas with certain elements of mainstream musical and religious culture in early-twentieth-century Britain. Music critics panned Foulds's music, mistaking its attempt to cultivate spiritual resonance as a lack of musical invention. The *Observer*'s music critic found the work "extremely dull" and pointed to its "lack of harmonic variety and melodic vitality."[117] It was, however, the antipathy of the *Daily Express* newspaper that, in the end, caused the British Legion to withdraw its support from MacCarthy's Festival of Remembrance. The *Express* objected to the religiosity, solemnity, and internationalism of *A World Requiem*. Its nationalist stance and support for Empire protectionism led it to be deeply suspicious of Foulds and MacCarthy's internationalist ideals. In 1927, the *Express* took over the running of the Festival of Remembrance and replaced the *Requiem* with military bands and patriotic community singing. The format remains relatively unchanged to this day.[118] Foulds and MacCarthy were so outraged by their ousting that they eventually moved permanently to India, where Foulds became director of music at All-India Radio and MacCarthy continued her mystical investigations of magical sound. MacCarthy's phono-therapy project met with a similar fate. In 1933, the *John Bull* magazine ran a damning exposé that rejected out of hand the esoteric basis upon which phono-therapy was based. It accused MacCarthy of quackery and mocked the assorted Theosophical texts and images present at her phono-therapy clinic. "A very queer mixture of mysticism exists at this clinic," warned the *John Bull*, "and it is hardly necessary to add that it is not registered as a nursing home or in any way recognised by the medical profession."[119] Occultism, thus, sometimes met with vigorous opposition from those discursive paradigms—such as nationalism and conventional medicine—which it openly challenged. However, this should not lead us to assume that the project of re-enchantment lacked influence or importance in early-twentieth-century Britain. Discursive clashes such as those that MacCarthy encountered with the *Daily Express* and the *John Bull*, especially when considered alongside the *Daily Mail*'s more sympathetic reporting of phono-therapy, are suggestive instead of the "unresolved tension between the spiritual and the secular," which Alex Owen has identified at the heart of British modernity.[120]

In Tune with the Infinite: Self-Help for the Soul

The idea that magical sound vibrations could counteract the threat of noise can also be found in the advice given to those suffering from nervous afflictions. While occult theories of the spiritual self may not ultimately have found a place in mainstream medicine, they flourished on the early-twentieth-century border between popular psychology and occult investigation, a frontier occupied by self-help writers such as Edwin Ash. These self-help writers mediated between the secular disenchantment of rational science on the one hand and popular alternative spiritualities on the other by fusing the principles of psychology with occult methods of healing. The notion that musical vibrations could counteract the damage done to the body by noise, although it originated in esoteric teachings, was taken up with enthusiasm by writers of popular psychological self-help books for the nervous. Self-help authors such as Ash strayed outside the territory of conventional medicine and psychotherapy in their efforts to bring the widest possible range of present-day health theories to sufferers from nerves. They embraced unconventional spiritual ideas and openly subscribed to the argument put forward by occultists such as Besant that modern science had not yet uncovered all of the forces at work in the natural world, particularly where the psyche was concerned. They also openly propagated, and popularized, the idea that a spiritual influence could be brought to bear in the art of healing and in the maintenance of good health.

Because sound, and musical sound in particular, had been invested with so much mystical potential by occult investigators such as Besant and Mac-Carthy, it featured as a suggested therapeutic agent in self-help literature, mirroring warnings that noise was among the most destabilizing factors in modern life, indeed often appearing adjacent to these very warnings. Writings on neurasthenia and other functional diseases of the nervous system, as

Chapter 1 pointed out, often contrasted the arrhythmic character of man-made noise, as a cause and symptom of nervous illness, with the essentially rhythmic qualities of the natural soundscape. In the writings of the original theorist of neurasthenia, George M. Beard, and the most prolific British medical writer on noise, Dan McKenzie, music was evoked as ordered sound, allowing noise to be categorized as its other, sonic disorder. Both Beard and McKenzie noted that musical sound might be considered a therapeutic influence on the nerves, an antidote to the "nerve-jangling" effects of modern urban noise, but neither men devoted any sustained attention to music's healing powers. Yet, for the self-help writers who, as Chapter 1 detailed, considered noise to be an especial threat to the nerves, and who often likened the nervous system to a musical instrument, musical vibrations had a unique ability to calm the nerves and "restore their tone."[121]

W. Charles Loosmore's *Nerves and the Man: A Popular Psychological and Constructive Study of Nervous Breakdown* (1920) was among the most emphatic of such self-help books on this point. Loosmore argued that "music has a far deeper meaning than is generally supposed" and that it plays "an important part in reorganising the mental faculties and enabling the mind to function in a healthy and balanced manner."[122] H. Ernest Hunt, author of *Nerve Control: The Cure of Nervousness and Stage-Fright* (1915) and *Self-Training: The Lines of Mental Progress* (1918), advocated in his advice to sufferers from nervousness that music has a mysterious power to bring the nerves to order in, among others, his 1932 book, *The Spirit of Music*.[123] Hunt proposed that "Music exists as a permanent witness to the reality of the intangible, and to the power and pre-eminence of qualities which no money can purchase and which Time is powerless to destroy."[124] Self-help writers agreed with McKenzie that music, unlike noise, brought an orderly and rhythmic vibration to bear upon the nervous system, but they also, significantly, identified music's most powerful effects as being essentially *spiritual*, rather than physical, in character. This set them apart from conventional physicians such as McKenzie. Their concern was with physical and mental breakdown, but they thought that such illness was intimately connected to the health not only of the body or the mind, but also of the soul.

Self-help writers such as Ash, Loosmore, and Hunt were in the vanguard of those who popularized psychology and psychotherapeutic treatment to a mass audience in early-twentieth-century Britain. Ash's 1911 book, *Nerves and the Nervous*, for example, was one of the early commercial successes of publisher Mills and Boon, appearing alongside popular titles on children, cookery, the home, and travel as well as the romantic novels for which the publisher later became so well known.[125] Distinct from practical psychoanalysts and professional psychologists, popular psychological self-help writers such as Ash, Loosmore, and Hunt brought a variety of expertise and backgrounds to the field. In Ash's case, this background was medicine, but Loosmore and Hunt had in common a particular interest in the relationship between psychology and spirituality. Loosmore had the more conventional religious background having practiced as a Congregationalist minister in the North of England.[126] Hunt, a schoolteacher, was a spiritualist, who, having published several texts on psychology and the nerves (including *Nerve Control*, which was aimed specifically at stage performers), went on to teach psychology in specialist music colleges in addition to maintaining his prolific publishing career in psychological and spiritualist matters.[127]

While canonical pioneers of psychoanalysis such as Freud may have dismissed religion as a "delusionary system designed to keep men and women from understanding the true nature of their instinctual drives," the relationship between psychology and religion was in fact much closer than might immediately be assumed in early-twentieth-century Britain.[128] Man's inner life had, prior to the claims of psychologists, been in the jurisdiction of the churches and their ministers, but, as Graham Richards argues, a direct clash between the two "did not in fact materialise in Britain."[129] Rather, Christian ministers often recognized that the techniques of psychology could aid them in their pastoral work. Psychologists, for their part, were by no means universally dismissive of religion, and many of them in fact came to think of religious belief as "the natural outcome of healthy psychological development."[130] The famous American psychologist William James, author of *The Varieties of Religious Experience* (1902), was among those who came to this conclusion.[131] Nervousness, as the malady par excellence of the period 1890–1930, was rethought in this context as a symptom of disrupted psycho-religious well-being. Petteri Pietikainen has argued, in the case of Sweden, that a consensus emerged between psychologists and Lutheran pastors that secularization was itself at the root of the spread of nervousness in the modern age and that religious belief should play a central role in combating neurasthenia by aiding the maintenance of a healthy mind.[132]

While conventional psychological and religious authorities came to a friendly compromise over claims to speak for man's inner life, the relationship between followers of alternative spiritual practices and the new psychology was closer still. Theosophists and spiritualists were attracted to psychology as a potential science for the soul and, in turn, their theorization of the occult power of the mind influenced psychological theory, particularly in the informal sphere of self-help writing.[133] This was a dual process that Hanegraaff has described as the "psychologisation of religion and sacralisation of psychology."[134] "Alternative therapy," the offshoot of this process, was one of the occult revival's most durable and influential legacies, Hanegraaff points out, guiding the path taken by alternative medicine and self-help writing throughout the twentieth century.[135] "The popular impact of psychology," completes, for Hanegraaff, "the series of transformations by which an esoteric religious worldview was gradually adapted to contemporary society."[136] Esoteric religious ideas found their widest audience and applicability, in other words, through popular psychological self-help books such as Ash, Loosmore, and Hunt's. Although the following pages focus on these three writers by way of a case study, their blending of occult psychology with medical psychology and their advice about the magic effects of musical sound was typical of a wider trend in early-twentieth-century self-help culture.

Those who wrote self-help books for the nervous in early-twentieth-century Britain, as Chapter 1 pointed out, were part of a phase in the history of psychiatric medicine in which neither somatic nor psychosomatic explanations had come to fully dominate in the treatment of mental illness. Belief in a spiritual basis for nervousness had a role to play in this transitional period. It stood to reason to self-help writers that functional nervous diseases, including conditions such as neurasthenia, which had no obviously visible organic cause, might be linked to the invisible workings of the spirit. Self-help literature's discussion of neurasthenia and nervousness was indeed interwoven with Theosophical and spiritualist ideas about the body and about self-realization. Alfred Taylor Schofield was another author who, like Ash, Loosmore, and Hunt, became interested, simultaneously, in psychotherapeutic therapy in the treatment of nervousness and in occult spirituality, the two being essential counterparts in the progression of medicine and the treatment of nervous disorders. Like Ash, too, Schofield, published self-help books that ranged across these topics.[137] Self-help writers agreed with conventional psychotherapists that techniques such as suggestion and autosuggestion could be adopted in the resistance of nervous illness, but that the effectiveness of such treatments was, at root, an indication of the inner divinity of all human beings. The psyche, for religiously inspired writers like Ash, was not simply a subconscious store of memories whose troublesome intrusions into consciousness could be corrected by therapy and suggestion, but a higher, spiritual self that could be cultivated in such a way as to harness the spiritual powers latent in man, including the ability to establish the health of the physical body.

Throughout the history of medicine, Ash argued, a realization gradually developed that illness could be cured by divine forces. "From the most ancient times down to the present day," argued Ash, spiritual healing has evolved "from the grossest rites of superstition to an increasing realisation of spiritual power as an expression of a divine principle of love."[138] Starting out as "invocation of helpful gods to exorcise and destroy evil demons," this divine principle, explained Ash, is now conceived "as the workings of pure spirit in matter."[139] Explicitly adopting the Theosophical theory of the subtle body, Ash believed that man's spiritual existence was no less real than his material existence, and that the one could be caused to influence the other in medical practice and self-help. "All life is spiritual," argued Ash, and "in its inner working all healing is spiritual, whether manifested through the physical, the mental, or the spiritual—whether expressed in results of Body, Mind or Spirit."[140] Hunt, similarly, described healing as emanating from an "innate divinity" that "works from within outwards."[141] "The mind moulds the body," he explained, but this process works, according to Hunt, not as do sense impressions from the outside world through the physical nervous system to the brain, but from the soul, the higher inner self, outward through the "subtle body" identified by Theosophists.[142] The subtle, spiritual, body was, in such theories, an interface between the higher self and the physical body. If one could cultivate a higher spiritual selfhood, then the subtle matter of the body would bring to order its physical counterpart.

Hunt explained to his readers that we live in "two bodies," one natural and the other spiritual. "There is no particular difficulty in picturing how this can be," Hunt continued, "for both worlds are to an extent material but of a different grade of vibration; we have to get away from the idea that the two things cannot occupy the same space at the same time."[143] Indeed, according to Hunt, "The reality of the invisible is surely one of the things to which the thoughts should grow accustomed" in the cultivation of nervous well-being.[144] Hunt argued that the body reacts to the vibrations sent to it from the mind: "The vibration rate of the body," he wrote, "is largely determined by the thoughts."[145] These vibrations may inculcate nervousness if the individuals in question have shut themselves off from the reality of their higher spiritual self. In this case, the vibrations emanating from the subconscious mind are irregular, arrhythmic, and thus damaging to health. In order to cultivate a higher selfhood capable of setting the healing vibrations of the spiritual body in motion, Hunt argued that the conscious mind must train its subconscious counterpart in the "knowledge of spirit, of ourselves and our friends as spirit-actors in the spirit-drama of the world." Only this knowledge can "give us stability in the time of trouble."[146] For those whose thoughts vibrate at the higher rate of spiritual self-realization, the body is calmed, according to Hunt:

> Death, accident, disease, blows, wounds, and hardships may assail the body, like the storms that beat and rage about the house, but quiet within—for spirit is ever calm—is the thinker living on another plane of being, vibrating at a

higher rate than these can ever reach, intrinsically unaffected by these coarser happenings.[147]

This was a technique of healing which, Ash pointed out, had been understood by ancient civilizations but had been excluded from modern medicine and psychotherapy. "Man seems to have lost knowledge of, and touch with, what is the most marvelous part of his complex organisation," wrote Ash, "and is only now beginning once more to take an interest in, or to understand, the vast capacities of his inmost self."[148] Explicitly adopting Theosophy's critique of materialist science, Ash wrote:

> The great fallacy of modern science has been the assumption that the occult powers and influences upon which the ancients laid so much stress either do not exist or are of no importance. True it is that because we have no definite means of measuring these things they have scarcely come within the province of physical science, nevertheless these influences are there not only to be studied, but to be made use of by those who by training or natural aptitude are fitted to purpose the ancient wisdom.[149]

Ash argued that modern psychotherapy, to its credit, had begun the task of investigating the occult properties of man's "subconsciousness," but he went on to criticize psychologists for failing to take account of the full potential of psychic healing.[150] He complained in relation to psychotherapists that, having uncovered a small part of the occult power of mind through techniques such as suggestion and autosuggestion, that they then rushed to explain their findings within the narrow parameters of conventional, materialist science.[151] It is for this reason, Ash argued, that psychologists have made less progress in the art of healing than have occult investigators. "We have to face the extraordinary fact," he wrote, "that scientific psychotherapy has rarely been able to effect the same widespread healing results as have frequently been achieved by comparatively untrained workers inspired by a strong faith in their own powers to control psychic forces far wider in scope and influence than those of simple suggestion."[152]

Although he was probably unaware of her work, Ash could easily have been writing here about Maud MacCarthy's experiments in phono-therapy. "Scientific" psychotherapists, as Ash described them, make the mistake of analyzing only the mind and its effects on the physical body without considering the spirit and its connection to the vast, but invisible, world of subtle matter, "the dim vistas stretching out on all sides of us."[153] Ash believed that in order to fully cultivate the power of the mind to overcome nervous illness, psychologists would need to understand not only how to plant simple suggestions into the subconscious, but also how to awaken spiritual selfhood by harnessing the innate divinity of man's higher self. "In the desire to link ourselves up with a far wider life of mental power that comes from a world associated with but not immediately manifest to the ordinary experiences of human life we are definitely leaving the orthodox psychological camp," acknowledged Ash.[154] But, he continued, "we must not be afraid to adventure with the magi and the prophets and the poets if we want greater knowledge and greater power to control our nerves and to live more abundant lives."[155] Ash noted that even if we cannot easily explain the experiences of the spiritualist, for example, these experiences indicate the existence of "forces of extraordinary potency as regards human mind," which have the potential to yield vital clues in modern man's struggle against nervous illness.[156]

In addition to this direct reference to spiritualism, Ash's 1912 book *Mental Self-Help: A Practical Handbook* directly referenced Theosophical ideas in its attempt to explain the difference between mental and spiritual healing, the difference, that is, between what scientific psychotherapists do and the techniques practiced by occultists. Ash proposed that psychotherapeutic treatments such as suggestion operate on the mental plane, but that there is also "a far higher plane than the mental, and it is from that higher psychic plane that we can look for the greatest benefits in the regeneration of mankind, either mentally or physically."[157] This was a reference to Theosophy's theory of the seven planes of existence, with the intuitional and divine planes higher up the spiritual hierarchy than the mental. Confirming Theosophists' assertion that individual men and women could cultivate higher forms of intuitional and divine selfhood, Ash argued, "What we have to study now from the practical standpoint is, how we can best get into touch with the great reservoir of psychic energy that seems so near and yet so difficult to reach."[158] He concluded that "the study of treatment through mind" must now encompass not only the standard tactics of suggestion and psychoanalysis, "but go farther and attempt to understand how and on what basis prayer and appeals to the highest spiritual instincts of mankind have curative value."[159]

The occult vibrations of the mind and the occult vibrations of music were held to be of essentially the same subtle matter by Theosophists and their followers in the emerging popular psychological self-help industry. For this reason, music was identified as one of the occult forces at work in nature that had the power to set the soul vibrating in those higher registers that led to true selfhood. Hunt explained that subtle matter existed not only in the human body, but also all around it in the natural world. "Just as the physical body is but the outer form of inner and finer selves, so also the physical world represents but the shell of inner worlds of finer graded matters."[160]

The latter could, given proper training, be caused to impact on the former, bringing the soul in harmony with God's universe. "Vibration is the key to the mystery," explained Hunt.[161] In *The Spirit of Music*, he argued that music "allies itself with the forces at work on the spiritual side." He agreed with Cyril Scott, John Foulds, and Maud MacCarthy that not all music had the power to aid the higher vibration of the soul, and that it was incumbent upon the initiated composer to write music that vibrated at the rate of the subtle, spiritual, matter of the world. "Sounds without sense or meaning are futile," explained Hunt, "notes without a heartfelt message are 'returned empty' as they were sent forth, and practice without purpose other than mere self-gratification, agility, or display, is a magnificent and glorious waste of time."[162] Foulds and others typically put jazz music and hypermodernist atonal music into this category. However, according to Hunt, "music, when its true underlying purport is discovered, is at once an inspiration and a most real means of achieving that fundamental object, for which our very existence here at this present moment is devised, namely spiritual growth and development."[163] Just as Hunt believed that one could plant spiritual ideas into the subconscious mind by the psychotherapeutic technique of suggestion, so he believed that, in essence, true art, including music, embedded itself as pure spirit in the psyche. "To explore the beauties of Art and Music," he explained, "is to add those beauties, by expression and the power of memory, to the self. Thus we may grow more beautiful, just as surely as by thinking ever in terms of pounds, shillings and pence, we grow more sordid and mercenary."[164] It is clear that Hunt was inspired by Theosophy because he held up Theosophist-composer Cyril Scott as an example of one whose music was designed to facilitate spiritual self-realization. Hunt's citation here was to Arthur Eaglefield Hull's writings on Scott.[165] Eaglefield Hull, a music writer and teacher, had, of course, been on the British Music Society committee that had originally recommended Foulds's *A World Requiem* to the British Legion, so it is evident that, among those conversant in Theosophical ideas, the priority to disseminate music with "vibrational purpose" was a shared and urgent one in early-twentieth-century Britain.

Loosmore's *Nerves and the Man* was similarly emphatic in its explanation of music as a stimulant of the spiritual self. "Common experience," explained Loosmore, "goes far to support the view that music has a strange and subtle power over the human mind, especially when the mind is labouring under stress or depression or excitement."[166] This is why music, he thought, could be a particularly useful therapeutic agent in the treatment of nervous illness. Loosmore argued that nervousness "is found only in the life of man. He alone has the power to become unnatural, and to upset the balance and rhythm which are characteristic of the natural world."[167] The solution to nervousness is, for Loosmore, "the natural world itself." "Nature," he explained, "is a living protest against nervous disorder."[168] Music, "just one mode of expressing that law of harmony which exists in and behind all life," is an emanation of nature, and thus has the power to restore the nerves to order.[169] But Loosmore, like Hunt, emphasized that music's effects on man were to be explained by spiritual rather than physical influence. "Music is perhaps the chief handmaid to religion," wrote Loosmore. Religion, he continued, "has much to do in stabilising and refreshing the mind. The intoned service, hymns, such as the *Te Deum*, the musical response, along with the deep-toned accompaniment of the organ, each and all of these are confessedly great aids in awing and quieting the mind of the worshipper."[170]

Loosmore acknowledged McKenzie's argument that music can also have a positive physical influence on the nerves. Returning us to the harmony of nature, "it is a reminder of the normal healthy state," and has a direct "stimulating effect" upon the nerves, leading to renewed health and vitality.[171] He encouraged the nervous patient to take up singing because the vibrations it caused in the throat and throughout the body had the effect of physically regenerating "tired and languishing nerves."[172] However, he also followed Hunt in arguing that music has direct access to our subconscious via the emotions. Since emotions impact in turn on "thought and action," the influence of music is to restore calmness of mind and relaxation of body. "It is possible so to appeal to the emotions by means of music," explained Loosmore, "as to influence for good not only the mind, but the whole man."[173] This was a form of psychotherapy, then, but a form of mind control brought about not by the suggestion of words but by the vibrations of musical sound. "Life would be far happier and more buoyant, not to speak of its being more efficient," Loosmore argued, "if we paid a little more attention to the appeal made to us by sweet and inspiring music."[174]

Indeed, Loosmore thought that failure to harness the restorative power of musical sound would put modern man at greater and greater risk of nervous breakdown. "We have no manner of doubt," he explained, "that, if we are to meet successfully the increasing stress and strain of the future, we shall do it best by availing ourselves more fully of the soothing and exhilarating influence of what has been called the healing art."[175] Loosmore thought that music had a special ability to calm the nerves specifically because it offers us "glimpses of the infinite" and a "feeling of kinship with the ultimate reality."[176] In supporting evidence, he quoted Thomas Carlyle, famous sufferer from noise, to the effect that music "is a kind of inarticulate, unfathomable speech, which leads us to the edge of the infinite and lets us for moments gaze into it."[177] Like Ash, Loosmore described this as a "high plane" of self-realization, evidence for some familiarity, at least, with Theosophical ideas.[178] Further evidence for this familiarity appears in Loosmore's list of the composers whose works he thought to have a particularly calming effect on the nerves. This list included not only Chopin, Grieg, and Sibelius, but also Cyril Scott, whose *Danse Negre* was identified by Loosmore as an especially good influence on the nerves.[179]

Of the three self-help writers under consideration here, though, it was Hunt who went the furthest in explaining to his readership the occult foundations of music's influence. To God, urged Hunt, "the Lord of Form, of Harmony, and Tune be praises ever sweetly sung by instruments of musick 'neath the hand of man; that Glory may be rendered as most justly due, to God, Creator of the Musick of the Spheres."[180] In Hunt's version of the Pythagorean theory of the constantly vibrating universe, man's higher self could become such an "instrument of musick." Although it could not produce any audible sound, its vibrations could nonetheless be in harmony with those of the heavenly realm. In *Nerve Control*, Hunt described the whole endeavor toward nervous well-being as essentially the art of getting "in tune" with the divine. He offered an analogy: "If a tuning-fork vibrates to D, it is impossible that it should respond to the call of a G fork."[181] Health is really a case of making our spiritual bodies vibrate at the correct pitch so as to be in tune with heaven. "If our whole attitude vibrates," continued Hunt, to the "lower tones of impotence and failure then the call of our divinity and high heritage may sound again and again and we shall be unable to hear. We have no spiritual ears to hear."[182]

Hunt borrowed this idea from the American self-help writer Ralph Waldo Trine, author of the best-selling work *In Tune with the Infinite*, first published in 1897 but followed by many reprints. This book argued that the "great central fact" of human life is the "coming into consciousness of our oneness" with the "Infinite Life" and "the opening of ourselves fully to this divine inflow."[183] Trine was part of the New Thought movement, which emerged in late-nineteenth-century America. Adherents of New Thought argued that one could take responsibility for one's own well-being by shifting the focus of life from the external, material world to the inner world of spirit.[184] Trine explained that each of us has the power to "open or to close ourselves" to "divine inflow." "This we have through the power of mind, through the operation of thought," he explained.[185] Also sometimes described as "harmonial religion," this movement emphasized the need to unite the inner self with the harmony of nature and thus, ultimately, with heaven, since, as Trine himself pointed out, "The word heaven means harmony."[186]

One tactic to get "in tune with the infinite," according to Hunt, is to use the power of thought and suggestion to "tune ourselves higher." Hunt likened this to an organ tuner, who, when "tuning a reed pipe . . . has another note sounding in order to give him the pitch, and he tunes up or down the scale through all degrees of dissonance until the pitch of his pipe nears that of the sounding note."[187] Since each of our conscious thoughts leaves "its indelible mark in raising or lowering the balance" of the mind, argued Hunt, "beyond question we possess the power of tuning ourselves upward in the direction of those ideals. This it is to vibrate to the higher tones of being," he continued, "and so to learn more of truth. This is the only learning that weighs anything in the truest scales."[188] In addition to suggestion and thought training, however, Hunt believed that hearing spiritually conceived music, vibrating in the required way, could facilitate mankind's tuning up to heaven. "The tuning of the body" to fine music, argued Hunt, "enables the spirit to express its melody the better."[189] Loosmore, too, suggested that neurasthenics were essentially out of tune with the divine vibrations of the universe. "The discordant note which is so often found in so many lives is unnatural. We are made for peace and calm, since we come of the calm source of all things."[190]

In the case of each of the self-help writers examined here, advice about the benefits of music followed shortly after warnings about noise. For example, Ash's warnings about noise and discussions of spiritual healing were adjacent to one another in texts such as *Nerve in Wartime* (1914) in which Ash advised his readership that "continual din produces effects which are physical and quite outside the direction of the victims' will power" but also that such effects can be resisted by "those whose faith is firm in the things of the Spirit."[191] Nervous resilience is, in fact, "steadfastness of the soul," according to Ash.[192] Describing nervousness as a "discordant note" was Loosmore's attempt to cast nervous illness as unnatural and caused by artificial stimulants such as mechanical noise. He aimed to show that the solution was to be found in the natural resources of God's universe, such as music, operating through the emotions and upon the spiritual self. Hunt put this argument most succinctly when he explained that, by cultivating the vibrations of the higher spiritual self and of the spiritual body, we can train the mind to reject the "coarser" vibrations of harmful sense impressions such as noise. This was a central part of his theory of "sense training."[193] Having set our body vibrating in tune with the divine, the lower vibrations of urban noise no longer affect us. Explaining how this process works in relation to the visual sense, Hunt wrote the following in his mystical text, *The Gateway of Intuition* (1934): "Sight cometh to a man through the light of his eyes and he beholdeth the multitude of things that are around him; but there is an inner vision which he may use for growth and his Soul's purposes."[194] Continuing with the example of sight, Hunt argued that "if he so desire, a man may close his vision to the outer world, so that the things of sense are curtained and concealed; then in a world within, amplified and from a thousand limits freed, his thoughts move with an unaccustomed grace."[195] We may do precisely the same with our sense of hearing, in Hunt's opinion, and this strategy was his solution to the threat posed by noise.

In Ash, Hunt, and Loosmore's self-help texts, therefore, the British public received clear advice that music written by certain kinds of spiritually inspired composers was among the most powerful antidotes to nervous decline and to the role that noise played in this process. Such self-help books prove that critique of noise did not lead only to disenchanted campaigns such as Lord Horder's for greater technical control over the urban soundscape. Critique of modernity, and of noise as the preeminent symbol of modernity's intrusion on the self, was also countered by those who sought modern re-enchantment. Self-help writing was in itself characteristically modern, under the terms of Alex Owen and Mathew Thomson's analysis, because it insisted on the existence of a psychological self that could be brought into view and acted upon by those with sufficient expertise in the workings of the psyche. Yet such expertise was developed not only in the disenchanted world of professional medicine and psychology, but also in the enchanted realm of occult investigation and the self-help culture that it inspired.

Conclusion

Self-help books such as those discussed above indicate the validity of Treitel's argument that "The occult is everywhere in modernity."[196] Occultism offered an expert discourse to early-twentieth-century Britons who might not otherwise have found a voice in the increasingly professionalized world of expert intervention. In overlooking it, as Owen has argued, "it is historians who are off-beam, ignoring or sidelining a phenomenon that was so obviously remarked upon and important at the time."[197] As Chapter 3 goes on to point out in relation to the case of professional psychology, modern occultism was sufficiently important to form a constitutive outside to the discourse of mainstream science as it came to take institutional shape and to increasingly divorce itself from esotericism over the course of the early twentieth century. This is surely reason enough to take occultism seriously in the history of modernity. However, among those seeking to make sense of their spiritual selves it is clear to see that occultism remained relevant and popular well into the twentieth century. In the aftermath of the First World War, spiritual guidance, esoteric or otherwise, was gladly welcomed by war-weary Britons. In contrast to Owen's focus on the pre-1914 period, this chapter adds to the work of Jay Winter and Jenny Hazelgrove in pointing to the continuing presence, and cultural importance, of spiritual and occult movements after the First World War.[198] To our growing understanding of alternative spiritualities in early-twentieth-century Britain, this chapter brings a sonic dimension: the "age-of-noise" narrative, I have argued here, prompted and structured esoteric engagement with the question of urban and industrial modernity. Unlike the leaders and supporters of the Anti-Noise League, Theosophically inspired sound magicians and self-help writers did not wish to return society to an earlier age of quiet, even though they were dissatisfied with the sensory conditions of city life. Realization of selfhood, spiritually defined, depended upon exposure to unfamiliar and mystical sounds, as Russolo's *Art of Noises* manifesto, quoted in the epigraph to this chapter, makes clear. In contrast to the pessimists of the Anti-Noise League, those in pursuit of re-enchantment strained to hear the sounds of the future rather than those of the past and embraced the potential of social vibration rather than rejecting it. Though they shared with noise abatement leaders a disdain for mechanical noise and a belief that such noises would cause a crisis of nervous illness in industrial societies, agents of sonic re-enchantment differed from their noise abating counterparts in the way they heard modernity. For followers of Theosophy, modernity was to be heard in the unfamiliar vibrations of magical music, vibrations that promised to lead humanity to a newly spiritualized life.

3 Creating the Sonically Rational

Modern Interventions in Everyday Aurality

I find your letters in the green-backed files
Signed long ago, and half expect to see
You with your pipe revolving caustically
Facts of acoustics, gels, and flooring tiles

—Inscription to the memory of building scientist Percy Barnett
in Hope Bagenal, *Practical Acoustics and Planning against
Noise* (1942)

For the sound experts under discussion in this chapter, sonic modernity was not an unhealthy problem to be overcome, nor a path to spiritual revelation, but rather a rational solution to problems inherited from a previous age.[1] The rapid and unplanned industrialization of the Victorian era was reimagined, in this rationalizing ethos, as a dead-end, discarded modernity.[2] Its chaotic material and social infrastructure was to be superseded by a rational world planned by expert professionals and imposed from above by the intervention of the state. Poverty, slum housing, underregulated working conditions and class division, necessary by-products of nineteenth-century free-market liberalism, were recast as irrational and unmodern in this context. Denis Linehan puts it thus in relation to early-twentieth-century attitudes to Victorian modernity, "The solution to this modern disaster was modernism."[3] Beginning with piecemeal interventions in working conditions, housing provision, and public health, but leading ultimately to the creation of the welfare state and the nationalization of industry after the Second World War, this mode of encountering the modern was modernist, in Linehan's sense, not primarily because of any aesthetic experimentalism, but because its proponents thought of modernity as the path to a perfect future rather than as the departure from an idealized past.

The First World War was the pivotal catalyst for this new way of thinking about modernity in Britain. The war necessitated a greater role for the state in the day-to-day lives of the British people than ever before. The turbulent two decades following the war, which included economic crisis and significant labor unrest, meant that elite support grew behind a new political consensus in favor of state planning and intervention.[4] What Anson Rabinbach describes as the post-1918 politics of "social rationalization," and a "vision of a society in which social conflict was eliminated in favor of technological and scientific imperatives," included a drive to rationalize the everyday soundscape.[5] Rabinbach has in mind the Fordist production techniques developed in the American workplace, but in Britain no less than in the United States, technical intervention in the minutiae of everyday life, including its sounds, became a prominent feature of early-twentieth-century governance. Historians and theorists of everyday life in early-twentieth-century Britain have tended to focus on the surrealistic inspirations of the anthropological and social survey organization Mass-Observation, an organization founded independently of the state in 1937.[6] Yet the real revolution in everyday investigation taking place in early-twentieth-century Britain was that being enacted by a raft of new state agencies, often under the auspices of the government's Department of Scientific and Industrial Research. These agencies were tasked with observing everyday life and of designing rational ways for the state to intervene in it. In contrast to the sound experts discussed in the previous two chapters, therefore, this chapter deals with sonic expertise developed on behalf of the technocratic state after 1918. These sound experts were often at pains to distinguish their modern, scientific approach from that of others. The Anti-Noise League's pessimistic outlook on modernity, in particular, was given short shrift by state experts who found no place for it in their own, future-oriented definition of sonic modernity. Indeed, it was for this reason that leaders of the Anti-Noise League so often found themselves frustrated in their efforts to convince public agencies of the health threat posed by noise.

This chapter examines two sites of state-led technocratic intervention in relation to everyday soundscapes: the workplace and the home. In part as a response to the intense lobbying of the Anti-Noise League and to the coverage gained by noise abatement in newspaper reporting, government bodies responsible for improving housing and working conditions sought to uncover hard-and-fast data about the effects of noise on the health and happiness of the British people at home and at work. Their application of twentieth-century scientific method to the noise problem, however, set them apart from antinoise campaigners such as Lord Horder, who relied upon the rhetoric of medicalized cultural critique, rather than on twentieth-century scientific methods, to come to their conclusions about noise. As one government scientist put it to the Secretary of the Anti-Noise League in 1937, noise should be treated "not as an individual problem, but as a public affair; I mean one wants to know whether the amount of social discord that is produced in this way is worth taking a lot of public notice of, or whether it is just the infrequent crank who sits up and howls about it."[7] An account of the noise problem that emphasized, however covertly, its especial concern for the "intelligent section" of society was insufficient, in other words.[8] State-sponsored investigations of sound's role in everyday life shifted emphasis not only toward new technical methods of investigation, but also toward the reconceptualization of sound as a facet of the social.

Although the post-1918 ethos of state intervention was a significant departure, expert problematizing of the social had evolved as a feature of British class culture from the early nineteenth century, according to Mary Poovey. The ability to "understand, measure and represent" the "social body," grounded particularly in knowledge of its poorest elements, became fundamental to expert authority as it emerged alongside the nineteenth-century middle class.[9] Those who adopt Michel Foucault's analysis of expert power in modern societies argue that objective expertise, operating at arm's length from the state, was part of liberal "governmentality" in countries like Britain. Nikolas Rose argues, "Expertise in the conduct of conduct—authority arising out of a claim to a true and positive knowledge of humans, to neutrality and efficacy—came to provide a number of solutions which were of considerable importance in rendering liberalism operable" as a political regime in the nineteenth century.[10] Rather than relying on direct force, regimes of truth created by autonomous experts, such as sanitary reformers, allowed liberal states to act in the apparently objective interests of *all* of their members, a situation which Patrick Joyce has described as "the rule of freedom."[11] Early-twentieth-century welfarism marked a significant advancement in the operations of this liberal mode of government, according to Rose. "This was not so much a process in which a central state extended its tentacles throughout society," he explains, "but the invention of various 'rules for rule' which sought to transform the state into a centre that *could* programme— shape, guide, channel, direct, control—events and persons distant from it."[12] Rose offers social workers as an example of expert agents of diffuse state power in liberal societies: "Political rule," he writes, "would not itself set out the norms of individual conduct, but would install and empower a variety of 'professionals' who would, investing them with authority to act as experts in the devices of social rule."[13]

One such device of social rule to emerge in early-twentieth-century Britain took the form of normative claims about rhythm and its sonic manifestations.

In contrast to Theosophists such as Maud MacCarthy, discussed in Chapter 2, who developed an individualized theory of sonic affect through vibration, experts working on behalf of the state in the post-1918 period were more inclined to pay attention to sound's rhythmical qualities. It was through its rhythm or lack thereof, they thought, that sound exercised its influence in social life. In the workplace, it was the rhythm, or otherwise, of industrial sounds that determined whether workers would be able to psychologically adapt themselves to noise. At home, rhythmically regular noises, and those identifiably part of a community's everyday life, were found to be entirely tolerable if not welcomed, as one acoustic researcher put it, as "a blessing in disguise" for their ability to drown out intruding irregular sounds.[14] Unexpected sounds that penetrated the home, on the other hand, were said to have "spoiled" the rhythm of daily life through interruption of leisure or disturbance to sleep.[15] The ability to define what constituted being in rhythm, or out of it, was the axis upon which expert sonic authority was exercised in early-twentieth-century Britain.

Cultural theorists, following in the footsteps of Henri Lefebvre, have emphasized the importance of rhythm in social and political life. Power, as Lefebvre claimed, "knows how to utilize and manipulate time."[16] State investigations of sound's role in everyday life reveal that rhythm was certainly of direct interest to those involved in constructing the norms of hearing and of sonic environments, confirming Tim Edensor's argument that "the rhythmic lineaments of everyday life are weighted with power."[17] Where rhythmic conditions were thought to be optimal, the failure of individuals to adapt to these conditions was diagnosed as psychological maladjustment to society, a deviation from the norm. In such cases, as well as in defining these norms in the first place, the private interiority of the mind became a legitimate realm of state knowledge and intervention. The hearing self was calculated and classified by newly professionalized psychologists in order to provide rational techniques for sonic governance. Rhythm was also, as the third section of this chapter proposes, a component of the state's cultural projection of sonic modernity. Dealing with state-sponsored public information films of the 1930s, this section argues that while government scientists were investigating sound's effects in the workplace and the home, state filmmakers concurrently went in search of modernist ways of representing the everyday soundscape and of promoting the positive value of its rhythmical qualities.

This chapter, therefore, follows Poovey and Rose in directing attention to the role of expert professionals in defining and acting upon the social in early-twentieth-century Britain. As Poovey argues, claims to expert agency depended upon knowledge of the mass working-class population, and the sound experts discussed in this chapter developed just such claims in relation to the effects and significance of noise in working-class life. These claims should not, however, be taken as historical evidence of working-class attitudes to noise. Working-class voices rarely emerge on their own terms in the noise investigations discussed in this chapter. Instead, they come refracted through the social scientific priorities of surveys, questionnaires, and psychological tests and thus reveal far more about the workings of expert discourse than they do about popular attitudes to noise. Although there are points in this chapter where noteworthy moments of disjuncture between investigator and investigated emerge, the primary aim here is to explain the ways in which sound was incorporated into the mode of liberal governance described by Rose. As the first section of the chapter makes clear in relation to the clash between those who supported and those who rejected the neurasthenic explanation for noise's health effects, expert groups had to compete for the attention and backing of the state. This process of competition significantly shaped the direction taken by the state in its management of everyday soundscapes.

Beyond Neurasthenia: Working Rhythms and the Rise of Industrial Psychology

Investigations of noise in the workplace were instigated during the 1930s as part of a newly emerged science of work. Aiming to improve both the efficiency and the well-being of those employed in British industry, this new science drew upon the expertise of physiologists, psychologists, and social scientists in an attempt to bring the human body into harmony with the machines it operated in the nation's factories and offices. Efforts had been made from the late nineteenth century to develop a scientific replacement for the dominant moral framework within which work and worker fatigue were discussed in Victorian Britain, but it was not until the First World War, when the state assumed responsibility for emergency munitions production, that questions of industrial efficiency and worker fatigue were researched in a systematic way.[18] A committee set up in September 1915 by the Prime Minister, Lloyd George, to investigate how best to improve munitions production concluded that increasing the length of the working day should no longer be seen as the most effective way of improving output, but that "understanding the physical and mental capacities of each worker" was necessary in order to maximize their efficiency.[19] In fact, a reduction of working hours and the introduction of rest pauses were found to improve efficiency.[20] There was a humanitarian as well as a business rationale for putting the worker and his or her needs at the heart of the efficiency question during the First World War. The government munitions committee claimed that it had "clearly shown that false ideas of economic gain, blind to physiological law, must lead as they led through the nineteenth century to vast national loss and suffering."[21] This sentiment exemplifies the new ethos of state responsibility, and of anti-Victorianism, which came to prominence after the First World War. Belief that the efficiency and health of the British worker could be improved by better knowledge of the physical and mental effects of work led to the establishment of the Industrial Fatigue Research Board (IFRB), under the joint auspices of the government's Department of Scientific and Industrial Research and Medical Research Council, in 1918.[22] The body was renamed the Industrial Health Research Board (IHRB) in 1926 in recognition of its holistic approach, beyond a pragmatic interest in economic efficiency, to the question of workers' welfare.

The IFRB and its successor provided the context within which the newly developed science of psychology, in particular, was transformed into a tool of state knowledge-gathering, applied for the first time to the mass population of working people. Industrial psychology, the subdiscipline devoted to understanding the relationship between work and the human psyche, developed as a specialist field of practice as a result of the IFRB and IHRB's financial support. These bodies gave industrial psychologists a legitimate, state-sanctioned presence as observers of everyday life in Britain's workplaces. Female psychologists were employed, such as May Smith, to gain the trust of the many women workers who entered industrial employment during the First World War and who remained an important part of the British workforce thereafter.[23] Smith spent time working in a laundry, for example, before embarking on her study of fatigue in the workers of that industry. Smith and her colleagues reported that their working-class subjects were usually open and willing to talk about the experience of work and its effects on their mental health.[24] Such qualitative information was collected, in the form of interviews, alongside quantitative data.

The inclusion of psychologists in the work of the IHRB was lent urgency in 1935 following a report published by the Regional Medical Officer for Scotland, James L. Halliday; the report claimed that the percentage of workers in receipt of National Insurance benefits in Scotland due to psychoneurotic disorders was 33 percent, not the official figure of 2 percent.[25] Mathew Thomson points out that this report led to "a significant episode of social alarm" in Britain about the psychological damage done to workers by industrial working practices.[26] With the shell shock epidemic fresh in the memory, it was widely feared that industrial work was creating a population unfit for work, or, for that matter, for defending the nation in what now seemed a possible future conflict in Europe. Industrial psychology was thrust, therefore, on to the frontline of national defense. Yet this crisis was manufactured, to some extent, by industrial psychologists themselves, in the interests of their own disciplinary expertise. During the early 1930s, industrial psychologists had become increasingly vocal about the need to shift medical thinking on "nervous disorders" away from what they considered to be outmoded physiological explanations and toward more up-to-date psychological investigation.[27] It was time, they argued, to leave behind the neurasthenic paradigm. Workers who had been involved in an accident and whose mental fragility subsequently made them unfit for work were still regularly diagnosed in the 1920s and 1930s as suffering from neurasthenia, or from some other functional disorder of the nervous system, and were granted compensation in light of their physical ailment. Industrial psychologists launched a scathing attack on this practice and insisted that "nervousness" was a mental rather than a physical problem, deserving of psychological treatment rather than the stigma of permanent physical disability, which came with the neurasthenic diagnosis. The 1935 panic about psychoneuroses in industry was, therefore, part of a broader shift, promoted by an emergent class of professional psychologists, toward psychological modes of social intervention.[28]

Among the most strident voices of this new psychological profession was Millais Culpin. He pioneered the discipline of industrial psychology at the London School of Hygiene and Tropical Medicine and, in 1931, called for an end to the use of neurasthenia as a diagnosis in industrial health, describing it as a "mytho-pathology" belonging to an earlier medical age. He had earlier predicted that neurasthenia would "fall by the sheer weight of the load it has to bear, every mental disturbance short of certifiable insanity, and many bodily disturbances as well, coming under this almost useless title."[29] He was certain, by the early 1930s, that many of the symptoms diagnosed as neurasthenic, and thus as originating in the physiology of the nerves, should now be understood, instead, as part of "an emotional state, an anxiety neurosis, dependent not on any physical disturbance caused by trauma, but on a number of psychological factors."[30] The prominent physician, Sir E. Farquhar Buzzard, had lent his influential support to this line of argument in an article carried by the *Lancet* in 1930. He described neurasthenia as a "dumping ground" for a whole range of symptoms that, he argued, had now been shown to be caused by psychological, rather than physiological, disturbance.[31] Buzzard estimated that around half of workers diagnosed as suffering from functional disorder of the nerves were in fact affected by a psychoneurosis. Spelling out the difference, Buzzard argued that "It is

indispensable that the patient should realise that his mental state is responsible for, and not dependent on, his bodily ailments."[32]

Psychologists such as Culpin pointed out that, unlike neurasthenia, psychoneurotic conditions were treatable using the principles of psychotherapy.
Culpin argued that the patient diagnosed with neurasthenia had no choice
but to resign himself to ongoing debilitation and unemployment, "compelled
to cling to compensation as his only safeguard for the future." The principles
of psychotherapy, on the other hand, promised rehabilitation and return to
work.[33] Culpin argued that it was only right that those suffering from breakdowns should be given "a fair chance of recovery" even if the present legal
framework of compensation maintained a vested interest in the neurasthenic
diagnosis.[34] Culpin's psychological paradigm established itself as the primary
mode of intervening in industrial health after 1935. It was actively promoted
by industrial psychologists as a rational, modern, response to worker illness
and absenteeism through bodies such as the National Institute of Industrial
Psychology (NIIP) and through periodicals such as *Industrial Welfare*.[35]

Whereas the popular psychology of Ash, Hunt, and Loosmore, discussed
in Chapter 2, merged older neurasthenic with newer psychological theories
of nervous illness, professional industrial psychologists insisted upon investigations of the self based purely on the principles of twentieth-century
investigative science. Indeed, this insistence was at the heart of their conceptualization of modernity. Culpin was among those at pains to distinguish modern scientific psychology from what he saw as earlier, insuffi-
ciently rigorous, sciences of the self. His book, *Recent Advances in the Study
of the Psychoneuroses* (1931), argued that psychology's progress had been held
back by the "mechanistic" ethos of nineteenth-century science.[36] Psychology
remained remote from medicine in this context because doctors thought of
patients only as "a collection of bio-chemical reactions." They failed to see
that these bodily reactions "might be influenced by [the patient's] mental
state" and clung to mytho-pathologies such as neurasthenia as a result.[37]
Culpin admitted that attempts to understand the workings of the human
mind had progressed in the late nineteenth and early twentieth centuries
via investigations of the so-called "occult" undertaken by organizations such
as the Theosophical Society. However, he derided these investigations as a
"mixed ancestry of miracle working, charlatanry and misinterpreted empiri-
cal observations and experiments" and was resolute in his conviction that
the principles of rational, scientific psychology should now assume center
ground in a genuinely modern social pursuit of health.[38] Culpin, along with
his colleagues in the new profession of industrial psychology, thus rejected
both the neurasthenic paradigm discussed in Chapter 1 *and* the enchanted

experimentations outlined in Chapter 2 as ways of defining the modern experience. Both were unmodern, for Culpin and others, precisely because of the dubious and outmoded nature of their scientific methodology. While the religious and pseudo-rational underpinnings of magical cures rendered them inherently unsound, neurasthenic diagnoses were rejected because they lacked a proper "observational basis."[39]

What made industrial psychology modern, for Culpin, were the rigorous and objective scientific techniques it employed. In their joint investigation of telegraphists' cramp undertaken in 1927, for example, Culpin and May Smith evolved a scientific method that was to become typical of industrial psychology in the 1930s and which was used to analyze the effects of noise in the workplace.[40] This included two complementary modes of observation. First, detailed interviews were undertaken with workers in order to identify the presence or otherwise of neurotic symptoms. Questions about fear of the dark, for example, or about "uncomfortable sensations of being observed," as well as specific questions, such as "does anything in particular make you nervous?" allowed the interviewees to be classified according to the extent of their psychoneuroses.[41] Those without any symptoms were classified as 0, while those with increasingly severe psychotic symptoms were classified on a scale from 1 to 1+, 2, 2+, and so on. The second mode of observation allowed the "objectivity" of this classification to be tested. It required interviewed participants to undertake a test on the McDougall-Schuster dotting machine.[42] Invented by the experimental psychologist William McDougall in 1900, the machine tested the ability of participants to aim with a stylus at small circles moving at increasing speed in a spiral shape across a revolving disc. The test proved, according to Culpin and Smith's findings, that those with slight to severe psychotic symptoms performed progressively worse at this test than those without symptoms.[43] This, in turn, proved that psychosis, even of a minor variety, could impact upon the efficiency of work such as that undertaken by telegraphists. Culpin and Smith concluded, in opposition to the commonly held view that the conditions of industrial work *cause* fatigue and nervous illness, that preexisting psychoneurotic disorders *predispose* workers to conditions such as telegraphists' cramp.[44]

A. J. McIvor has argued that in its adoption of such methods and conclusions, industrial psychology was at the center of a shift in early-twentieth-century Britain toward renewed confidence in the ability of science and technology to solve social problems and toward placing rational science and technology at the center of a new definition of modernity.[45] McIvor points out that the findings of industrial psychologists and other state-sponsored experts were promoted to employers through the work of organizations such as the British Science Guild, among others, whose stated mission was "to convince the nation of the necessity of applying methods of science to all branches of human endeavour and thus to further the progress and increase the wealth of the Empire."[46] It is clear that, in their sponsorship of bodies such as the IHRB, government ministers were expressing their own confidence in investigative scientific methods as the basis for a socially interventionist state. This preference helps to explain why ministers and civil servants remained skeptical about the advice sent to it by the British Medical Association (BMA) and the Anti-Noise League in the late 1920s and 1930s, which pointed out the relationship between urban noise and neurasthenia. The government's own scientists, especially those employed through the IHRB, were offering starkly different conclusions about noise's health effects than those put forward by antinoise campaigners. The difference hinged on the waning fortunes of neurasthenia as a medical theory.

The lag between industrial psychology's new theories of neurosis and the increasingly outmoded dependence of those in the general medical profession on the neurasthenic diagnosis was exposed in an argument that Culpin sparked with the BMA in 1928 on the topic of noise. Culpin reacted with impunity to the BMA's 1928 campaigning and deputation to government on noise. He was especially critical of its use of neurasthenic theory to explain noise's effects on health. In an article for *Industrial Welfare*, Culpin wrote:

> Noise is receiving attention now, and many letters have appeared in the Press claiming that it causes nervous breakdown. Of that there is no evidence. . . . All we know is that to some nervous people some noises are very distressing; that may be a sound argument for diminishing noise; but that by some direct action upon nerves it causes breakdown is a speculation outside the realms of physiology.[47]

In keeping with the principles of industrial psychology, Culpin argued instead that those who were sensitive to noise were very often, as with sufferers from telegraphists' cramp, predisposed to be so by an underlying psychoneurosis. He argued that "Certain outside influences," such as noise, "are assumed to cause nervous illness but the easy acceptance of such explanations hides the fact that these causes by themselves are harmless."[48] Sensitivity to noise, or to other features of industrial work, are relied upon by the nervous patient to explain their poor state of health when in fact the cause of their sensitivity is psychological, rather than physiological, in nature. "What we call nervousness is to a great extent a liability to experience the emotion of fear in circumstances that should not arouse that emotion," Culpin explained.[49] His inference was clear: treat the underlying neurosis and one would also treat the sensitivity to noise. For Culpin, attacks on noise such as those launched by the Anti-Noise League exposed not a crisis of mechanical civilization, but rather the widespread incidence of psychoneurotic disorders in society, a problem that necessitated the intervention of clinical psychologists. Culpin quipped, in a clear jibe at BMA members' failure to adopt the principles of psychotherapy, that those suffering from sensitivity to noise would be better off avoiding the doctor altogether and seeking instead the assistance of an industrial welfare worker.[50]

Due to his involvement with the IHRB, Culpin's attack on the BMA amounted to a serious blow to the credibility of calls for noise abatement. The BMA was alert to this. Responding to Culpin's argument that "such unpleasant things as noise are, in short, convenient pegs on which the nervous subject hangs his symptoms" and that through psychotherapeutic treatment the nervous patient could adapt him or herself to noise, the BMA replied that there was in fact a significant difference between daytime noises, to which one might well be able to adapt oneself with effort, and those of the nighttime which disturb sleep.[51] "The hardened evolutionist," wrote the *British Medical Journal*, "may view without regret the gradual elimination of the nervously unfit by electric motor horns, open exhausts, rattling lorries, and pneumatic drills, but the practising doctor will continue to look upon noise as an evil, and will support any measures to mitigate the pandemonium which engineers have let loose upon us. Thus, while agreeing with Dr Culpin that too much emphasis is still laid on environment and too little on personal reaction to it, we shall continue to hope for less stimulation of the auditory centres along our uphill path to Utopia."[52] Culpin, however, rejected the argument that disturbance to sleep was in any way different to other kinds of noise sensitivity and retorted to the BMA that "if every pop should mean a shilling in my bank balance I could sleep happily beside a continued procession of motor cycles, and only wake up when the row ceased."[53]

As the academic discipline of industrial psychology grew in stature, Culpin's argument about the psychological basis of noise sensitivity gained ground, its place as scientific orthodoxy assured. The Cambridge University psychologist, F. C. Bartlett, argued in his book *The Problem of Noise* (1934) that the "main attack" of noise is "not directly physiological, but by weapons of an insidious and subtle psychological order."[54] He was more sympathetic than Culpin to the cause of noise abatement but was clear in his assessment that sensitivity to noise signified an underlying psychological problem rather than a physical sensitivity of the nerves. Bartlett recounted the case of a woman whom he had treated. She was worried about the lack of sexual intimacy in her marriage and had "become worked up into . . . a 'state of nerves.'" A newly married young couple had moved in next door and she could "hear everything that goes on . . . morning, noon and night." Bartlett implied that her neighbors' youthful sexual vitality was exacerbating this woman's own sexual neurosis. She complained that her nervous state had indeed been worsened by the new couple living next door but identified the noise caused by "the slamming of doors" as the causative problem. Bartlett concluded in relation to this, as well as to other similar cases, that "noise is made the burden of complaint that fundamentally has other and deeper causes."[55]

In terms of their relative influence on government decision makers, it is clear that Culpin and Bartlett's line of argument about the psychological causes of noise sensitivity held sway over that put forward by the BMA and the Anti-Noise League about neurasthenia. Having given the BMA's 1928 deputation on noise a cautious reception, the Ministry of Health turned instead to industrial psychologists such as Culpin for reliable evidence about noise's effects in everyday life. In response to the BMA's lobbying, Culpin set about gathering objective scientific facts about noise. His 1927 study of telegraphists' cramp had already indicated that noise affected working efficiency only in those with clearly identifiable preexisting psychoneurotic symptoms. Those free from symptoms, although they might object to noise, were shown to be able to adapt themselves to it without prejudice to their working performance.[56] A fuller investigation of the relationship between noise sensitivity and psychoneurosis was integrated into the IHRB report on *The Nervous Temperament* published by Culpin and Smith in 1930.[57] In order to establish the effects of noise in the workplace, Culpin and Smith observed four groups of workers: "a group of 30 girls working at or near a very noisy process called 'stamping'"; "a group of 19 typists working in one room"; "a group of 19 men students who worked under fairly quiet conditions disturbed at intervals by traffic"; and, finally, "a group of 156 men whose work is sometimes done to the accompaniment of much noise."[58] These workers were all subjected to the standard assessment for psychoneurotic symptoms. Each was also asked how they reacted when required to work in a noisy environment. Their answers were split into three categories: not affected; slight dislike; and seriously affected.[59] Culpin and Smith then cross-referenced these responses with each worker's assessment for psychoneurotic symptoms. They found clear evidence that those with increasingly severe psychoneuroses were progressively more likely to find noise disturbing in their working life.[60] On the other hand, they concluded, "most people free from nervous symptoms can become indifferent" to noise.[61]

The ability of most working people to adapt themselves to noise was related, in subsequent IHRB investigations, to the rhythmic qualities of the working soundscape. The reason that manual workers were unaffected by, and did not complain about, noise, according to industrial psychologists, was that their work was usually done in rhythm to the sounds produced by the machines they operated. Smith noted the case of a woman factory worker who explained that so long as the noises around her were rhythmically connected to the work she was performing, she didn't mind noise. However, "when an irregular click developed, which in no way affected the working of the machine, she found that extremely annoying."[62] Bartlett and K. G. Pollock undertook a number of experiments in 1932 in which test subjects were required to undertake tasks similar to those performed in industry to the accompaniment of various noises delivered via headphones. Their evidence suggested that while unsynchronized sounds did indeed have an impact on worker performance, "noise in general has extraordinarily little effect upon simple motor tasks."[63] They found that, while workers often experienced initial dislike of noise, they quickly adapted themselves so long as the noises were in rhythm with the work being performed. "There is generally an initial disturbance which is usually counteracted by increase of effort," wrote Bartlett and Pollock, "but following this comes a definite period of adaptation. During this period the organism appears to settle down to the noisy conditions, treating them as a kind of natural background of its task, so that in many cases even the subjective discomfort diminishes or passes away."[64]

The conclusion that manual work was not significantly affected by noise was supported by another experiment dealing with the effects of noise in a Lancashire weaving shed. Testing the impact of earplugs on worker efficiency, H. C. Weston and S. Adams found that an increased productivity of only 1 percent was attained by those using earplugs and that this increase could equally have been due to other environmental factors such as temperature.[65] Industrial psychologists were led as a result of these conclusions to reject the argument frequently put forward by supporters of noise abatement that noise acts as an insidious background drain on bodily energy through its physical effects on the nervous system. Mental adaptation to rhythmic noise was said to be part of a normal psychological makeup. Bartlett and Pollock confirmed Culpin's argument that adaptation to noise was a matter of psychological "attitude" rather than "a change of sensorial reaction in any physiological sense."[66] Those who could not adapt themselves to noise were described by Smith as suffering from "faulty emotional adaptation to the environment" rather than any intrinsic fatigue brought on by sound.[67]

When drawing these conclusions, industrial psychologists often added bristling critique of the popular clamor for noise abatement. Bartlett and Pollock argued that popular fears about noise's effect on working efficiency had been "greatly exaggerated" by organizations such as the Anti-Noise

League and accused noise abatement advocates of manufacturing a social panic about noise.[68] "There is no question that noise is very generally disliked," wrote Bartlett and Pollock, but, they added, "when all kinds of popular statements about the baleful effects of noise are prevalent, it becomes very easy for any person who is 'off colour,' or who fails to adapt himself to the social group, to make noise the butt of his grievance. We are convinced that it is this fact, coupled with the great influence of social suggestion, which accounts, to no inconsiderable degree, for much of the popular prejudice against noisy conditions of work."[69] Smith, likewise, criticized the "lurid detail" with which antinoise campaigners described noise's effects. She also identified the antimodern tenor of noise abatement in her observation that its supporters often harked back to "a 'golden age,' usually any period other than their own, when noise was unknown."[70] Industrial psychologists' efforts to expose the irrational and antimodern basis of noise abatement rhetoric were part of a wider campaign to establish their discipline as a rational, even-handed, modern method of social intervention.[71]

Supporters of noise abatement were sensitive to these criticisms. Dan McKenzie, author of the 1916 book *City of Din*, wrote a scathing review of the research undertaken by Bartlett and Pollock in a desperate attempt to reclaim ground for the noise abatement movement. He rejected the method of psychology out of hand ("It seems that the moment a psychologist utters an opinion it straightway becomes a fact!") and was utterly incredulous that psychologists were claiming to have solved "the problem of noise by denying that there is any problem."[72] He goaded Bartlett by arguing that any sensible physician knows only too well of the *physical* pain caused by noise. He likened psychologists' denial of the causative link between noise and illness to the claims of the Christian Science movement that disease could be cured through prayer, no doubt aware of the association between the new psychology and modern occultism. The worst insult of all to McKenzie was that Bartlett's research should have been sponsored by the IHRB: "How broad-minded of the Medical Research Council," he wrote, "to sponsor and to promulgate views so closely akin to Christian Science!"[73] This last-ditch attempt to persuade government authorities to listen to the Anti-Noise League rather than the IHRB was futile. The tide had already turned in favor of psychological expertise.

Yet industrial psychologists shared more than they might have liked to admit with supporters of noise abatement. One of the central findings of industrial psychology in relation to noise was that the noise-sensitive minority, more often than not, identified noise's violation of their right to privacy as the source of the problem. This "mental effect" was, according to Culpin and

Smith, a matter of "resentment, the noise being regarded as an assault on their right to quietness."[74] Yet such complaints about noise also had a clear social profile, according to industrial psychologists. Culpin and Smith found that objection to noise was commoner in factory overseers than in factory workers. In a study involving three "very noisy industries"—chocolate-shaping, tin-stamping, and printing—Smith found that when workers were asked about noise "the opinion of the majority was that they got used to it. In each case, however, it was the manager who objected. . . . The explanation was, I think, that the workers were helping to make it, while the manager was forced to hear it but was powerless to prevent it."[75] Industrial psychologists explained this social difference with reference to their theory of working rhythm. Because managers were often involved in mental work not directly related to the rhythmic sound of the machines surrounding them, they were more likely for this reason to be affected by noise, according to Bartlett and Pollock. Unlike their manual worker counterparts, those involved in mental work were, in general, found to suffer significant diminution in working efficiency in noisy conditions, irrespective of the noise's rhythm. Because mental work was "discontinuous" compared to more-or-less simple manual work, noises of either a rhythmic or an arrhythmic character were likely to reduce efficiency in mental work, according to Bartlett and Pollock.[76]

Industrial psychologists thus unwittingly reproduced much of the social politics of noise abatement. In their conclusion that mental workers were more likely than those involved in manual work to complain about noise, they found some accidental common ground with antinoise campaigners such as Lord Horder, who identified noise as an especial disturbance to the "intelligent section" of society.[77] While they may have disagreed with Horder about the medical causes and effects of noise sensitivity, industrial psychologists were ultimately caught up in the same social politics of sound as antinoise campaigners. A clear tendency emerged in the discourse of industrial psychology to identify manual workers as possessing something akin to a collective, social self that evolved in time with the shared rhythms of the industrial work they performed. Brain workers, on the other hand, tended to be associated with an individualized, interior selfhood that worked to its own temporal rhythms and depended for its well-being on the ability to separate itself from the surging pulse of industry.[78]

Thus, one way or another, the argument that brain-working people required sonic isolation from the rhythmic soundscape of the working masses remained a powerful one in the 1930s. The advert for Underwood Noiseless Typewriters shown in Figure 3.1, for example, is typical of this social politics of everyday sound. The advantages of the noiseless typewriter are presented, in this advert, as primarily benefiting the male brain worker rather than his nearby female typist. Although industrial psychologists found no particular difference between men and women in terms of sensitivity to noise, because women were more likely to be employed in manual work than in a brain-working capacity, adverts such as this one tended to gender the noise-sufferer as male—as did, of course, the Anti-Noise League's prominently used logo. On the other hand, the second female figure in Figure 3.1—a client rather than a worker—is shown to be as appreciative of the quiet afforded by the new Underwood typewriter as the male figure. This is suggestive of the fact that working status, rather than gender, tended to be seen as the determining factor in noise sensitivity. Whereas female typists adapt themselves to the rhythmic sound of their work (a study by Smith had proven this fact), women not involved in manual work were as liable as brain-working men to find the noise of the typewriter disturbing.[79] Adverts such as those in Figure 3.1, and the one for Newalls Insulation Company in Figure 3.2 which also centralizes the acoustic needs of the brain-working man, were ultimately part of the same rational, scientific modernity as industrial psychology because they promised to solve the noise problem through advances in modern technology, but by emphasizing the needs of brain workers over those of manual workers with respect to noise, a clear overlap emerged with the discourse of noise abatement.

In contrast to brain workers, whose work, according to industrial psychologists, was best undertaken in quiet conditions, manual workers could in fact be stimulated by the presence of certain kinds of sounds. One of Bartlett and Pollock's findings was that "automatic work," such as that performed in factories, is actually aided by the presence of rhythmic noise. If some kinds of industrial work were performed better with background rhythmic noise, it stood to reason to Bartlett and Pollock that introducing certain kinds of *music* into factories could potentially aid productivity.[80] In terms of its long-term influence, this was early industrial psychology's most significant finding in relation to noise. Industrial psychologists concerned with the impact of boredom on the productivity of factory workers took up Bartlett and Pollock's suggestions about music with enthusiasm and subsequently developed sophisticated data about the relationship between certain kinds of music—popular, rhythmical dance music—and the performance of industrial work in factories. The presence of music was found by IHRB scientists to counteract boredom's tendency to reduce worker productivity.[81] As a direct response to the IHRB's findings, the BBC designed its famous "Music while You Work" radio program which, beginning in June 1940, was piped into industrial workplaces across the nation in order to aid worker

A QUIET OFFICE...

with an
UNDERWOOD
N·O·I·S·E·L·E·S·S

In presenting their New and Latest Model Noiseless Typewriter, Underwood takes pride in making this very valuable contribution towards noise elimination, and, at the same time, presenting to the World of Commerce a still better Typewriter.

An Underwood Standard Noiseless Typewriter offers greater speed and accuracy; enables the Typist-Secretary to do more and better work without fatigue, and gives that absolute quiet so essential for clear thinking and undisturbed concentration.

For personal writing the ideal machine is the Underwood Noiseless Portable. Strong, dependable, noiseless—all the exclusive Underwood features combined with complete portability. So light—it can be carried everywhere. So quiet—it can always be used without disturbing others.

For thirty-five years the name " UNDERWOOD " has been world famous, as the recognised standard of typewriter efficiency. Over five million have been sold, so with the dawn of every business day millions of Underwood Typewriters are put into use " Speeding the World's Business."

UNDERWOOD STANDARD NOISELESS
For Office use

UNDERWOOD NOISELESS PORTABLE
For Personal use

UNDERWOOD NOISELESS TYPEWRITERS

UNDERWOOD ELLIOTT FISHER, LIMITED
Typewriters. Accounting Machines. Adding Machines. Carbon Paper. Ribbons and other supplies.
120, QUEEN VICTORIA STREET, LONDON, E.C.4. Tel.: CENTRAL 1080.
and 40 fully equipped Branches and Service Depots throughout the country.

FIGURE 3.1 Advert for the Underwood Noiseless Typewriter in *Noise Abatement Exhibition: Science Museum, South Kensington, 31st May–30th June 1935* (London: Anti-Noise League, 1935), 75.

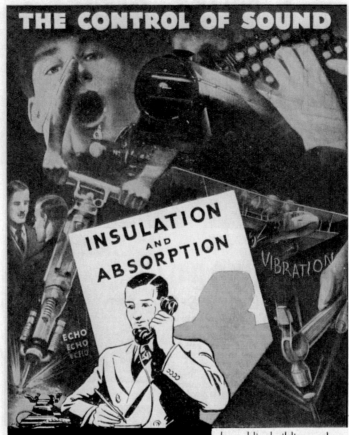

FIGURE 3.2 Advert for Newalls Insulation Company in *Noise Abatement Exhibition: Science Museum, South Kensington, 31st May–30th June 1935* (London: Anti-Noise League, 1935), 76.

morale and efficiency. Insights about the psychological effect of industrial noise on manual workers were thus transformed, as Keith Jones has put it, into a musical "technique for control of the productive self" during the Second World War and after.[82] Having transformed the working self into a scientifically knowable object of state intervention, industrial psychologists used their insights about the psychological effects of the rhythmic soundscape to lessen the friction between the working environment and the working self in the case of manual workers while maintaining an older tradition of aligning brain work with quietness. Industrial psychologists' insistence that noise sensitivity was a matter of individual psychological maladjustment to society rather than of any danger inherent in the mechanical soundscape meant that the Anti-Noise League remained frustrated in its desire to transform noise into a public health priority. Industrial psychologists normalized the sounds of industrial modernity and allowed them to persist.

Privacy, Interiority, and the Meanings of Home

The workplace was not the only site of state intervention in everyday aurality. The home, too, was the subject of expert knowledge-gathering in this period. As well as setting the stage for government interest in the psychological effects of workplace noise, the First World War was also the catalyst for a shift toward state intervention in housing, which included, as one of its core principles, an attempt to perfect ideal sonic conditions for domestic life. New home building ground to a halt in the wartime conditions of 1914–1915 and rents rose considerably as a result. Under pressure to take action, the government stepped in to control prices.[83] Having made this initial move toward central regulation, momentum grew in support of greater state responsibility. "Homes fit for heroes" proved to be a popular rallying cry at the end of the war and, in response, the 1919 Housing Act set in motion the construction of a million local authority-owned council homes and a further three million private houses in the period to 1938.[84] It was hoped that a new role for the state in directing this activity would ensure a rational approach to home building in contrast to the profit-driven haste of Victorian urban development. The government established the Building Research Station (BRS) as a branch of the Department of Industrial and Scientific Research in 1920. It was tasked with establishing rational principles for home building and disseminated its findings to local authorities, architects, and the building industry via regular bulletins. The modernist ethos of rational state-led planning was embodied in the BRS and its sister organization, the National Physical Laboratory (NPL). Among other projects, these two bodies cooperated in producing detailed scientific research about sound in the home, facilitating, as the IHRB did in the case of industrial psychology, the growth of the new discipline of architectural acoustics.[85]

At the heart of these organizations' work was a guiding principle: the home, irrespective of the social class of its occupants, should provide a private, quiet, sanctuary from the sounds of the outside world. While adaptation to rhythmic noise was classified as the norm in the industrial workplace, in the case of the home the threat posed by environmental and neighbor noise was taken altogether more seriously as a threat to mental health. After all, periods of rest away from the rhythms of the workplace were part of the wider rhythmical logic of the working week. Noise, in the domestic context, meant disruption to the rhythm of rest. Quietness at home was thus constructed as part of the normative rhythmic operation of everyday sonic life. The greater interest in soundproofing the home in comparison to the dismissal of the need to quieten the factory can also be attributed to one of industrial psychology's central findings in relation to noise: if, as Culpin and Smith argued, noise's psychological disturbance was experienced primarily as a violation of personal privacy, then it stood to reason that the private home, rather than the public workplace, should be the real site of concern for the socially interventionist state.

Bartlett was also among those who argued, in contrast to his skepticism about the impact of noise on workers' welfare, that it was in the home rather than in the workplace that noise posed its most genuine threat to public health. "Sound, like love," he wrote, "'laughs at locksmiths,' and has a most disconcerting habit of finding its way through or across all manner of defences."[86] Deftly conflating physical and psychological space, Bartlett implied that noise's intrusion on the privacy of the home intensified its attack on the private interiority of the mind. Indeed, he thought of the home environment, and its soundscape, as being inextricably linked to the maintenance of psychological health. To the case of the neurotic housewife tortured by her door-banging neighbors he added "an old lady, desperately poor, unbendingly independent," whose mental fortitude in the face of poverty was severely tested by the sound of next door's gramophone loudspeaker. Its sound signified to her not only an invasion of domestic privacy, but also the material inequality between herself and her neighbors.[87] Sound had the potential, in other words, to extend the psychological strains of social life into the individual privacy of the home. Given his involvement with the IHRB, Bartlett's warning about domestic noise and his suggestion that "the builder, the builder's constructor and the architect" should urgently do all that they could to protect the nation's psychological well-being goes some way to explaining why domestic sound was a more urgent issue for the rationalizing state in this period than workplace noise.

In contrast to the workplace, where it was argued that only brain workers required separation from the auditory rhythms of industry, a quiet home was seen as necessary to the well-being of all classes of people. The social survey organization Mass-Observation (M-O), which contributed a good deal to the expert understanding of home life in the 1930s and 1940s, pointed to the importance of securing quiet conditions in the home. This quote from one of M-O's respondents was found to be typical, across the class spectrum, of responses to a 1943 survey on "What does Home mean to YOU?": "On the whole what I want from a home is privacy . . . being able to choose my own company, quietness and my own things around me." Home, M-O concluded, is defined as "a place of peace and rest, a place where one can be oneself, where one belongs by right, and where one can be free and alone."[88] The yearning for privacy which M-O uncovered evolved in response to the overcrowded slums and cramped boarding houses of the interwar period. Young couples desperate to set up home for the first time, as one 1940s home-guidance pamphlet put it, longed for "an escape from parents and landladies, from cinemas and dance halls, from back alleys, dark lanes, or the back seat of cars."[89] Those lucky enough to have secured somewhere suitable to live cherished the privacy they found there. "Whatever people may think of their neighbors in the street or the people they meet shopping or going down town, they definitely like to have their home to themselves," explained M-O. "The desire for privacy, for keeping oneself to oneself, is a powerful motive in modern society."[90]

This desire, although it was often expressed in connection with a wish to have "a front door of one's own" was shown by M-O to be a matter of emotional as much as of physical space. The *feeling* of privacy was maintained not only by bricks and mortar but also, more importantly, by the sensory separateness which one could attain at home. Quietness featured prominently in people's definition of home in M-O surveys. "It does mean somewhere you can get away from the outside world and enjoy books, music, intimacy, privacy and quiet," replied one respondent.[91] Another answered, "Home means . . . Leisure, quiet, privacy" and "forgetfulness of . . . muddle, hurry and noise and squalor and discomfort, anxiety and worry."[92] When noise disrupted the privacy of the home's interior, the blow could be severe: "Our life have been crushed out of us," wrote one elderly working-class woman. "Wireless, piano, doors banging, water heater, gossiping women, dogs barking, that's just a few of what we get," she complained. "What a blessing it would be if we could have soundproofed houses."[93] If the home was a place where one could be oneself, a place in which selfhood could be realized and maintained, then it was also a potential site of acute disruption to the self, according to M-O investigations.

The building scientists and architectural acousticians assembled at the Building Research Station and the National Physical Laboratory were thus far keener than their colleagues in the Industrial Health Research Board to promote the age-of-noise narrative within government. This was not just because of M-O's findings about the value placed on a quiet home across the class spectrum. A noisy world, after all, was a world in need of a building scientist and an architectural acoustician. BRS officials claimed that the private building companies driving the post-1919 housing boom had failed to sufficiently grasp the importance of noise as a concern in the design of healthy homes.[94] Private developers were accused of putting economic concerns above the imperatives of rational planning. In particular, the BRS warned that new homes were being built using the cheapest rather than the best materials. Its researchers argued that the majority of post-1919 homes were in fact, for this reason, acoustically inferior to those built in the Victorian and Edwardian periods. Architectural acousticians Hope Bagenal and Alex Wood led the way in making this argument, insisting in *Planning for Good Acoustics* (1931) that "cheap rapid domestic building," using materials such as gypsum plaster and thin tympanum walls and flooring, had resulted in modern homes that were, without doubt, more prone to noise-nuisance than their predecessors.[95] For Bagenal and Wood there was a terrible irony in this situation: just at the moment in history when "the noise of the motor-bus, the jazz band, the lift motor and gate, and the loud speaker" invaded the home, the architect and builder had left the inhabitant "naked to noise."[96] This issue was also at the heart of Bartlett's psychological discussion of domestic noise. He criticized the tendency in post-1919 homes to create "interiors that look bright and clean" but which "throw back all the sounds made inside them from every surface upon which they strike, and that transmit from all quarters the noises made outside."[97] Bartlett pointed out that it was no good creating homes designed for better physical health if an unintended consequence was to produce homes more likely to damage their inhabitants' mental health as a result of noise.

Bagenal and Wood argued that not only was the world outside the home a noisier place, but the modern home was filled, from the inside, by sounds emanating from all manner of new domestic technologies: "The force pump of the heating system, the electric transformer, the ventilating fan, the refrigerator, the vacuum cleaner," all contributing "their various screams, hums, and tappings."[98] In a report commissioned by the BRS, Bagenal found, to add to this list, that technological innovations affecting the material fabric of the home, including radiators, indoor toilets, and telephones, allowed sound to circulate more freely than before through "the holes, ducts, and chases required everywhere for pipes and wiring."[99] These factors, Bagenal thought, should have led to higher, rather than lower, standards of acoustic design in post-1919 home building. Yet the evidence to the contrary was incontrovertible. For example, in a government survey undertaken in Scotland of those living in new homes, it was found that "the poor construction of many of the new houses was commented upon, particularly from the point of view of noise." Respondents were nostalgic for the "thick walls" of their previous homes.[100] The Health Organization of the League of Nations lent its weight in 1937 to the conclusion that modern buildings "are for the most part deficient in adequate sound insulating building properties" and that their poor acoustics "destroy the amenities of home and life."[101]

Claims about the acoustical inferiority of post-1919 building practices prompted the government to fund a program of sustained acoustical research, undertaken at the BRS and the NPL, into materials and designs that would alleviate the noise problem in the modern home. From the 1933 BRS bulletin "The Reduction of Noise in Buildings: Recommendations to Architects" by Bagenal and P. W. Barnett to the comprehensive report "Sound Insulation and Acoustics," published in 1944 by the Ministry of Works, the state took a detailed technical interest in how it might provide the best sonic conditions for psychological well-being at home.[102] This program of research intensified in the early years of the Second World War when the government decided to put in place plans to develop another four million new homes, to begin as soon as the conflict was over, in recognition of fact that the "homes fit for heroes" scheme, in its various manifestations, had largely failed to alleviate the problem of slum living in major towns and cities.[103] The majority of the new suburban homes built after 1919 had been bought by middle-class families, and the expected "trickle-down" effect had not materialized. It was decided that many more social housing developments in urban areas would be needed if anything were to be done about slums.[104] Reports such as the Ministry of Health study *Construction of Flats for the Working Classes* (1937) had already begun to put these plans in place.[105] That this report, and others like it, devoted a significant proportion of its attention to the issue of noise is suggestive of the centrality of acoustics in the desire to build homes fit for the future in the 1930s and 1940s. Research into the principles of the sonically rational home became a prominent feature of the state's technocratic intervention in everyday life during this period.

While the IHRB's investigation of workplace noise exposed serious tensions between the rationalizing modernism of state-funded industrial psychologists and the sonic nostalgia of the Anti-Noise League, the case of the BRS's domestic acoustics research reveals no such clear-cut dichotomy. Where industrial psychologists were at pains to separate the modernity of their investigative methods from those of noise abatement supporters, architectural acousticians found it useful to draw upon the groundwork laid by the Anti-Noise League in promoting the necessity of their expertise. Hope Bagenal is a useful case in point. He sat on the Executive Committee of the Anti-Noise League and shared his fellow members' critique of "mechanical civilization." In his professional career, Bagenal nevertheless subscribed to the modernist principle of science-as-solution that underpinned the BRS's work.[106] Bagenal used the 1935 Noise Abatement Exhibition held at the Science Museum as an opportunity to capture his fellow architects' interest. He secured the cooperation of the Royal Institute of British Architects (RIBA) in designing and building the prototype soundproofed home for the exhibition and, under Bagenal's supervision, RIBA's *Journal* published "Interim Recommendations on Planning against Noise." The article included a diagram of RIBA's own London headquarters at 66 Portland Place (a striking art deco building completed a year earlier in 1934) as an example of good practice (Figure 3.3).[107] In the same way that the Anti-Noise League's logo (Figure 1.1) stands as a visual summation of the modernity-as-crisis narrative discussed in Chapter 1, RIBA's diagram of its own headquarters usefully emblemizes the modernist ethos under discussion in this chapter. The noise emanating from the three motor vehicles at the bottom of the diagram is rendered powerless by the modernist design of the building: none of its windows face the road, while its "brain" (the top-floor council chamber) is shown to repel the weak sound waves of the motor traffic by virtue of its lofty position and reinforced walls. It is an architectural metaphor, though probably an unintentional one, for the noiseproofed self detailed in the writings of popular psychological self-help writers such as Ash, Loosmore, and Hunt. Bagenal extended this architectural logic to the case of home building: "Much can be done," he explained, "by proper planning. The modern dwelling . . . ought to turn its back on the street, like the Roman house and the Mediaeval convent."[108] In presenting such apparently effective solutions to the noise problem, Bagenal might easily have undermined the Anti-Noise League's claim about the seriousness of noise's threat, as did Millais Culpin, for example. If noise could be so easily contained by the modernity of "proper planning," then, under the terms of this logic, there might have been no need for a noise abatement campaign at all. Instead, Bagenal drew upon the Anti-Noise League's work as a way to raise the status of architectural acoustics as an expert discipline. He found it useful, in other words, to play upon the age-of-noise narrative in order to promote the value of architectural acoustics as

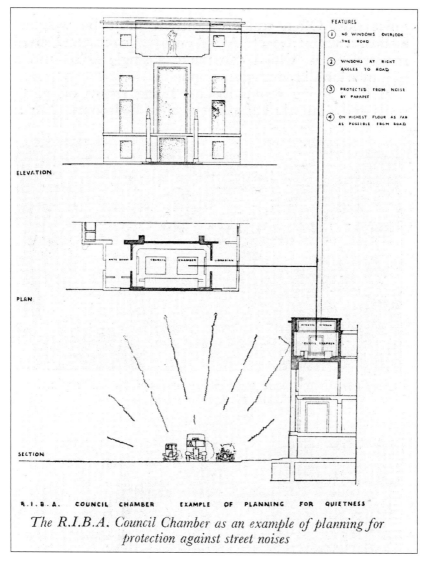

FEATURES

① NO WINDOWS OVERLOOK THE ROAD

② WINDOWS AT RIGHT ANGLES TO ROAD

③ PROTECTED FROM NOISE BY PARAPET

④ ON HIGHEST FLOOR AS FAR AS POSSIBLE FROM ROAD

ELEVATION

PLAN

SECTION

R.I.B.A. COUNCIL CHAMBER EXAMPLE OF PLANNING FOR QUIETNESS

The R.I.B.A. Council Chamber as an example of planning for protection against street noises

FIGURE 3.3 Illustration of Royal Institute of British Architects headquarters at 66 Portland Place, London, from "Interim Recommendations on Planning against Noise," *Journal of the Royal Institute of British Architects* (June 1935): 7. RIBA Collections.

a form of professional expertise. Therefore, while competing ways of hearing modernity were sometimes pitched in sharp contrast to one another in early-twentieth-century Britain, as in the case of the neurasthenic versus the psychasthenic paradigms in relation to workplace noise, they could in other instances—such as this—overlap and even support one another.

RIBA's "Interim Recommendations" on noise set out a two-pronged approach to home acoustics, which also underpinned the approach taken at the BRS and the NPL. First, new housing developments should, it was said, pay attention to the siting of homes in relation to possible external sources of noise. RIBA's *Journal* included diagrams that pointed to the value of organizing communities so that residential areas were built away from noisy industrial and recreational areas and away from major roads and railways. A community so planned, argued RIBA, had obvious advantages to flawed "ribbon developments" in which homes were planned lining busy roads.[109] Such principles had formed a central part of the garden city movement since the nineteenth century, but in the interwar period they were taken up and repackaged as a solution to the acoustic problems of the age. As plans for a significant new wave of home building developed during and immediately after the Second World War, the newly established Ministry of Town and Country Planning incorporated these principles into its work. The concept of sonic "zoning," in particular, was adopted as a principle of postwar planning.[110] Bagenal was among those who actively pressed the government to adopt such principles. In 1947, he warned the Department of Scientific and Industrial Research that postwar new towns must avoid the "sandwich cities" chaos which blighted Britain's major urban centers, "where works have grown up in back gardens, where factories and housing estates come next to each other and where the working-class population are bred and inured to noise."[111]

In the 1930s and early 1940s, however, far more research was dedicated to the second prong of RIBA's recommendations. Here, the material fabric of the home itself, rather than its situation in relation to the rest of the town or city, was the focus of attention. Establishing precisely how much sound penetrated through the walls and floors of different kinds of homes necessitated not only finding new ways of measuring noise (using the recently standardized measures of the decibel and the phon[112]) but also distinguishing between two different kinds of sound transmission: airborne and structure-borne. The latter included footsteps and other sounds caused as a result of physical contact with the building. The former included, for example, speech and music.[113] The NPL built replica partitions in its laboratory (Figure 3.4) in order to develop precise measurements relating to the sound insulating

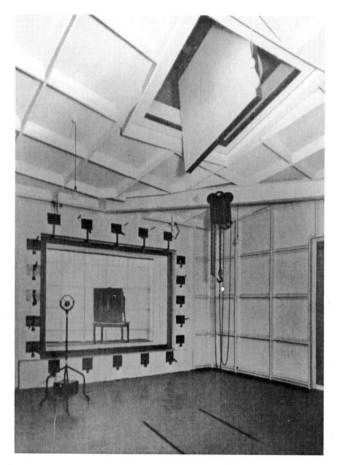

FIGURE 3.4 Photograph of "Rooms at National Physical
Laboratory for Measuring Transmission of Sound through
Partitions (loud-speaker visible through test aperture)" from
A. H. Davis, *Noise* (London: Watts and Co., 1937), 106.
Photograph originally published in the National Physical
Laboratory Annual Report, 1934. Courtesy NPL.

properties of various different types of walls and floors. Ideal materials for
sound insulation were recommended, as were ideal thicknesses of partition.
The innovation that the BRS remained most proud of was the "floating floor"
concept which involved a concrete floor being insulated from the structural
floor below it and the walls around it by rubber or felt pads.[114] This was
especially useful in designing quieter flats. A version of it, adopted by H. W.
Cullum and Co., is shown in Figure 3.5. In addition to structural innovations,

FIGURE 3.5 Advert for Cullum Soundproofing System in *Noise Abatement Exhibition: Science Museum, South Kensington, 31st May–30th June 1935* (London: Anti-Noise League, 1935), 77.

acoustic planners working at the BRS and the NPL recommended new ways of arranging rooms within houses and flats. Figure 3.6, for example, details the attempt to lessen the auditory intrusion of the indoor toilet cistern. In example B, bathrooms have been planned against bedrooms and above the living room. This leads, according to the report's authors, to unnecessary disturbance of leisure and sleep caused when the toilet is flushed. Example A shows ways of avoiding this problem by planning bathrooms away from bedrooms and living rooms.[115] In semi-detached houses and flats, it was also recommended that living rooms should be planned so that they adjoined the neighboring living room, and the same with bedrooms, so that the auditory rhythms of daily life would be synchronized from one dwelling to the next. Concerns about noise thus had a significant impact on how home interiors were organized from the 1930s onward. They also contributed to the development of new building designs, especially for blocks of flats. Figure 3.7 shows two such designs. Residents of Example A are exposed to the full force of traffic noise on one side, and, on the other, from the internal courtyard, to the sounds of milk delivery, refuse collection, and neighbors' loudspeakers. Example B avoids these problems by removing the courtyard and setting windows back from the street at right angles.[116]

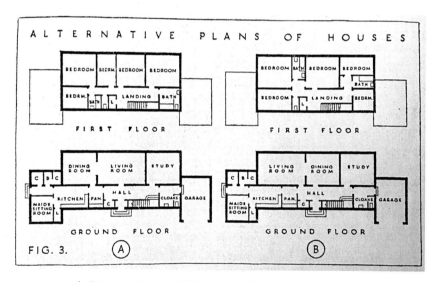

FIGURE 3.6 Diagram from A. H. Davis and C. J. Morreau, *The Reduction of Noise in Buildings, Building Research Special Report No. 26* (London: His Majesty's Stationery Office, 1939), 6. Courtesy of Building Research Establishment.

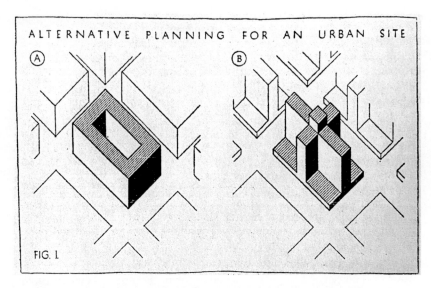

FIGURE 3.7 Diagram from A. H. Davis and C. J. Morreau, *The Reduction of Noise in Buildings, Building Research Special Report No. 26* (London: His Majesty's Stationery Office, 1939), 4. Courtesy of Building Research Establishment.

However, what neither of these two solutions to the domestic noise problem could account for was the psychological variation between home-dwellers in terms of their sensitivity to sound. The NPL could accurately measure the amount of sound transmitted by various sources through a variety of different types of walls and windows but was faced with the problem that people seemed, according to anecdotal evidence at least, to vary quite radically in their tolerance of noise in the home. Determining ideal standards of insulation was not simply a matter of which building materials to use, as BRS researchers R. Fitzmaurice and William Allen found in their attempt to specify the thickness needed in walls and windows for different kinds of domestic activities (Figure 3.8). In order to claim, for example, that a house affected by "moderate traffic" would require 36-inch brickwork to allow the right acoustic conditions for study or sleeping (as the diagram in Figure 3.8 suggests), it was also necessary to determine what constituted a "normal" psychological attitude to noise. "The aim," wrote Fitzmaurice and Allen, "has been to set the [noise] reduction levels of various forms of construction to a point where ordinary people would not complain, but it has to be appreciated that hypersensitive people on the listening side may consider the reduced level still a source of objection."[117] Fitzmaurice and Allen were

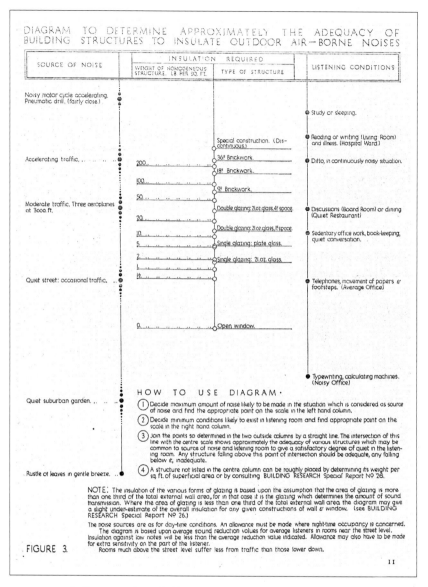

FIGURE 3.8 Diagram from R. Fitzmaurice and William Allen, *Sound Transmission in Buildings: Practical Notes for Architects and Builders* (London: His Majesty's Stationery Office, 1939), 11. Courtesy of Building Research Establishment.

not equipped to base their assessment of psychological normality on firm evidence, since none existed. Surprisingly, psychologists had not undertaken studies of home noise during the 1930s in the same way that they had of work noise. It nonetheless became increasingly apparent to building researchers that the collection of such data would be necessary if the sonic home were to be optimized to its fullest extent.

The gathering of objective data about people's psychological relationship with domestic sound finally emerged alongside the plans being put in place for new social housing developments to alleviate slum living in the early 1940s. Blocks of flats had been identified as the best format for new social housing developments, but experience had shown that, on the whole, British people were generally reluctant to live in flats. For example, an M-O study found, "There can be no doubt ... that flats are unpopular with the great majority of English people."[118] In this same report, M-O confirmed what planners feared most about working-class people's antipathy to flat living: "The main trouble is the noise ... wireless going and children playing round the yard. You can hear everything going on," as one interviewee put it.[119] Indeed, the "chief positive" complaint about flats, M-O reported, was the noisiness of neighbors.[120] BRS investigators feared that if they could not solve the problem of noisiness in flats, then working-class Britons would never be persuaded to live happily in them. The problem of slum living would persist and the vision of a modern urban future would not be realized. A visual rhetoric of anti-Victorianism was promoted in films and posters during the 1930s and 1940s encouraging working-class people to see flats as part of a future worth fighting for (Figure 3.9). Public information films such as *Housing Problems* (1935) reinforced this message, visually juxtaposing dilapidated Victorian houses with clean, modern flats. This film also emphasized that new flats were being built with the noise problem specifically in mind: the futuristic design of Quarry Hill flats in Leeds, for example, was said to provide ideal sonic surroundings.

Nevertheless, the BRS knew that it still faced an uphill struggle in convincing working-class Britons to accept flats. In 1943, the BRS commissioned the Wartime Social Survey—the government agency responsible, as part of the Ministry of Information, for monitoring morale and social attitudes—to undertake a study of everyday hearing in the British home. Dennis Chapman, a lecturer in social science at the University of Liverpool, who had previously conducted surveys on domestic heating and lighting on behalf of the BRS/ Wartime Social Survey, was given the task. Chapman's survey, published initially under the title *Sound in Dwellings* (1943) and subsequently as *A Survey of Noise in British Homes* (1948), was based on interviews undertaken with 1,528 women and 487 men from 2,017 individual households in locations

FIGURE 3.9   Army Bureau of Current Affairs poster designed by Abram
Games, 1942. The caption on the right reads "Clean, airy and well planned
dwellings make a great contribution to the Rehousing movement. This is a fine
example of a block of workers' flats built in London in 1936." Wellcome Library,
London.

across England, Scotland, and Wales, including several districts of London.[121]
More women than men were involved because Chapman considered the
home to be a primarily feminine domain. He noted, however, that there
was no significant difference between men's and women's responses to his
survey. The targeted homes were all of "small and medium size, of the kind
likely to be built in large numbers after the war" (1,480 were houses and 537
were flats).[122] The survey focused on three different kinds of sounds: those
originating within the home, those coming from a neighbor's home, and
those originating outside the home. For each, interviewees were asked to
comment on what kind of sounds they heard, whether they found them to
be troublesome, and whether they disturbed their sleep. The design of the
research reflected the priorities of the BRS in contrast to the more whimsi-
cal surveys undertaken by M-O. For example, Chapman had clearly been
instructed to ascertain whether the noises people heard in their homes were
airborne or structure-borne, a key concern of building scientists. When asked
this question, however, most interviewees were more or less at a loss to find
an answer. It is a shame, in some ways, that Chapman stuck so closely to
such utilitarian priorities, since a more wide-ranging M-O approach would

have certainly uncovered a greater depth of qualitative information about people's sonic experience of home.

Chapman's survey nevertheless represents a noteworthy willingness on behalf of the state to undertake statistical research about psychological attitudes to domestic sound. Chapman found that the "hypersensitive" minority to which Fitzmaurice and Allen referred numbered a not inconsequential 25 percent in terms of sounds originating within the home and 30 percent in terms of sounds from a neighbor's home.[123] Of these sounds, Chapman found that people were far more likely to object to discontinuous noises, such as the banging of doors, than to the sound of a neighbor's wireless set. Among such discontinuous sounds, the most prominent was the toilet cistern.[124] As a relatively new innovation, the indoor toilet was both a discontinuous and a relatively unfamiliar sound to which people found it hard to adjust. The percentage of those troubled by sounds originating outside the home was higher still at 40 percent. The sounds likeliest to trouble in this respect were children playing in the daytime and traffic noise at nighttime.[125] However, by far the starkest finding in the report from the BRS's point of view was the startling difference between those who lived in houses and those who lived in flats regarding sensitivity to noise: 95 percent of flat-dwellers said that they were aware of the sounds surrounding them while 34 percent said that their sleep was disturbed by sounds coming from neighboring flats, compared with only 19 percent of house-dwellers.[126] The BRS concluded in 1948 that the main contribution of Chapman's survey had indeed been to provide "useful figures for the common observation that modern flats are thought to be unreasonably noisy."[127] However, Chapman's study was far less useful to building scientists than it might have been because, due to financial constraints owing to wartime conditions, the researchers were not able to record the decibel levels relating to the sounds commented upon by their interviewees.[128] It did not, in the end, contribute much in the way of establishing the objective psychological norms for noise sensitivity that Fitzmaurice and Allen had identified a need for.

Chapman may also have come to regret that his noise survey stuck so closely to architectural questions such as the issue of airborne versus structure-borne noises. By 1955, he acknowledged that a significant shift had taken place in expert discussions of housing away from the building science approach promoted by the BRS and toward a greater concern with community cohesion, which evolved within the new Ministry of Town and Country Planning. Identifying Walter Gropius as the godfather of this approach, Chapman explained that "the creation of 'neighbourhood spirit'" was now seen as the cure for "widespread unhappiness" in towns and cities rather than ever-greater technical knowledge about building materials.[129] Indeed, a 1944 Ministry of Town and Country Planning report noted, "It is now a commonplace to say that the solution of the housing problem does not lie wholly in the provision of the number of dwellings which may be required, however well-planned, well-designed, well-constructed and well-equipped every one of these dwellings may be."[130] The report concluded that it is necessary, in addition, to understand the role played by neighborhood and community.

The shift in emphasis from building science to neighborhood unit planning brought with it a new conceptualization of the noise question. Town and country planners suggested that the problem of noise lay not so much in the poor soundproofing of dwellings as it did in the breakdown of sonic communities. "During the past hundred years the larger towns have absorbed smaller communities and coalesced with other towns. The physical result has caused a partial breakdown of that feeling of neighbourhood or community which is one of the fundamentals of social well-being," explained the 1944 report. "Despite the benefits of continuous technical invention," it continued, "the life of many town dwellers is filled with unnecessary difficulties created through an unorganised physical environment." Among these difficulties was noise. With the ever-greater road traffic passing through urban areas, sonic communities had been drowned out by traffic noise. If the local neighborhood was ever to be a "comprehensible entity" to its inhabitants, then sonic space as well as physical space would have to be carefully planned. Similar arguments had been made, of course, in RIBA's original 1935 recommendations on planning against noise, but there was, without question, a marked novelty in the emphasis that 1940s town and country planners laid on the importance of a community's ability to hear itself as a community rather than just on the intrusion of noise.

The implications of this insight for British town planning were not put into practice until the major new town schemes of the 1950s and thus lie outside the scope of the present study. However, evidence collected by M-O is sufficient to suggest that town and country planners had hit upon a valuable way of reconceptualizing the noise question. M-O reports indicate that the word *noise* was more often used to refer to sounds that were perceived by the hearer to emanate from a social Other than to the mechanical sounds that so exercised the Anti-Noise League. Such accounts were particularly common in the responses of those working-class people who had moved to new blocks of council flats. M-O explained that working-class flat-dwellers often objected to the way in which "all sorts" were housed together in one block. One respondent, for example, complained that "You'll find the railway people are quite different from the others. We stick together and like to keep ourselves quiet. But these others, they're always popping in and out, and their children the same. The noise they make is awful. You can't alter them, they'll never be altered now."[131] Another commented upon "the people in the flats above me and next door! The language was awful, and the noise! They was a rough lot, those."[132] Quietness, in these accounts, does not equate to an absolute absence of sound, nor to the intrusion of mechanical sounds from outside of the home, but rather to shared codes of sonic respectability. Yet the BRS's domestic acoustic research was undertaken in the 1930s on the basis that the maximum attainable quietness should be striven for in home-building practices. Chapman himself identified the flaw in this plan: "Strangely," he wrote, "there seem to be quite a lot of noises which people like to hear."[133] The noises with positive associations were those that connected the hearer to sonic community. If the BRS had been more inclined in the 1930s and 1940s to undertake social surveys about attitudes to domestic sound rather than follow the age of noise logic about the negative effects of mechanical sounds, then it might well have placed less emphasis on soundproofing and more on sonic community. This is an instance where clear hints of a schism between investigator and investigated emerge in the social interventionism of early-twentieth-century Britain. Building scientists and architectural acousticians were keener in the 1930s than their counterparts in the industrial health movement to construct a sound-sensitive working-class subjectivity, but they did so in a way that projected the middle-class preoccupation with mechanical noise and with absolute sonic privacy at home onto these subjects. M-O reports suggest just enough for us to see the shortcoming of such an approach.

Keep in Rhythm: Everyday Soundscapes and the Documentary Film Movement

Beyond the realms of work and home, a quite different kind of state-commissioned sound expertise was emerging. Public information filmmakers, with the new technology of sound cinema at their disposal, were tasked with the question of how to officially represent everyday sound and its rhythms on screen. The opening lines of W. H. Auden's poem, *Night Mail*—

> This is the Night Mail crossing the border,
> Bringing the cheque and the postal order,
> Letters for the rich, letters for the poor,
> The shop at the corner and the girl next door.

—epitomize a sonic communitarianism, built around the shared rhythms of national life, which came to distinguish British public information films of the period. This section returns to the theme of rhythmic attunement begun in the first part of the chapter and argues that documentary filmmakers, like industrial psychologists, attempted to present the rhythmic sounds of modern life as rational and unifying. Auden's poem was written for inclusion in *Night Mail*, a film produced by the General Post Office (GPO) Film Unit in 1936.[134] The GPO, a publicly operated service since the seventeenth century, was in many ways the public face of the British state.[135] Its long-standing ability to connect one home to another across the length and breadth of the British Empire via the medium of postal communication was a daily reminder of the relationship between state and citizen.[136] As Auden's poem concludes: "None will hear the postman's knock / Without a quickening of the heart, / For who can bear to feel himself forgotten?" The GPO was also, in the 1930s, an institutional pioneer of innovative public information filmmaking. *Night Mail* charts the overnight journey of a Post Office train transporting letters and parcels between London and Scotland. It was a filmic celebration of the relationship between state and citizen made possible by the post. Its release, and associated publicity material (Figure 3.10), coincided with efforts to

FIGURE 3.10 Poster designed to advertise the GPO Film Unit film *Night Mail* by Pat Keely, 1939. © Royal Mail Group 1939, courtesy of The British Postal Museum and Archive.

rebrand the GPO (and by association, the state itself) as a forward-looking institution at the forefront of modern innovation.[137] If the IHRB and BRS's work represents the scientific hard edge of the British state's modernist rationalism in the interwar period, then GPO public relations initiatives such as *Night Mail* are characteristic of its growing interest in the cultural projection of modernity at this time.

Part of a realist tradition of documentary filmmaking established by John Grierson in the late 1920s, *Night Mail* was typical of the films made under Grierson's influence at the GPO in the 1930s.[138] Gathered initially under the auspices of the Empire Marketing Board (EMB), an organization formed by the government in 1926 to promote the consumption of British Empire goods, Grierson's film unit was transferred to the GPO in 1933 where it was given license, under the encouragement of public relations pioneer and civil servant Stephen Tallents, to educate the public via the medium of film about a broad range of topics.[139] GPO films were screened in schools, in town halls, at exhibitions (including the 1938 British Empire Exhibition), and even in Post Office branches. For their part, Grierson's filmmakers were motivated by a desire to represent the realities of everyday social life (and in this respect shared a good deal with members of Mass-Observation) as well as to harness film's potential to enhance democratic citizenship. In addition to fulfilling these social democratic aims, EMB and GPO films captured the modernist spirit of the age by celebrating advances in science and technology. Along with its oversight of BBC radio services, the GPO was directly responsible for operating and promoting new communications technologies, including the telephone. These sound-rich subjects were the most common topic of GPO films in the period to 1939.[140] Films such as *Conquering Space: The Story of Modern Communications* (1934) and *We Live in Two Worlds* (1937) feted man's domination over space and time through the rapidity and reach of telecommunications. *BBC—The Voice of Britain* (1935), *Calendar of the Year* (1936), and others cultivated an imaginative bond between British national identity and the synchronicity of the GPO's sound communications systems.[141]

It was precisely because of the auditory subject matter of GPO films that they developed a distinctive, celebratory, approach to the representation of the modern industrial-technological soundscape. *Night Mail* may have had the most traditional of communications technologies as its topic, but it is nevertheless the outstanding example of trends and techniques that characterized the GPO Film Unit's cinematic work. First and foremost, *Night Mail* was remarkable at the time (and remains so today) for its representation of everyday noises. Auden's poem is fondly remembered for its ingenious rhythmic mirroring of the unmistakable triplet crotchet beat of the steam locomotive in full flight. Yet the sequence in which the poem is used, alongside a score by the young Benjamin Britten, accounts for only the final 3 minutes of a 22-minute feature.[142] The preceding 19 minutes consist of what sound designer Alberto Cavalcanti called the "orchestration of noise."[143] The rhythmic sound of the train's progress on its journey through England provides the background to a range of other mechanical noises on the sound track, including the rattling and banging surrounding the GPO workers sorting mail inside the train; the bells, buzzers, rattling, and clanging that accompany signal and station work; and keynote sounds associated with particular industries that the train passes by—a buzzer for the mines of Wigan and metallic clanging of different pitch for the steelworks of Warrington and the machine shops of Preston.

The GPO Film Unit was born concurrently with the birth of sound cinema and, in addition to pioneering ideas about "actuality" film, Grierson was determined that his filmmakers would be at the forefront of the documentation of everyday sound: "The microphone, too, can get about in the world," he enthused. "By doing so, it has the same power over reality as the camera had before it. It has the power to bring to the hands of the creative artist a thousand and one vernacular elements, and the million and one sounds which ordinarily attend the working of the world."[144] GPO Film Unit sound recordist Ken Cameron recalled, "With my gigantic new beauty of a sound truck I travelled the length and breadth of Britain."[145] The Film Unit, he said, always went "to great lengths to record the actual noises heard in everyday life."[146] Cavalcanti, who had been hired by Grierson to oversee the GPO Film Unit's approach to sound, insisted that the socially realist documentary film must combine three elements in its sound track: speech, music, and effects.[147] With respect to the third of these, using the actual noises of everyday life as effects was especially useful because, as Cavalcanti explained: "Pictures are clear and specific, noises are vague. . . . That is why noise is so useful. It speaks directly to the emotions. Babies are afraid of loud bangs, long before they can have learned that there is any connection between noise and danger—before they even know there's such a thing as danger. Pictures speak to the intelligence. Noise seems to bypass the intelligence and speak to something very deep and inborn."[148]

Mechanical and electronic noise was used to signify modernity in GPO films, but it was also intended, as Cavalcanti suggests here, to enhance the emotional resonance of reality film for audiences by enveloping them in realistic everyday soundscapes. In *The Song of Ceylon* (1934), for example, the noise of radio static, Morse code bleeps, and the sound of a ship's horn are juxtaposed with the traditional working rhythms of Ceylonese tea pickers in order to draw attention to the contrast between modern and traditional working practices. In *Spare Time* (1939), the rattling and buzzing of the South Wales mining industry is set alongside the sound of a male voice choir to make a point about the contrasting temporalities of work and leisure in working-class communities. Cameron believed that in its use of sound, the GPO Film Unit had transcended standard definitions of documentary film: "Something else has crept in, something indefinable," he wrote. "Perhaps this something might be called imagination, or humanity, or simply a knowledge and observation of how the people of this country live and work, think and act."[149]

Given the controversy about noise in 1930s Britain, the GPO Film Unit's approach to the representation of modern soundscapes was always likely to attract negative comment. Predictably, the use of everyday noises in GPO films did not meet with the approval of the Anti-Noise League. In 1939, the League's journal *Quiet* published an article by the film producer Andrew Buchanan arguing that, far from adding to the emotional resonance of film, everyday noises were unnecessary on a film sound track, especially given the danger they posed to health. "Documentary film-makers sometimes reproduce the actual noises made by sawmills, drills and machine-shops, and the results are diabolical, though very true to life," complained Buchanan.[150] "I would prefer to watch an industrial process accompanied by illustrative music," he explained, "rather than hear the dreadful din which really should surround it."[151] He elaborated:

> I know that orchestras are not to be found playing in a factory of noiseless machinery, but when I go to a cinema, I do not expect to experience factory conditions. Occasionally, news-reels reproduce heavy gun-fire. Unfortunately, many of us know what gun-fire sounds like, and we don't want to hear it introduced into an evening's entertainment. We like to see what is *really* going on in the world—if we can—but we need not have our ear-drums injured in the process. Our imagination is quickly kindled by pictures of guns firing. It is dulled by the actual sound of them.[152]

GPO filmmakers believed, on the contrary, that realistic sound was of equal importance to realistic images in the production of documentary film.

Night Mail's presentation of the railway soundscape's intricacies should also be set in the context of a long tradition in Britain, and elsewhere, of identifying trains, and the noise made by trains, as the preeminent symbol of mankind's fundamental incompatibility with machine. "Railway spine," the neurasthenic condition arising in those especially sensitive to railway travel, was the modern nervous ailment *par excellence* in the nineteenth century.[153]

In its 1862 special issue on railway spine, the *Lancet* reported, "The rattle and noise which accompany the progress of the train create an incessant vibration on the tympanum, and thus influence the brain though the nerve of hearing."[154] This was no less a contributory factor in creating the "condition of uneasiness, scarcely amounting to actual fear, which pervades the generality of travellers by rail" than the rapidity of visual information passing by the carriage window.[155] In 1873, *All the Year Round*, the periodical formerly owned and edited by famous sufferer of railway spine and supporter of street noise abatement, Charles Dickens, ran an article entitled "Sound and Fury—Signifying Something," in which the unnamed author associated railway sounds with the creeping crisis of nervous illness in modern society: "Whenever I arrive at, or depart from, the London Bridge terminus of the South-Eastern, and of the London, Brighton and South Coast Railways, my ears are perpetually assailed—I might, without exaggeration, say pierced—by the short, sharp, sudden shriek of the steam-whistle, notifying the egress or ingress of a train. The sensation sends a pang through my nervous system; my teeth jar, and my hands involuntarily rise to my ears to deaden the excruciating sound."[156] For Dan McKenzie, author of the 1916 book *City of Din*, the sonic vibrations that accompanied the railway journey were also a special case in point.[157] "Now in railway travel," he explained, "a rolling stream of loud noise is incessantly battering naked unprotected nerve-endings, a hyper-excitation that, like pain or anxiety, keeps the nerve-centres in the brain on the stretch for hours together."[158]

In this context, the decision of *Night Mail*'s directors, Basil Wright and Harry Watt, to include such extensive use of train noises takes on an additional significance. *Night Mail*, along with other GPO films that depicted everyday working soundscapes such as the coal industry feature *Coal Face* (1935), were self-conscious attempts to reorient the dominant negative view of industrial and mechanical noise in Britain. GPO films presented noise as a progressive and socially unifying force. In *Night Mail*, the train plays the part of modernity. Its speed and rhythm, the qualities that establish it as modern, are indicated primarily by noise. Two key scenes involving the piercing sound of the train whistle underline the association between the train's noise and its modernity. First, at a local station where a passenger train has stopped to let the postal train overtake, the camera remains on the faces of two men on the platform as the screaming whistle of the postal train is heard approaching. As the heads of the two men turn to watch the speeding locomotive pass, the moving train is represented only by the noise it makes as it passes through the station. Second, after the narrator explains over the continuing clatter of train noises that postal trains from across the Midlands connect at Tamworth, Rugby, and Crewe, the film slows its frenetic pace to show traditional rural life taking place by the side of the railway tracks. A man leads a shire horse to its stables and the sound track is notably silent except for occasional birdsong. Then, as the man takes out his pocket watch, the sound of the passing train's whistle becomes audible again, punctuating the passing of time. The postal train noisily hurtling by represents the penetration of modern temporality into the traditional structure of rural life, underlined by the falling of a newspaper from the train's window.

Supporters of the Anti-Noise League, and those who continued to subscribe to its medicalized critique of modernity, would surely have interpreted such scenes as revealing the disruption caused by "mechanical civilization" to the timeless natural rhythms of human life. GPO filmmakers instead celebrated a modern harmony between man and machine in postal work and a national unification made possible by GPO services. In *Night Mail*, railway workers press their ears to telephones in order to coordinate the arrival and departure of connecting trains at stations. In signal boxes, workers' fingers tap out Morse code on the telegraph system while bells ring to signal the response. The telegraph wires that stretch along the side of the railway tracks carry messages from one signal box to another, the nervous system of the railway network. The office full of telephones at the station office is the metaphorical brain. Noise is shown to be fundamental to the healthy, rhythmical "body" at work in the transportation of post across the country. It stands for progress, efficiency, and standardization. No less than industrial psychologists, then, GPO filmmakers did a good deal to shift noise away from its association with neurasthenic illness.

In order to demonstrate the compatibility of man and machine and the rational nature of mechanical noise, *Night Mail* paid particularly close attention to the automated system in which sacks of mail are attached to a trackside device that releases as the train passes, dropping the mail into the moving carriage. The train in turn deposits sacks at the trackside in a similarly automated manner. Sound and its temporal qualities are essential to this process, as one senior operative explains to an apprentice on board the train. As they prepare to deposit a sack of mail at a drop-off point, the senior operative explains how to time the maneuver in relation to the passage of the train toward this moment. "You want two bridges and forty-five beats," he explains. The train then passes under a bridge, which causes an intense burst of noise as the steam hits the stonework. At the second of these intense bursts, the senior operative begins counting to forty-five in time with the beat of the train's turning wheels. A rapid montage sequence cuts between close-up shots of the baskets in which the mailbags are held on the side of the train and the turning of the wheels whose noise makes the timing of this complex operation possible. In contrast to McKenzie's claim about the inherent incompatibility of man and machine, *Night Mail* suggests that sound unifies man and machine in a shared and mutually beneficial rhythm. Although they were probably unaware of the IHRB's work, GPO filmmakers ultimately put forward a very similar argument about the usefulness of rhythmic noise in working life. Rhythmic noise represents collective, social, endeavor in GPO films such as *Night Mail*.

In addition to presenting this positive view of working soundscapes, GPO films also tended to celebrate the rhythmic qualities of wider social life.[159] For example, the 1937 GPO film *Trade Tattoo*, made in support of a "post early" advertising campaign encouraging people to post their letters by 2 P.M., explicitly urged its audience to "Keep in Rhythm" with the greater sonic community of the British Empire. Rather than use everyday noises to make this point, as *Night Mail* had, *Trade Tattoo* shows scenes of industrial work from across the Empire accompanied by Cuban dance music. Everyday life was rendered thus as a pulsating dance. Such films were intended to encourage people to imagine their daily working routines (as well as their postal habits) as rhythmically synchronized to the national, and imperial, community. Although it does not contain noisy sound effects, *Trade Tattoo* maintained the trend in GPO filmmaking of presenting a positive interpretation of everyday soundscapes. Through its absence, industrial noise was presented as if it were the equivalent of the dance music heard on the sound track. Indeed, Cavalcanti's approach to film sound often blurred the distinction between music and noise. In particular, the GPO films scored by composer Walter Leigh, such as *The Song of Ceylon*, tended to blend traditional musical elements with noisy sound effects in what fellow documentarian Paul Rotha described as early attempts at "musique concrète."[160] This was part of the conscious attempt at the GPO Film Unit, under Cavalcanti's influence, to reposition noise as something of social and artistic worth.

Toward the end of the 1930s, the GPO Film Unit began to take a somewhat different approach to the representation of everyday noise. Grierson had moved on, and Humphrey Jennings, whose well-known association with the surrealist movement was at odds with the Griersonian model of actuality film, became the primary director associated with the Unit.[161] *Spare Time*, a documentary about the leisure pursuits of industrial workers made for exhibition at New York's 1939 World Fair, was his first major film and usefully underlines the difference in approach that Jennings brought to bear. The film presents a detailed comparison of the work-leisure rhythms of three major British industries—steel, cotton, and coal. In contrast to the blending of noise and music that characterized films such as *Night Mail*, *Trade Tattoo*, and *The Song of Ceylon*, *Spare Time* insists on the absolute separation of the two in order to present a more critical stance on industrial working practices than had previously been the case in GPO films. The pastimes represented include playing darts, the walking of whippets, watching football, racing pigeons, visiting the zoo, dancing, visiting the fairground, playing cards, watching a puppet show, but above all, music. As the British Film Institute's *Monthly Film Bulletin* noted, "The subtle differences in atmosphere in the three industries are really felt and heightened by their own uses of music—the more aggressive, downright music of the steel-workers' silver band, the haunting, peculiar rhythm of the Manchester cotton-workers' carnival band, and the sad yearning of the miners' songs."[162]

Jennings used music in *Spare Time* to represent the freedom of leisure time. Noise, on the other hand, was used to signify the temporality imposed on the worker by his employer. "This is a film about the way people spend their spare time," opens the commentary, with a shot of an industrial landscape in the background. "Between work and sleep comes the time we call our own. What do we do with it?" inquires the voice-over. The starkest contrast between music and noise comes in the section dealing with coal workers. It opens with shots of a Welsh mining village and the sounding of the siren that indicates the end of the working day. From the sound of the siren there is an immediate cut to the music of a funfair. Next comes the rehearsal of a male voice choir accompanied by a woman at a piano. Scenes of men in the pub follow, with the music continuing in the background. The piano, in need of tuning, makes a hollow sound, which, in contrast to the sooty faces of the men drinking beer, makes for a scene of exceptional pathos. This is followed by an extended scene of the male voice choir performing hymns, which cuts to a YMCA basketball match and then in equally quick succession to a miner at home with a cup of tea being poured for him by his wife. The tranquillity that the viewer has been lulled into by the performance of the choir is brutally disrupted by the cut to the sound of a factory horn and the image of the coal mine's exterior coming to life. Miners with torches make their way to work in the dark, and the sounds are those of metallic clattering. "As things are," returns the voice of the omniscient narrator, "spare time is a time when we have a chance to do what we like, a chance to be most ourselves." The miners cram into the cage-style elevator that takes them into the pit. A final scene of chimneys and industrial landscape concludes the film.

Although he was by no means in the pessimistic camp occupied by supporters of the Anti-Noise League, Jennings believed that human happiness could be preserved only by the balancing of animal and machine forces. His documentary history of Britain's industrial revolution, published posthumously as *Pandæmonium, 1660–1886: The Coming of the Machine as Seen by Contemporary Observers*, was a philosophical treatise, of sorts, on this theme.[163] For Jennings, music was an animal force. Noise was a machine force. The two had, in his view, to be carefully counterbalanced. In *Pandæmonium*, he quoted Hugh Miller's 1846 book, *First Impressions of England and its People*, as proof of his theory that, during the nineteenth century, industrial workers cultivated musical pastimes in order to balance out their noisy working life. "In no town in the world are the mechanic arts more noisy" than in Birmingham, wrote Miller. "The noises of the place, grown a part of customary existence to its people—inwrought, as it were, into the very staple of their lives—exerts over them some such unmarked influence" and as a result, when the factories close for the evening, "they seek to fill up the void by modulated noises, first caught up, like the song of the bird beside the cutler's wheel or coppersmith's shop, in unconscious rivalry of the clang of their hammers and engines."[164] Jennings was not involved in the production of *Night Mail*; if he had been, the project would probably have taken a different course in its representation of noise. He was less optimistic than Cavalcanti about the possibility of man's unity with machine. Jennings's distinctive use of music to represent the endurance of the human spirit in an age of mechanical noise was at the forefront of the Second World War Ministry of Information films for which he is best remembered. These films, discussed in Chapter 4, used sound as the primary means of encouraging communality of purpose on the home front during the war.

In the work of state documentary filmmakers there was, therefore, a difference of approach in the representation of everyday noise. Films such as *Night Mail* attempted to project a rhythmic togetherness at the heart of Britain's industrial and technological soundscape. In their celebration of rhythm and noise, filmmakers such as Cavalcanti extended the logic of industrial psychology by representing noise as a force that connected working-class people to the temporal synchronicity of their nation. Jennings was altogether more reluctant to celebrate noise as a facet of working-class life and insisted that the noise of machines must be kept in balance with the musical sounds of human life. Although these differing ways of representing noise in documentary film were not direct modes of expert intervention in everyday soundscapes in the same way as industrial psychology and building science were, they were nevertheless part of the elite reimagination of the social, and of what the social should sound like, in early-twentieth-century Britain. Through both of its divergent strategies of representing everyday noise, GPO filmmaking contributed, in an imaginative sense, to the opening up of everyday sound worlds as legitimate and knowable realms for expert intervention.

Conclusion

Tim Edensor argues that the "diffuse forms of power" operating in liberal political contexts "often seek rhythmic conformity and spatio-temporal consistency." He adds, with a view to the contemporary world, "The rigour of school and work hours, regulations about commercial opening hours and the sale of alcohol, the time when noise is labelled 'antisocial,' along with many other beats that we are expected to follow, establish 'good habits,' often laid down by the state."[165] These "good habits," in the case of early-twentieth-century Britain, included adapting oneself to the rhythm, and in turn to the sounds, of industrial work. Such adaptation was identified as a psychosocial norm by the professional experts of the newly emerged industrial psychology movement. Documentary filmmakers, too, promoted the sonic rhythms of technology as part of a new, rational, planned modernity. The home was imagined, in the rationalizing ethos outlined in this chapter, as a place of rhythmic pause, where a separation between private quietness and public sound should be protected. Nevertheless, the overriding logic remained: noise, so long as it was controlled by experts and so long as it conformed to rhythmic norms, was part of the regular, rational, functioning of social life.

4 National Acoustics

Total Listening in the Second World War

This has been a quiet day for us, but it won't be a quiet night. We haven't had a quiet night now for more than five weeks. They'll be over tonight.

—Voice-over, *London Can Take It!* (1940)

The Second World War, with its bombing of civilian populations, brought a greater transformation of the everyday soundscape than any of the other forces of change at work in early-twentieth-century Britain. Total war on the home front altered what people heard in their daily lives and how they listened. The quote that opens this chapter is from the film *London Can Take It!* which was produced in 1940 by what had been the GPO Film Unit (now renamed the Crown Film Unit) under the direction of the wartime Ministry of Information.[1] The narrator, American journalist Quentin Reynolds, is presenting a day in the life of Britain's wartime capital city. "Now it's 8 o'clock," he says, followed by the chime of Big Ben. "The searchlights are in position. The guns are ready." The air-raid warning siren sounds. "The nightly siege of London has begun." The menacing sound of approaching enemy airplanes is heard on the sound track, followed by loud explosions. "These are not Hollywood sound effects," Reynolds explains. "This is the music they play every night in London, the symphony of war." The visuals cut from the flash of explosions and searchlights to men playing darts and an elderly couple sleeping, people stoically going about their daily lives despite the noise of the blitz that envelops them.

Codirected by Humphrey Jennings and with sound recording by Ken Cameron, *London Can Take It!* continued a tradition begun in 1930s GPO documentary filmmaking of telling the story of everyday British life through sound. In the context of nightly bombing raids, documentary filmmakers' desire to realistically represent the modern soundscape took on new significance. War films such as *London Can Take It!* gave GPO documentarians an opportunity to develop and extend their ideas about sonic community at a time when the resilience of community had become a matter of urgent importance. The sound of Big Ben chiming, the noise of antiaircraft guns firing or a group of nurses singing quietly at their station were used to poetically encapsulate the war effort on the home front in Crown Film Unit films. Audiences were encouraged to hear the "symphony of war" with pride and national commonality of purpose. Humphrey Jennings and Stewart McAllister's *Listen to Britain* (1942), which, through a montage of everyday sounds, "blended together in one great symphony . . . the music of Britain at war," is the outstanding example of wartime documentary film's projection of national unity through sound. In fact, as this chapter argues, both within and beyond the filmic efforts of the Ministry of Information, national identity and everyday sound were deliberately and powerfully bound together during the Second World War in Britain.

This chapter offers an auditory perspective on the politics of nationhood by identifying the ways in which certain sounds were designated as sources of authentically national culture and how certain habits of listening were codified as essential to national citizenship in Britain during the Second World War. Historians of sound have often treated the nation and national identity as secondary concerns on the basis that urbanization and technological development, the two forces responsible for material changes in the acoustics of modern societies, were shared across national borders. While it is certainly true that noise abatement campaigns, for example, were a common feature of modern European and North American cities, it does not follow that noise abatement was seen to be desirable for the same reasons in Berlin, Paris, and New York as it was in London or Manchester. Clare Corbould and Mark M. Smith have demonstrated, in the American context, that discourses about urban and industrial noise were dependent on a specifically American politics of racial difference.[2] This was not a structuring factor in the cultural politics of early-twentieth-century Britain in quite the same way. In Britain, claims about class, as previous chapters have suggested, were more likely than race to be evoked explicitly as sources of sonic difference and hierarchy. Variations between national contexts, in other words, alter how social sounds are experienced, discussed, and managed. More importantly, the ideological and imaginative project of nation building was itself based, as this chapter argues in relation to the case of wartime Britain, upon the conceptualization of a nationally specific acoustics. An individual's resonance with, or resistance to, the sound-space of the nation was, and remains, a marker of insider/outsider status. Wartime situations heighten the politics of belonging and, in turn, amplify its sonic underpinnings.[3]

Before the outbreak of the Second World War, the most obvious attempt to strengthen the underlying acoustic pattern of the nation was the project developed in late-nineteenth- and early-twentieth-century art music to create specifically national schools of composition. From the 1860s onward it became common practice across Europe to claim that certain composers and musical idioms were uniquely national and that this specificity was a product of a composers' familiarity with the nation's folk music traditions. In Britain, a movement evolved between 1860 and 1940 that attempted to establish a distinctively English music to counter the reliance on foreign, particularly Germanic, composers. Known as the English Musical Renaissance, it was championed by men such as Sir Charles Groves who encouraged English composers to write specifically English-sounding music. A peculiarly national sound was to be achieved by drawing upon the folk music traditions of the English countryside, which, in a parallel "folk music revival," were being championed by collectors such as Cecil Sharp.[4] Composers including Hubert Parry, Charles Villiers Stanford, Edward Elgar, and Ralph Vaughan Williams adopted the call to incorporate English folk idioms into their compositional works and, together, they formed what has come to be known as the pastoral school of English music.

The English Musical Renaissance sought to ground national culture in the apparently timeless and culturally unique acoustics of the English countryside. "Rather than just providing a backdrop or context," as George Revill has argued, "musical sounds themselves played a distinctive part in the cultural politics of Englishness in the early twentieth century, legitimating specific landscapes and histories."[5] The rural soundscape was identified by proponents of the English Musical Renaissance as a reference point for national identity, in contrast to the rural sounds of other nations, but also, as Revill points out, in opposition to urban and industrial soundscapes. Revill describes the pastoralism of composers such as Vaughan Williams as a "spatial ordering of sounds," which, privileging the countryside, marked out "appropriate subjectivities for the nation."[6] The specific rhythms of rural life upon which folk music was based (of preindustrial labor processes, for example, or the dances of courtship rituals) were extended as rhythmic underpinnings of national subjectivity in the music of English pastoral composers.

This process of privileging the past over the present and the rural over the urban as sources of authentically national culture was reversed in the relentlessly modernist Soviet Union, where the state encouraged machine music and noise orchestras to reflect the cultural legitimacy of factory production over rural traditions as a source of collective, Soviet, identity.[7] A similar process was at work in British documentary filmmakers' representation of technological soundscapes in the 1930s, discussed in Chapter 3. Although their films were in no sense anti-rural, these filmmakers attempted to rele-gitimate the rhythm of industrial noise as a reference point for national belonging because, as state employees, they had been tasked with presenting a new, more positive, image of British industry. Identifying and promoting sources of aural reference for national identity is, in other words, part of the politics of national belonging, no less in liberal contexts such as Britain than in more culturally centralized settings such as the USSR.

Times of war, as Sonya O. Rose has argued, often serve to intensify and accelerate the "ideological work" of nation building.[8] This was certainly true in Britain on the home front during the Second World War where, famously, a "people's war" spirit is said to have come to fruition.[9] In addition to iden-tifying the processes of exclusion that took place in the wartime imagining of "the people," Rose points to the deliberate rhetorical and symbolic work that went toward constructing the people's war: "Even though it may seem self-evident that war heightens the significance of the nation as an object of identification," she explains, "the process of national identity formation is not automatic."[10] The nation must be actively "imagined," as Benedict Anderson puts it.[11] Sound, as Revill has argued in relation to the English Musical Renaissance, has a powerful role to play in this process of imagining. While Rose acknowledges that "a complex potpourri of sounds, especially the loud and deep wail of air-raid sirens, the droning planes overhead, and the frightening whistle of a bomb as it plummeted through the air" play a central role in how the people's war is remembered in Britain, she does not include sound in her analysis of the ideological work of wartime nation building between 1939 and 1945.[12] As examples such as *London Can Take It!* begin to reveal, however, the sounds of the home front during the Second World War structured not just the memory of the conflict but also played an active part in the imagination of national community during the war itself.

Second World War strategies for defining the meaning of sounds and for shaping practices of hearing were framed by debates and modes of expert intervention, which had already emerged in response to the challenge of the age of noise. Each of the three distinct ways of hearing modernity outlined in the previous chapters remained active during the war: expert discourses about noise and "nerves," about maintaining the soul's steadfastness in the face of potentially damaging vibrations, and about techniques for keeping in rhythm, were reformulated after 1939 as contributions to the national war effort. This chapter does not, therefore, outline another way of hearing modernity but rather examines how the alternative ways of hearing modernity discussed in previous chapters came to refashion themselves after 1939 as contributions to the ideological work of nation building. The Second World War prompted confluence rather than proliferation in expert claims about sound. Although spiritual self-help writers and government scientists, for example, did not find any new scientific common ground during the war, they did agree that techniques of self-management were necessary for the greater good of the nation-at-war. Discursive constructions of sonic modernity in the diverse modes of sound expertise at work in early-twentieth-century Britain gave way during the years of the war to discursive constructions of hearing nationally. In both official and unofficial capacities, the sound experts discussed throughout this book became mediators of national sound and of the acts of hearing that qualified one for inclusion as a member of "the people."

Among the most striking features of the sonic imaginary in Britain during the Second World War was the extent to which rural sounds, and the quietness of the countryside, came to signify the essence of the national homeland. A rural imaginary was squarely at the heart of cultural attempts to establish what the nation sounded like during the war, not so much in terms of its national music but in terms of everyday soundscapes. The reservation of church bell ringing to indicate enemy landings prompted a public debate, conducted on the letter pages of national newspapers, about the sonic essence of the nation in which the loss of rural church bell ringing in particular, as a signifier of the nation-at-large, was mourned. Certain keynote sounds of the nation, often those associated with the countryside, such as the peal of rural church bells, were thus elevated to new cultural significance after 1939. The Anti-Noise League was revitalized in this cultural context. It was renamed the Noise Abatement League in an effort to reorient the cause of noise abatement toward national, rather than class, interests. Lord Horder insisted that "we are not antis.!" in an effort to throw off the cranky, elitist, image which his organization had gained during the 1930s.[13] During the war, the League operated a scheme to take "over-strained" civil defense workers out of cities and into the countryside for quiet rest breaks. Quietness, and the conditions for self-reflection that rural quietness afforded, was aligned with strength of national character in the face of the noisy enemy invader by the Noise Abatement League.

A body of historiography has categorized the rural preoccupations of early-twentieth-century British culture as a nostalgic reaction against modernity.[14] Situating twentieth-century Englishness as "nostalgic, deferential and rural," it has been argued, set the tone for the backwardness of British cultural and economic life in the twentieth century.[15] Arguing against this analytical tradition, Peter Mandler prefers to describe early-twentieth-century Britain as a "post-urban" rather than as a rurally nostalgic society. Suburbanization, the motoring boom, and the rambling movement—all features of interwar culture—were more likely to bring the city to the country than the other way round, he argues.[16] Mandler's rejection of the ruralism thesis is a useful contribution to the debate about cultural modernity in early-twentieth-century Britain, but one of the overarching arguments made throughout this book has been that alternative modes of experiencing modernity, and its sounds, coexisted and overlapped in early-twentieth-century Britain. So it was in the Second World War. Documentary filmmakers could celebrate the sonic modernity of factories and radio broadcasts while at the same time contributing, in their films, to the idea that the quiet rural soundscape constituted the sonic quintessence of the nation. Indeed, Sonya Rose has argued that, during the war, while depictions of the countryside came to symbolize the "historical permanence" of the nation, depictions of the city tended to signify the nation-at-war.[17] Therefore, *both* urban sounds and rural sounds could be codified as national in this context, and this process of sonic imagining is clearly at play in prominent war films such as *Listen to Britain*.

Sound also came to be subsumed into the "total war" approach adopted by the wartime state.[18] At the outbreak of war, the government hurriedly took on emergency powers to control every aspect of the audible environment, giving bells, whistles, and sirens specific wartime meanings and tightly controlling their use. The streets of Britain were otherwise eerily quiet, since creation of noise by anyone other than official war personnel was designated a criminal offence. The *Lancet* commented in 1940, "In this war, life is controlled, food is controlled, and even noise is controlled."[19] Listening—to radio broadcasts, warning sirens, and other wartime sound signals—became a fundamental requirement of the wartime citizen,[20] as did knowing when *not* to listen: a restful night's sleep made possible by the wearing of earplugs became a patriotic act. Lying in bed at night, the sleepless were no longer troubled by noisy roadworks. Instead, they listened out, ready at any moment for the undulations of air-raid sirens. The auditory culture of total war bound the hearer to the nation in ways that would have been inconceivable outside the conditions of aerial bombardment and fear of invasion.[21] Before 1939, sound had been the concern of private individuals distracted by noise, or of those who were concerned with making daily life more efficient in the workplace and the home. During the war, hearing became a matter of national as well as of individual well-being. In all their guises, debates about wartime sounds and national identity were inseparable from discourses about the effects of sound, positive or negative, on the human mind and body. Certain sounds were considered to be damaging to morale, others as contributing to the health of the nation and thus to its resilience in wartime.

The Soundscape of Total War

As part of the total war approach, which had its origins in the state's response to the First World War, the government took unprecedented steps in 1939 toward centralized regulation of the sonic environment.[22] Because the sound of air-raid warning signals had to be unmistakably audible at all times, sounds that might distract the civilian population's attention or falsely raise the fear of an attack were silenced or tightly regulated by the Emergency Powers (Defence) Act, 1939, passed shortly before the outbreak of the war. The Act included the Control of Noise (Defence) Order passed on September 1, 1939, which outlawed the public use of sound-emitting objects. Included in the list of banned items were sirens, hooters, whistles, rattles, bells, horns, and gongs.[23] The only people permitted to make widely audible and public sounds with such instruments were local officials, including police constables and air-raid protection wardens, and even then they would be allowed to do so only in tightly regulated ways. The Order stated:

> Subject to the provisions of this Order, no person shall, in any area in Great Britain, sound any instrument or cause or permit any instrument to be sounded, except—
> For the purpose of making a signal, in accordance with directions given by the local authority or chief officer of police for the area, to indicate that an air-raid by the enemy is expected or is in progress or has ceased, or that noxious gas is present, or that danger from such gas has ceased; or
> In such circumstances that the sound of the instrument is not liable to be mistaken for any such signal as aforesaid; or
> For the purpose of testing the instrument, or carrying out any exercise, in accordance with directions given by the local authority or chief officer of police for the area.[24]

Legislation of this kind could only have been dreamed of by Lord Horder's Noise Abatement League in their campaign for stricter noise control legislation in the years before 1939.

It was necessary for the Control of Noise Order to legally prohibit a wide range of mechanically produced sounds because specially manufactured air-raid sirens had been installed only in major areas of population such as London. Elsewhere, factory hooters or other preexisting loud noise systems were co-opted as air-raid warning signals, which meant that the types of sounds that could conceivably have been permitted as distinguishable from air-raid warnings would necessarily differ from one place to another across the country.[25] The only exceptions made by the Order were for sounds considered essential to the safe working of certain industries, of which shipping and the railways were among a small number of examples.[26] In addition to making air-raid warnings the only widely audible sound in a given area, control of noise was also, as with the control of light, intended to minimize the enemy's ability to identify areas of population, especially in the case of ground invasion, in which case civilians' ability to distinguish between sounds made by their own civil defense officers and those made by invading forces would also be of critical importance.

The Control of Noise Order tangibly altered what Britain sounded like during the years of the Second World War. The crescendo and diminuendo of the air-raid siren has come to signify the war in post-1945 popular memory, but equally significant during the war itself were the noticeable auditory absences caused by the Order. One effect of the Order, for example, was to outlaw the use of the hooters and buzzers that were still widely used to signal the beginning and end of the working day in industrial workplaces. Employers wrote to the Home Office throughout the war complaining that, because they now had no way to signal the start and end of shifts, their workers arrived late and left early, damaging productivity.[27] In October 1944, a representative of the Wales Civil Defence Region, for instance, wrote to the Home Office arguing for a reversal of the ban on colliery hooters in the South Wales mining region because their absence, and the absenteeism that this caused, was in large part responsible for falling coal production there.[28] Another letter from the Welsh Regional Controller of the Ministry of Fuel and Power stated that "I have no doubt that if Colliery Hooters could be again brought into use for their normal peace-time purposes, it would have a very material affect upon the time keeping and absenteeism of the men."[29] The extent of such complaints, which came from all parts of the United Kingdom and from all types of industry, indicates the continued importance of audible signals in the regulation of Britain's everyday working and living rhythms. Their sudden absence disrupted the work-discipline of industrial temporality.[30] In November 1944, partly in recognition that the frequency of air raids had lessened, the government relaxed the restriction on the use of factory hooters in cases where they were not being used as air-raid warning signals. A Home Security note explicitly explained that this alteration to the Control of Noise Order was intended to boost industrial productivity by allowing "large, industrial concerns, if authorised to do so, to sound their hooters at stated times to indicate to their employees the approach, beginning or end of a period of work."[31]

The most controversial application of the Control of Noise Order was its use in June 1940 to designate the ringing of the church bell, banned until now under the Order, as a warning of imminent enemy ground invasion. During the initial drafting of the Control of Noise Order in 1939, ministers and officials had been in two minds about whether to explicitly exempt the ringing of church bells from the Order. It was ultimately decided that including a clause exempting church bells would "increase rather than diminish" the difficulties of policing the Order because it would lead to other requests for exemption. Officials would be "on much weaker ground in turning them down, if the order already contains an exemption which [is] entirely unnecessary," it was felt.[32] Thus, the ringing of church bells was banned until June 1940, at which point emergency planners decided that a sound distinctly different to the air-raid siren or local air-raid warning sound was needed to indicate the parachuting down of invading German servicemen.

The Church of England's network of church bells was unique in its ability to provide a solution to this problem. Not only was the sound of a church bell instantly recognizable as such, but the presence of a church building complete with bells in almost all of Britain's towns, cities, and villages meant that this was also already a national sonic infrastructure. The presence of such a network meant that the state could avoid expending valuable time, effort, and money on providing a second auditory warning system to complement air-raid sirens. Church bells provided a ready-made communications infrastructure, which was both national in its coverage and local in its applicability. These qualities were enormously valuable to the wartime state and remained so in the Cold War context: in 1959, the government considered commandeering church bells again, this time to indicate the danger of fallout after a nuclear missile attack.[33] In both the Second World War and Cold War cases, Church of England officials were reluctant to allow their network of bells to be used for the purposes of war. The decision of 1940 was forced on the Archbishop of Canterbury and the Church of England Assembly, despite their protestations, by the Home Office. The *Church Times* satirically reported on June 21, 1940:

> In the parishes of England last week vicarage maids-of-all-work were knocking on their master's study doors and saying, "Please, sir, the policeman to see you." On being admitted to the sanctum (with that geniality which animates all members of the great undetected in the presence of the Law) the policeman explained that he had come to communicate an order from the Government prohibiting the use of church bells except to give warning of the imminent descent of enemy parachutists or air-borne troops.[34]

There were several cases of false alarms during which church bells were rung, sparking panic in local populations. Newspapers were keen to report sensational stories about the ringing of church bells throughout the war. Under the terms of government instructions, church bells should be rung if twenty or more parachutists were sighted above any given parish. It was reported in September 1940 that during a recent night of bombing, church bells had been rung in Wales and in the Northeast and Southwest of England. The *Manchester Guardian* reported that "All Home Guards in a Southwest town were called out about midnight on Saturday night. Some were called by loudspeakers in the streets and others by messengers. In a residential suburb church bells were rung."[35] Despite this panicked sound making, no evidence of invasion was found, and the incident remained a mystery. Accounts such as these suggest the potential for a sudden shift from eerie quiet to frenzied sound making on the streets of Britain during the blitz. Newspaper reporting of the simultaneous ringing of bells in several different parts of the country, more significantly, served to remind readers that although they experienced the threat of invasion locally, people were experiencing the same terrifying ordeal right across the land, the most striking commonality being the sounding of the church bell. Unlike air-raid alarms whose sound varied from place to place, the ringing of church bells now signified the same thing to all Britons: invasion. This gave the sound of the church bell a particularly chilling potency in wartime propaganda and fiction. The Ministry of Information film *Miss Grant Goes to the Door* (1940) and the Ealing Studios feature *Went the Day Well?* (1942) directed by onetime GPO documentarian Alberto Cavalcanti, for example, both included fictional imaginings of German invasion accompanied by the tolling of parish bells.

Alain Corbin's study of bell ringing in nineteenth-century rural France notwithstanding, there has been relatively little work undertaken by historians on the cultural and social significance of bells.[36] Prior to the installation of civic clock towers and the widespread ownership of personal watches (a shift to visual modes of telling the time), bells were the foremost means by which communities marked the passage of time, both on a seasonal and on a day-to-day level. Corbin also draws attention to the ways in which nineteenth-century French villages used the sound of bells to determine their spatial identity: being within earshot of the village bell meant that one was still within the territory of the village.[37] Although modern twentieth-century societies relied much less upon bells for their spatio-temporal coherence, church bells remained an important reference point, at least in imaginative terms, for the spatialization of identity. In wartime Britain, the sound of church bells, and especially rural church bells, was evoked as an auditory metaphor of the nation. As the countryside became ever more potent as a symbol of the nation's permanent essence, the sound of the village bell increasingly came to be described as a force uniquely capable of binding the individual self to the collective nation, reminding battle-weary Britons of their shared history and culture. Anglican clergymen were especially keen to encourage this line of thinking, but it is evident from diary entries, newspaper letter pages, and social surveys that many people regretted the silencing of church bells during the war and welcomed their eventual return as an expression of triumphant nationhood. The *Church Times* linked the silencing of church bells to the conditions of blackout: "What a blaze of light, what a clangour of bells there will be on the day—pray God, not far distant—when victory and peace are proclaimed!"[38]

A community's bells have been shown to be important as material objects as well as producers of sound. Richard L. Hernandez points out that in the case of rural Russia, the casting of new bells was often undertaken throughout history to mark important events and that the entire community was involved in the process by, for example, adding inscriptions to the bell's exterior. The metal for new bells "came from the villagers themselves in the form of old pots, mugs, and other scraps. Melting these contributions together," Hernandez explains, "made the bell a tangible, if mysterious, embodiment of the village."[39] The presence of a bell in each locality meant that it also became a "peculiar bearer of Russian national identity" linking the locale to the nation via the Russian Orthodox Church.[40] When the Bolsheviks attempted to remove and destroy church bells in the 1930s, the widespread resistance of Russian villagers transformed the bell into a symbol of national resistance. A similar process was at work in Britain during the Second World War. Church of England authorities worried about the effect of the war on the material condition of church bells. Not only might bells be destroyed by falling bombs, but their inexpert use by civil defense officers could also cause untold damage: "Bells may easily be damaged by those who may have temporary authority to ring them under the invasion warning scheme, but who have never learnt how to do so," reads a Church pamphlet about the care of church buildings in wartime.[41] Church bells were priceless precisely because they physically embodied the nation and its history. The *Norwich Diocesan Gazette* pointed out that many church bells dated from the fifteenth century and others from the thirteenth, and that "they have probably escaped the ravages of time more completely than any other part of the church's furniture, and are irreplaceable in their original state if destroyed."[42] The church bell signified, in reports such as these, the longevity and permanence of Church and nation. For this reason, Church of England clergymen remained vehemently opposed to the state's use of their bells.

Church officials also pointed out that inexperienced bell ringers would be incapable of producing peals recognizable to local communities as their own. Not only were bells themselves particular to local communities, so were the idiosyncrasies of those who rang them. Hernandez points out that Russian villagers came to recognize not just their own bells, but also the work of their own bell ringers, whose variously "mournful, warning and celebratory" peals were immediately decipherable. If the church bells of wartime Britain were to be rung by untrained officials, then the expressive bond between a community and its bell ringers would be broken. The *Church Times* noted the difference between a musical peal produced by trained bell ringers and the noisy tocsin that would be produced by a civil defense worker with no knowledge of how to ring a church bell. "The authorities seem to be ignorant of the fact that bell ringing is a difficult art, calling for no little skill, and unmeasured patience in the pursuit of it," argued the *Church Times*.[43] Senior figures in the Church of England were all too aware that church bells had, throughout British history, been used to create *both* celebratory peals *and* warning tocsins, meaning that banning the normal use of church bells for Sunday service should have been unnecessary.

The decision to use church bells as an invasion warning was controversial not just among Church of England clergy, however. It sparked a flurry of letters to the national press. Such letters argued that without the sound of church bells the spirituality at the core of British national identity would ebb away. A June 22, 1940, letter to the *Times*, for instance, stated, "In my opinion it is essential for the nation's spiritual uplift and staying power that the church bell should summon us to the House of Prayer."[44] Another exclaimed, "Surely the authorities have not thought what they are doing? They have silenced the daily reminder throughout the country of the one thing that can give us power in the long run to win this struggle against evil—prayer."[45] Such letters suggest that church bell ringing, although officially banned by the Control of Noise Order, may have continued in some places until June 1940; otherwise, such outrage would have seemed curiously belated. It is also possible, though, that those who felt strongly about church bell ringing used this opportunity to bring the issue to the wider public's attention. They did so in a manner that placed strong emphasis on the ability of church bells to unite the nation in both a spiritual and a spatial sense.

The Home Office was sensitive to the criticism that followed the new directive on church bells and kept a file of press cuttings relating to it. One letter cut out from the August 9, 1940, edition of the *Daily Mail* was from the Rev. E. N. Needham-Davies, who pleaded for the restoration of church bell ringing and underlined the argument that the church bell peal should be thought of as a keynote sound of the nation: "Let this song of England ring out again each Sunday, ring of home and ring of country, ring of peace that was and yet shall be; ring of a Faith that never dies and of a victory that none can take away."[46] Needham-Davies's letter explicitly linked nation with "country." Such was the strength of feeling among Church of England clergymen in particular on this matter that one vicar, the Rev. Robert Grant Colvin Graham, ignored the Control of Noise Order and rang his church bells in Old Bolingbroke, Lincolnshire, on July 16, 1940. He claimed that the letter from his Bishop had not fully explained the legislation, but upon prosecution he was nonetheless found guilty of willfully ignoring the Order and sentenced to four months imprisonment. He was released after one month following the upholding of an appeal.[47]

The link that Anglican clergymen and other letter writers made during the war between the sound of church bells, spirituality, and nationality adds weight to Matthew Grimley's claim that, during the interwar period, popular notions of "national character" had become more closely associated with a "tolerant, undemonstrative form of Protestantism." The tendency to link national and religious identity extended, as Grimley points out, beyond those in the Church who had a vested interest in maintaining it. Anglican church buildings became a familiar symbol of the nation in wartime art, film, and propaganda just as the peal of church bells came to represent it in sound.[48] This was especially true of the country church building. Despite the fact that the Church of England had invested heavily in building urban churches, particularly in London, during the mid-Victorian period, a clear connection was made in popular discourse during the Second World War between the village church in its idealized rural surroundings and the timeless nation. In the letters sent to national newspapers, those who bemoaned the loss of church bell ringing especially lamented its absence in the countryside. "I assure you as a country person this muzzling of the bells casts a weakening gloom on the countryside" reads one of the letters to the *Times*.[49]

The church bell peal was evoked more explicitly as an auditory metaphor of the nation in the public debate that followed the government's decision in 1942 to allow church bells to be rung on the morning of Sunday November 15 in celebration of victory in the Battle of Egypt. Diarist Clara Milburn enjoyed hearing the sounds of Coventry Cathedral on the Sunday morning wireless news: "I must say the familiar bells playing the tune 'O God Our Help in Past Ages,' followed by a wild peal, caught at my heartstrings."[50] Fellow diarist J. L. Hodson's entry for the same Sunday recorded the following upon hearing the church bells again: "That in me which has kinship with the soil and woods begins to stir; I seem to be aware of older generations dead and gone moving within me. Home and England and wooded Lancashire come welling up and much of the shell I've grown since boyhood begins to drop away and I feel young and small. I am aware of a boy in an Eton collar going to church to sing in the choir."[51] Hodson's diary entry offers compelling evidence of the emotional power that could be attached to the sound of church bells in wartime Britain. Typical of the tendency to designate the countryside as the source of national identity, Hodson made it clear that the sound of church bells located the hearer in both the local specificity and abstract generality of the nation.

Newspapers also offered a positive reception to the return of church bell ringing on November 15, 1942. Their reporting was no less effusive in underscoring the national significance of synchronized church bell peals across the land. The *Evening News*, for example, rejoiced in the decision to allow the bells to ring: "To-morrow's peals," it enthused to readers on November 14, "echoing in the Sunday silence of the cities and in the quietude of the placid valleys, exulting over vast factories and ship-lined docks, are more eloquent than Hitler's trumpets. For they speak not only of present battles. They are the voice of all this pleasant land and of all its age-old story."[52] The spatial reach of church bells across the nation was also emphasized by the *Manchester Guardian*, which explained to its readers: "From Shetland to the Scillies these victory bells will sound both in celebration and as a 'call to thanksgiving and renewed prayer.'"[53] Church bells became a sonic embodiment of the nation in these reports, geographically and spiritually, in a way that the physical geography of roads and railways could never be.

In May 1943, once the threat of invasion had lessened, the government amended the Control of Noise Order to allow the normal ringing of church bells. This followed a concerted campaign by senior figures in the Church of England to have bell ringing reinstated, in particular by the Archbishop of York, Cyril Forster Garbett, who raised the question in the House of Lords on March 31, 1943. He explained that members of the Church of England had always regretted that bells could no longer be used to summon congregations to prayer, but pointed out that even those with no interest in religion "miss the bells," thus emphasizing the importance of bells to national as well as religious culture. The Archbishop added that bell ringing was especially missed in the countryside where it was a more central aspect of everyday life than in cities. He stated, "Psychologically I am quite certain this silence of the bells has a very bad effect on the people."[54] In a March 1943 letter to Prime Minister Winston Churchill, the Archbishop of Canterbury, William Temple, made the case for allowing the ringing of church bells on Easter day and also pointed to the absence of rural bell ringing as a particular problem. "The absence of the bells, especially in country districts, is a very real loss," he wrote.[55] A familiarly rural-national imaginary underpinned newspaper reporting of the government's decision to end the ban on church bell ringing. The *Manchester Guardian* wrote that "this year a walker in the country who finds himself on a Sunday morning leaning on a stile and looking across one of our small valleys may hear again, breaking the silence of the drowsy summer air, coming from some steeple hidden in a nest of trees, the quiet sound of distant church bells."[56] The emphasis on the quietness of church bells in this report aligned their sound firmly with the countryside in opposition to the noisiness of towns, cities, and modern industry.

Government propagandists were alert to the emotional appeal of church bells and promoted their association with victory in war and with images of the countryside. Figure 4.1 shows a London Underground poster, "The Day Will Come when Joybells Will Ring Again," produced in 1944. The scene

FIGURE 4.1 London Underground propaganda poster, "The Day Will Come when Joybells Will Ring Again," by Anna Katrina Zinkeisen, 1944. © TfL from the London Transport Museum collection.

is of a family reaching out from the darkness of wartime toward the light of peace. The peaceful horizon is located in the countryside, and contained within it is the tolling of a church bell. Although the bell is not depicted visually, its sound is indicated by the quote, attributed to Churchill, at the foot of the poster: "The day will come when the joybells will ring again throughout Europe, and when victorious nations, masters not only of their foes but of themselves, will plan and build in justice, in tradition, and in freedom." The tradition alluded to by Churchill is that of the church bells' toll. The campaign conducted by the Archbishops of York and Canterbury to have church bell ringing reinstated, and the support that followed in the press, had evidently persuaded Churchill of the propaganda value of the church bell as a signifier of national identity.

In contrast to the fascination with rural church bells, which pervaded newspaper reporting and which featured in the Church of England's lobbying of government, Mass-Observation (M-O) commissioned a report to gauge Londoners' feelings about their return in 1943. From a representative sample, 59 percent of men and 66 percent of women said that they liked hearing the church bells again in London. Twenty-three percent of men and 7 percent of women were indifferent, but only 9 percent of men and 3 percent of women said that they disliked the bells' return. Of those who disliked hearing the bells, a majority were apparently drawn from the "unskilled working class," according to M-O.[57] Without knowing their religious persuasion, it is hard to draw a definite conclusion about why these people disliked hearing the bells. A possible explanation is that, by 1943, many unskilled workers were alienated from organized religion. This would fit the sizable historiography that highlights the gradual decline of religion in Britain between 1850 and 1950,[58] but another explanation, more in keeping with Sarah Williams's revisionist account of urban religion, is that those who disliked hearing the church bells belonged to dissenting religious groups for whom bell ringing was associated with the hegemony of the Church of England.[59] It may also have been that the return of church bells, along with factory hooters and buzzers, signaled to unskilled workers the return of a prewar social order and time-discipline through sound. The majority of all those asked by M-O were nonetheless pleased to hear the return of church bells, and it is clear from their responses that they associated the sound with the triumph of British national spirit in the war. A forty-year-old middle-class woman said, "I enjoyed it very much; it was delightful. Silly, of course, but it made one feel the war was as good as won."[60] Others laid emphasis on the familiar association between church bells, the countryside, and the nation. A fifty-year-old upper-class man, mirroring the *Manchester Guardian*'s reverie about quiet country bells, stated, "I thought it was very pleasant. I was away for Easter, and they sounded quite charming across the fields—they made one feel positively sentimental."[61]

Rest for Damaged Nerves: The Noise Abatement League's War Work

Of course, the soundscape of the Second World War was marked not only by the absence of familiar sounds, but also by the introduction of new ones, notably those associated with air raids. The sound of warning sirens, enemy fighter planes, exploding bombs, and collapsing buildings became an unavoidable part of the everyday soundscape during the war. During the early years of the war in particular there was widespread concern that the bombing would bring about mass neurosis in the civilian population. The blitz would re-create the conditions of First World War trenches on the streets of Britain, it was feared, and shell shock would become an epidemic in the civilian population. Because the noise of bombs had been identified as a major contributor to hysterical and neurasthenic illness in First World War servicemen, the noises associated with the blitz were taken seriously in the early years of the war as a significant threat to civilian health and morale. Although the industrial psychologists discussed in Chapter 3 had done a good deal to undermine the credibility of neurasthenia as a psychiatric category by the outbreak of the Second World War, the imaginative link between noise and nervousness was well-established enough to play an important part in fears about home defense in the early years of the war. The prominent neurologist and member of the Noise Abatement League, Sir James Purves-Stewart, was one of those who warned at the beginning of the war that the terrifying noises of the blitz could bring about mass shell shock in urban populations. He wrote extensively on the physiology of nervous illness in the years immediately after the First World War and his account of Second World War noise was cautionary in the extreme.[62] He evoked "the hum of aeroplanes at a greater or smaller height, the scream of the falling air-bomb; and the zoom of the low-flying dive bomber plane often accompanied by the splatter of machine-gun bullets . . . these noises are familiar," he continued, "not only to the members of our fighting forces, on land, at sea, and in the air, but also to most of our civilian population, exposed to the same risks and the same noises as the fighting men themselves."[63]

The Noise Abatement League set itself the task of providing a solution to the potential crisis of nervousness on the home front. Having found it difficult to secure the support of government ministers and officials in the 1930s, the League might well have quietly given up on its quest to eliminate "needless noise" during the war. The 1939 Control of Noise Order had, after all, initiated the sort of legal controls over city sounds that the League had been established to promote in 1933. Lord Horder admitted that the outbreak of hostilities meant putting aside his noise abatement campaign in the interests of the national war effort.[64] Horder himself was busy organizing humanitarian medical relief on the home front on behalf of the Joint War Organization of the British Red Cross and Order of St John. Yet, by March 1940, when the League's journal, *Quiet*, resumed regular wartime publication, he and his members had changed their minds. The experience of the first few months of the war led them to the conclusion that educating the public about the dangers of noise was in fact more urgent than ever before. For the many men and women involved in war work on the home front, "reasonable quiet when they need it," Horder argued in *Quiet*, "is perhaps the difference between standing the strain of this War or becoming a casualty to the tension of emergency."[65] Because more people were now working in shifts to meet the needs of the war effort, Horder continued, the maintenance of restfully quiet conditions during the day and night had become more than simply a matter of sociability and consideration; it was now one of national security: "Every effort to suppress needless noise," he wrote, "whether it be from shrill motor horns, dirty motor exhausts, barking dogs, jingling milk carriers, wireless loud speakers, or from any other source, is a contribution to the resistance of the nerve force of the individual, and therefore a contribution towards winning the war."[66]

Noise continued to be cast by the Noise Abatement League as an energy-wasting threat to the healthy and productive wartime citizen. "This war," wrote Horder, "more than any emergency that has yet confronted our people, is a war of attrition on nerves, especially the nerves of those living in towns and cities. As never before, it is necessary to conserve the nervous resources of the individual."[67] Horder's use of the word *attrition* implied the physical threat he thought dangerous sound vibrations posed to the human nervous system. It is indicative of the fact that, despite the vociferous claims of industrial psychologists (that noise sensitivity was a mental rather than a physical condition), noise abatement leaders maintained their attachment to neurasthenic discourse right through the Second World War. Apart from the fact that the question of noise could now be more convincingly set up as one of national solidarity, the other significant departure from prewar noise abatement discourse was the extra emphasis placed by noise abatement campaigners on undisturbed sleep as a means of staving off nervous exhaustion. "Great strains are placed on body and on mind," wrote Horder, "and sleep is more necessary now that it may be broken."[68] After the full extent of the blitz was realized in 1940–1941, supporters of noise abatement were more assured than ever in their conviction that the preservation of quiet, and understanding of the effects of noise on health, would be critical to the preservation of morale in wartime urban Britain. The Noise Abatement League stuck stubbornly to the theory that noise caused physical damage to the nerves and that it brought about nervous illness as a consequence.

The journalist Joan Woollcombe, *Quiet*'s founding editor, played a central role in coordinating the wartime activities of the Noise Abatement League. Woollcombe had, until this point, played the part of the noise-sensitive woman in the public work of the Noise Abatement League. Her involvement was intended to indicate to middle- and upper-class women that noise abatement was a cause for them as well as their husbands. She wrote articles in *Quiet*, for example, on soundproofing techniques for the housewife to try at home. During the war, however, Woollcombe took on a leading role in the organization while Horder was busy with the British Red Cross. Reflecting on the war in 1940, Woollcombe wrote that "the rigid pattern of social and civic life [will] get its jolt and shift into a fluid kaleidoscope: and—we might 'get things done' in the general muddle, that would be worth doing. Among them, strangely, *noise control*. Because from being the fad of a few, [it] has become the vital concern of the majority."[69] If the noise of motor cars and gramophone loudspeakers had been thought to pose a threat to nervous well-being in the 1930s, then the sounds of total warfare—"the growling, roaring crackle of an incendiary bomb on a burning building; the high-pitched tinkle of breaking window-glass; the crash of falling bricks, roofs and masonry" as Purves-Stewart put it—were a potential public health crisis of an entirely different magnitude.[70] Concern for the nervous health of the urban civilian population became the raison d'être of the Noise Abatement League during the Second World War. The war offered noise abatement supporters the chance, as Woollcombe put it, to redefine noise as a problem for "the majority" of people rather than just individual complainants.

Woollcombe spent the war working as a Red Cross transport officer in London. It was while working on the streets of the war-torn metropolis that she decided it was up to her to draw attention to what she considered the unquestionably damaging effects of war noise on her fellow civil defense workers. During the first months of the initial air raids in autumn 1940, she concluded that the noises of the bombing were so exhausting and destabilizing that the Noise Abatement League, uniquely placed to appreciate the problem at hand, should step in to provide respite. Up until this point, the League had been dedicated to the "suppression of unnecessary noise." Now, following Woollcombe's lead, it dedicated itself not only to an antinoise agenda but to securing the provision of quiet spaces in which civil defense workers could recuperate from the auditory bombardment of the war. Woollcombe believed that recuperation in quiet conditions was essential to the health of the civil defense workforce.

At first, the scheme to provide these quiet spaces was set up on an ad hoc and voluntary basis by Woollcombe herself:

> In the first crazy days of the September air attacks on London, as I—a Red Cross Officer on duty in a building that offered no sort of protection—was endeavouring to sit through the tenth successive night of bombing with as much dignity as possible—among the good resolutions that I made . . . was one about making peace, that is "quiet," available to those men and women with me, who, unlike myself, had no country home to which they might go for 24 hours rest on the problematical morrow.[71]

Woollcombe thought that the strain of listening for falling bombs and the traumatic experiencing of hearing bombs falling nearby would lead to an eventual nervous breakdown in civil defense workers. She began by offering to take some of her poorer Red Cross colleagues out of London for a night to her country home in Sussex so that they could rest and recover. "Here, surely, was a job for a member of the Noise Abatement League," she wrote, "more practical than preaching peace and more immediately necessary than most other activities open to civilian enterprise."[72]

When Horder found out about this, he handed Woollcombe £10 to put toward getting more of her civil defense coworkers out of London for quiet rest and pledged his support to enlarging the initiative into a fully blown "Country Residency Scheme" for all civil defense workers. Horder was an influential man. In addition to heading the home-front medical operations of the Red Cross and Order of St John war organization, he was also advising the Ministries of Health and Food at this time. So taken was he by the idea of creating the possibility of quiet rest breaks for civil defense workers that he wrote to the *Times* on October 15, 1940, stating in the firmest possible terms that Air Raid Protection workers should from now on be treated as "frontline fighters" who, if their crucial work was to be maintained, needed to be offered a "rest pause."[73] "I recently saw a small-scale experiment undertaken by a single-handed Red Cross transport officer," he wrote, "who transported personally as many of her colleagues as she could to hospitable quarters within reach of London for one night."[74]

Horder did not explicitly make the case against noise in this letter, but there is no question that it was at the forefront of his mind. He reported that "Tired, bomb-haunted women returned in new heart and better health as the result of the leeway of sleep being made up, the memory of one night's rest between sheets, one day's food in quiet, and a sight of the English scene instead of bricks and mortar."[75] This reference to the "English scene" is indicative of the rural ideal that had underpinned Horder's noise abatement campaign from its earliest days. The Luftwaffe's assault on British cities was only the latest form of technologized, and specifically urban, cacophony from which the countryside could provide restorative respite. With the exception of Ainslie Darby and C. C. Hamilton's *England, Ugliness and Noise* (1930), the countryside's quietness had remained an implicit reference point in prewar noise abatement literature, which had focused largely on the noisiness of towns and cities.[76] The rural imaginary summoned as a cultural response to the Second World War caused the noise abatement movement to lay far more emphasis than it ever had on the quietness of the countryside as an antidote to overexposure to loud noise. Just as church bells "quietly" reminded the nation of its enduring rural traditions, so could the quietness of the countryside as a whole be used to revive those upon whom civil defense depended. Rural landscapes were both peculiarly national and bringers of good health in this context.

After Horder's intervention, the Country Residency Scheme took on a more formal guise. Well-off people with large houses in the countryside were urged to offer beds for one or two nights to civil defense workers with no country homes of their own. Writing to the *Times* ten days after Horder's letter, Woollcombe let it be known that generous offers had indeed flooded in, as had large donations of money to cover the cost of travel for poorer civil defense workers.[77] Writing a year later in an article for *Quiet*, Woollcombe recalled that Horder's "letter to the *Times*, and my own that followed it, brought us some 300 offers of hospitality and a substantial sum in money for fares; and, perhaps most valuable of all, an S.O.S. from an Ambulance station in hard-pressed Bermondsey, after the Surrey Dock fire. Their people deadened and deafened, wanted a let-up; and we could give it to them. We did! . . . we got those workers away to quiet and countryside just as soon as we could, and we are still getting them away."[78]

So successful was the Country Residency Scheme in the six months after October 1940 that Horder recommended the scheme be officially integrated into the work of the Joint War Organization of the British Red Cross and Order of St John, whose job it was to provide medical relief to military personnel. In April 1941, the Joint War Organization made a grant of £1,064 to be spent on operating a national network of rest houses for an experimental period of three months and, this experiment having been a success, in June 1941, the Country Residency Scheme became a fully fledged department of the Joint War Organization under the new name of the Civil Defence Workers' Rest Department.[79] This new department was chaired by Horder and directed by Woollcombe. It was effectively, therefore, a de facto branch of the Noise Abatement League inside the British Red Cross and Order of St John. In May 1941, a dedicated rest house in Buckinghamshire, Little Missenden House, opened for the use of 25 men and 25 women while the owners, Mr and Mrs Dumas, lived in the gardener's cottage. It was described by the *Times* as "a blissfully quiet spot."[80] In August 1941, the Ministry of Health released 1,000 beds for the use of resting civil defense workers that had been intended for convalescing soldiers, and by November 1941, the annual expenditure of the scheme was calculated to be a sizable £10,430. Similar levels of financial support were maintained throughout the war.[81] Sir Arthur MacNalty of the Ministry of Health wrote to Lord Horder in 1943 to confirm that "by providing these rest houses for properly selected cases, you are making a notable contribution to the national war effort, for I am certain that in this way you are preventing many cases of serious breakdowns in health which would have required hospital treatment . . . you are enabling civil defence workers to carry on invigorated and refreshed."[82] The map in Figure 4.2 shows the extensive national network of country rest houses that had developed by the summer of 1943. Green trees represented the scheme's own rest houses, while red crosses indicated where beds had been made available for civil defense workers in military convalescent hospitals. Black stars marked the regional offices of the scheme at which civil defense workers could sign up for their rest break. The map, which was circulated among civil defense workers across Britain, was a visual equivalent of the power ascribed to church bells to reconnect the noise-weary self with the authentically national quietness of the countryside.

The scheme was not without its problems, however. Given that, as Horder explained, the rationale of the rest house was based on the principle of "preventative medicine," civil defense workers sometimes found it difficult to explain to their superiors that, although they were not ill and were not applying for sick leave, a night's rest—as Lord Horder had explained to them—was essential to avoid future nervous breakdown. Records suggest that the problem of convincing superiors of the need for a rest break limited the scheme's use by fire workers, for example. One Chief Fire Officer noted in 1944, "The existing procedure in this service is that a woman must be placed sick and obtain a medical certificate to that effect before she can be sent to a rest house."[83] Horder and Woollcombe, of course, thought that a rest pause was necessary primarily as a preventative measure of, rather than as a cure for, mental and physical illness. Horder and Woollcombe tried to

FIGURE 4.2   Map circulated in the publicity material
of the Civil Defence Workers' Health Department of
the Joint War Organisation of the British Red Cross
and Order of St. John, August 1943.

overcome this problem by creating a "Medical Certificate of Rest" which civil
defense workers could take to their GP. The doctor would be asked to certify:
"I am of opinion that the above named person is suffering from strain due
to the present blitz conditions and should be given facilities to go to a Rest
House for a short period of recuperative rest."[84] Nonetheless, the Executive
Committee of the Joint War Organization expressed considerable concern in
1943 that the rest house scheme was open to misuse and insisted that those
applying for a place should be carefully scrutinized by medical professionals
for evidence of potential ill health.[85] This is further evidence of the disjuncture between the medical claims of noise abatement supporters and those
for whom sound was not such a great obsession; preventative medicine, as
far as noise was concerned, was Horder's hobbyhorse, and the rationale for

it was not always immediately obvious to others, especially in the context of the later war period in which panic about blitz conditions had receded.

Further evidence of the disjuncture between noise abatement campaigners and those who did not directly support their campaign can be found in Woollcombe's account of those who made use of the rest houses. Newspaper reporting of their availability did not necessarily emphasize quiet as the primary benefit of a night's holiday in the country, yet it remained clearly at the forefront of Woollcombe's mind as she worked tirelessly for the scheme throughout the war. "The four years of war," she wrote in 1943, "have given the writer ample opportunity for, but no time to record, the observations forced upon her of the reactions of the ordinary people to noise—devilish noise; and also to the provision of refuge from noise given to tens of thousands of sufferers by her Department."[86] To her disappointment, however, the reactions of many of the men and women who stayed at rest houses showed, in her opinion, a marked lack of appreciation for the quietness of the countryside. "The appeal of a 'rest in the country' is enormous when it is made," wrote Woollcombe, but it is "not so great" when people actually "arrive in the silence and peace of the country and least of all, in the winter silence and peace: the great majority of those who are fit to get around, demand immediately the nearest town, the pub and the flicks."[87] Woollcombe's social prejudice is barely concealed in this account. The men and women who made use of the rest houses, by necessity of a lower social class than Woollcombe herself because they had no access to country homes of their own, were held in contempt for their inability to appreciate quietness. In particular, "younger or middle aged men" had "no resources in themselves," according to Woollcombe, by which she meant an incapacity to pass the time without some form of "noisy" amusement. She wrote of these men: "A reasonable rest and 'time to stand and stare' are unexplored: and they are not at all attracted by the idea." She bemoaned that such people were still produced by "our costly educational system."[88]

Presenting rest house users in the language of class difference, indeed of bare disdain, was entirely in keeping with interwar noise abatement discourse, which had often, as Chapter 1 points out, identified the source of noise as being the vulgar technological apparatus of the unthinking and uncultured urban masses. Indeed, Woollcombe's writings on the quiet rest break during the Second World War reveal the full extent of the early-twentieth-century noise abatement campaign's investment in notions of sonic class difference. The Country Residency Scheme was the Noise Abatement League's attempt to incorporate the quiet rest pause into the imaginative construction of "the people" and their needs. It was an attempt to show that the majority of people, rather than just the "intelligent section" of society, appreciated the value of quiet.[89] To have succeeded in this endeavor would have put the League on stronger ground in its lobbying of government ministers and civil servants who, as Chapter 3 points out, required evidence relating to the social, rather than just the individual, effects of noise. However, while it is evident that the civil defense workers who took up the Country Residency Scheme were attracted by the idea of a break from their duties, and probably also by the prospect of a break from bomb noise, they did not necessarily share Woollcombe and Horder's specific investment in and conceptualization of quiet as a resource of self-formation.

Woollcombe was nevertheless undeterred in believing that quiet country rest for those who otherwise had no access to the countryside was of great health benefit. The problem was simply that quiet rest's positive effects had yet to be fully demonstrated to the majority of the British people. "Given a chance to show the ordinary man and woman after the war *that rest and quiet pay* in terms of money, health and enjoyment of life, we may (after several decades) notice a trend toward *using quiet as a positive factor* in normal enjoyment of life," she explained.[90] Indeed, both she and Horder hoped to extend the use of rest houses after the war to all those working in noisy occupations. In a letter written to the *Times* in March 1943, Horder sought to build on the positive reaction he had received to the Country Residency Scheme and suggested that "there seems no reason why the principle should not be applied in industry" in order to treat and investigate cases of "sub-health" in the workforce.[91] Speaking at a training course for rest house wardens later in 1943, he added, according to the *Times*, that "he had no doubt whatever that the resthouse had come to stay as a fundamental necessity of preventative medicine of the future."[92]

In making their case for the postwar extension of the Country Residency Scheme, however, Horder and Woollcombe had all but given up on their attempt to construct working-class people as active seekers of quiet. In their suggestions for the extension of rest houses to industrial workers after the war, economic considerations, rather than humanitarian ones, were at the forefront of the argument. Horder pointed out: "We 'service' our taxi-cabs, and how rarely do we see one 'break down'? Is it not time that we began to 'service' our workers?"[93] Woollcombe put it even more starkly when she explained that "recuperative-rest is an economic idea in manpower, money, morale and medical services."[94] The postwar noise abatement campaign, under new leadership, took a somewhat different direction, partly due to the need to campaign against the expansion of civil aviation in the postwar period. Woollcombe, nevertheless, maintained a lifelong interest in promoting the "rest pause." In a 1968 feature for the *Times* entitled "Beating a Peaceful Retreat," she extolled the virtues of a quiet holiday in a convent, monastery, or similarly silent religious residence: "Reasonable comfort, good food and complete quiet cost relatively little and can be found in a number of places," she explained.[95] She gave the example of St. Helena's Retreat House in West Ealing, which was run by the Church of England. An alliance between a noise abatement supporter and the Anglican Church was natural enough given the emphasis put on quiet contemplation by both organizations. Although its Second World War rest break scheme was a success in some respects, the Noise Abatement League did not in the end make much headway in terms of transforming this class-bound ideal of quiet retreat into an imperative of objective sonic governance. Much of the damage, in this respect, had of course been done by industrial psychologists' attack on the noise abatement campaign in the 1930s. But, during the war, too, state experts took the study of noise and its effects in social life in a different direction to that of the Noise Abatement League.

"A War of Nerves": Aurality, Citizenship, and the Politics of Fear

The effects of blitz noise on civilian health and morale were a matter of concern beyond the confines of the Noise Abatement League. In contrast to the nationally unifying sound of church bells, bomb noises came to be thought of during the war as a sound that divided the embattled British population. The division was between those who stoically acclimatized themselves to the sound of falling bombs and got on with their day-to-day lives on the one hand, and those who became fearful in the presence of bomb noises or anxious while listening for the sound of air raids on the other. Government medical experts gradually came to the conclusion that the blitz was not causing mass psychiatric breakdown and found evidence that civilians could adapt to living in noisy conditions if they chose to do so.[96] Purves-Stewart, despite his allegiance to the Noise Abatement League, suggested that stoicism rather than shell shock was in fact winning the day across Britain. He argued that people living in bomb-hit cities "soon become acclimatised to the noise of the heaviest bombardments."[97]

As official panic about mass psychiatric illness lessened, acclimatization to blitz sounds was constructed as a moral duty of the patriotic wartime citizen. Acclimatization could be cultivated by various means, including the use of earplugs and the adoption of psychological "nerve training." It was, in other words, a *choice*. Those who allowed themselves to succumb to fear and noise-induced neurosis were said to be making a conscious decision to undermine the national war effort by failing to adopt such strategies and opening themselves to the threat of mental breakdown. Their fear came to set them apart from "the people." Joanna Bourke has argued that while emotions such as fear are felt individually, their construction as discursive categories has historically been part of a process in which the emotional individual has been categorized socially. This has especially been the case during times of war, she suggests. "Emotions such as fear do not only belong to individuals or social groups," argues Bourke, "they mediate the individual and the social. They are about power relations. Emotions lead to a negotiation of the boundaries between self and other or one community and another."[98] In the case of Britain during the Second World War, fear of noise separated bad citizens from good citizens, those who counted as fully national and those who threatened to destabilize the nation by failing to "hold their nerve."

The notion that one could choose to cultivate mental resistance to the effects of noise was promoted not just by home defense officials but was present also in popular self-help literature, the emergence of which is discussed in Chapter 2. The writer and journalist John Langdon-Davies, who had reported from the front lines of the Spanish Civil War, published a book entitled *Nerves versus Nazis* in August 1940 in which the need to cultivate resilience to noise was identified as the civilian's most important contribution to the war effort. "This is not only a war of machines," wrote Langdon-Davies, "it is a war of nerves. We must learn how to win the war of nerves."[99] Because Hitler himself was reported to have described the war in this way, it became common to use the phrase "a war of nerves" to describe the psychological experience of bombing.[100] Langdon-Davies emphasized that the blitz was primarily intended to bring about "fear, panic, and nervous exhaustion" and that in this respect, the noise of bombs was as damaging as the bombs themselves: "NOISE IS THE GREATEST ENEMY," he exclaimed.[101] "By perpetual bombing people can be kept awake, kept worried, kept restless, kept unoccupied," explained Langdon-Davies, "and this is exactly what is wanted. Noise is the way to do it. If there could be such a thing as a silent bomb certain to kill ten times as many people as the ordinary bomb, nobody would ever use it. It is the bark of a bomb that is worse than its bite."[102] *Nerves versus Nazis* was one of several self-help books published during the war that encouraged civilians to take practical steps to protect themselves against the damaging psychological effects of noise. It argued that fearing noise was irrational, because if the noise of a bomb was audible, then it meant that the bomb no longer posed any physical danger. Langdon-Davies proposed using the psychological tactic of mental suggestion. "Get into the habit of saying to yourself, *'Noise is not dangerous: noise is the proof that the danger is over. Since I have lived to hear the bomb explode, I am safe from the bomb.'*[103] He also thought it worthwhile to use earplugs to remove the threat of noise altogether.

Popular psychological and spiritualist writer, H. Ernest Hunt, explained that the noise of air raids, part of Hitler's psychological warfare against the British people, was intended to affect the subconscious mind and that, by training the conscious mind to resist this attack, the threat of noise could be lessened. Hitler's war of nerves was an attempt to subvert and overload the subconscious mind by means of sensory bombardment, according to Hunt. The subconscious, he explained, "does not touch the outside world direct, but receives the messages that the senses bring in, and stores them up. It is the mind of instinct and habit, the mind of feeling rather than knowing; the mind that comes with us into the world as soon as we are separate beings, enabling us to carry on the complicated business of living. . . . This is the realm of unchartered fears and unrecognized primeval emotions which Hitler sets out to disturb and exploit for his own ends."[104] Defeating Hitler's attempt to instill irrational fear in the subconscious mind involved the application of rational consciousness—the intelligent mind—which has the capacity to realize, for example, that "much of the raid noise is made by our own defence guns at their welcome work."[105] Hunt proposed that staying calm in noisy conditions was simply a matter of training oneself to rely on intelligence, which he gendered male, and resisting the feminizing effects of emotions emanating from the subconscious mind. In order to counter the criticism that not all Britons were equally intelligent, or indeed manly, Hunt pointed out that even horses "can be trained to remain calm," adding that "their imperturbable behaviour in the midst of a noisy and provocative crowd is marvellous. But if the horses can do it, why should we consent to remain at the mercy of a noisy environment? Have we not at least as much innate capacity as a horse?"[106]

For professional psychologists and psychiatrists, as opposed to popular self-help writers, the solution to the noise problem was not so obvious. While they had not as a rule committed themselves to Lord Horder's theory that noise was a cause of functional nervous disorder, they took seriously in the early part of the war the possibility that the sensory conditions of the blitz might bring about shell shock, or similar neurotic conditions, in the populations of targeted towns and cities. Amy Bell has argued that, in practice, the trench warfare of the First World War and the air raids of the Second World War were entirely different conflict experiences and that, over the course of the early 1940s, medical professionals came to realize this, which is what lessened their panic about the mental well-being of civilians.[107] Yet, during the early war years of 1940–1941, the fear that bomb noises would bring about shell shock symptoms in the civilian population had very real consequences for civil defense and led to a more sustained medical interest in noise on the part of the state than had ever been the case before the war.

The Prime Minister's own Private Secretary, J. L. Taylor, who had fought in the First World War, wrote to government scientists in May 1940 encouraging them to consider the distribution of earplugs to soldiers, because, as he explained, "The demoralisation of troops by shell fire or bomb burst is due to noise, not to the lethal power of the missile or to fear of destruction."[108] The impact of noise on soldiers' health and morale was closely observed by medical and governmental authorities during the Second World War, and this directly influenced how the question of civilian health was approached. The *British Medical Journal*'s "Survey of One Hundred Cases of War Neuroses," published in 1941, found that from three main groups of neurotic soldiers— the anxious, the depressed, and the hysteric—those with anxiety neurosis "showed tremors and jumpiness, especially to noises."[109] This was because, as another *British Medical Journal* article explained, "their neurotic breakdown was either determined or in part precipitated by the unaccustomed stress of noises, such as gun-fire, shell-bursts, exploding bombs, sirens, planes, and dive-bombing."[110] Such findings led to concern among home security officials about the impact of war noises on the civilian population, exposed for the first time, en masse, to the experience of mechanical warfare.

Warnings about the potential for mass war neurosis on the home front caused the government to instruct the Medical Research Council (MRC) in 1940 to undertake serious and sustained investigation of noise's effects on the mental well-being of civilians. The MRC's report concluded that the noises of air raids were in fact relatively untroubling to civilians, psychologically speaking, compared to the fear people felt in anticipation of air-raid noises.[111] It reported that, of those who could not sleep through air raids, there were two types: those who felt fear in anticipation of noise and those who stayed awake because they were actively listening for air-raid noises. This latter group, explained the report, "find reassurance in air-raid noises since each distant explosion is, to them, a sign of escape from possible death."[112] Anticipation of noise, and the fear that produced, rather than the noise itself, was damaging to people's mental health. The harmful psychological effect of prolonged fear was exacerbated by the sleeplessness it caused. The report pointed out that "almost all urban dwellers manage to sleep successfully in spite of the rattle and noise associated with the movement of traffic on towns." But in the war, it continued, "The main factor responsible for loss of sleep seems to be fear, and the tension which fear provokes." It was the effects of sleeplessness that most concerned the Medical Research Council. "Loss of sleep, whatever its cause, will eventually produce fatigue and a continuous feeling of strain which, as they become chronic, will make sleep even more difficult."[113] The MRC thus extended, in the war, the approach to noise developed by the Industrial Health Research Board (IHRB) in the 1930s. Like the IHRB's industrial psychologists, MRC researchers insisted—contrary to the claims of the Noise Abatement League—that noise itself was not a physical threat to health. Rather, as industrial psychologist Millais Culpin had always insisted, the fear preceding the hearing of a noise was the real problem.

An M-O report produced in September 1940 confirmed that loss of sleep was a widespread problem in the civilian population and argued that noise was at the root of this. "More and more evidence is coming in to show that the high degree of sleeplessness is largely due to noise, and especially to the tension connected with *listening* for a noise," wrote M-O.[114] Another M-O report, produced for publication in the *Lancet*, added weight to this conclusion: "A large proportion of those losing sleep or suffering from strain were listeners—people who listened for the plane coming, or for the bomb swishing, often without being able in any way to improve their position or increase their safety when they heard anything."[115] There is anecdotal evidence of M-O's assertion in Clara Milburn's August 24, 1940, diary entry. She recorded being unable to sleep the previous night because "One of our planes went over just as I was settling down, and that woke me up so thoroughly that I dozed for part of an hour. Then, after hearing 2 a.m. strike, I heard the enemy 'zoom-a-zoom-a-zoom' plane." A night in the "dugout" listening to passing enemy planes followed.[116]

It is interesting to contrast the conclusions of the mainstream medical profession with self-help literature's discussion of sleeplessness. In contrast to the secular-scientific approach taken by the MRC, self-help writers such as Hunt remained attached to spiritualized and occult theories of well-being. Hunt argued, "In the mental *blitzkrieg* perhaps one of the most dangerous assaults is upon the nation's sleep" but rather than emphasize fear of noise as the principal contributory factor, he made reference to the "spiritual" quality of sleep, continuing the trend in prewar self-help texts such as Edwin Ash's for the merging of scientific and spiritualized discourses about the body.[117] During sleep, according to Hunt, "the real self, the ego, partially withdraws from its close association with the body, and slips away, leaving the body to carry on its cleansing processes at a low subsistence level of vitality."[118] Like others influenced by the modern occult revival such as Maud MacCarthy,

Hunt was interested in the musical qualities of bodily well-being. He likened the ego, or the real self, to the battery of a loudspeaker set, which could be removed for recharging.[119] Continuing his auditory metaphor, he argued that sleep was part of the rhythmic order of nature, "for law, order, and rhythm are at the basis of the universe."[120] The body, for Hunt, was part of the vibrating Pythagorean universe:

> Our bodies have their rhythm in every organ; the heart-beat is regular, the breathing is regular also, and all the varied periodicities of the body in health are like the component tones of some great musical chord. When one organ is out of tune the whole harmony is marred, and then disharmony and disease occur.[121]

Working within quite different intellectual parameters, the MRC's solution to the problem of sleeplessness was to propose that the state manufacture and distribute earplugs as widely as possible to help civilians block out the sound of air raids. It was felt that the "employment of ear protectors of efficient pattern, whilst it could not be expected to render the sounds of air raids inaudible, might yet yield so great a reduction in incident sound" as to bring about "fear-extinction."[122] In the summer of 1940, 45 million pairs of earplugs were ordered by the Ministry of Home Security. Their mass distribution by air-raid protection wardens began in October 1940 and continued through the autumn and winter months of that year. The state-issued earplugs were an inch long and made of brown rubber.[123] The intention was that earplugs would become an essential appendage of the wartime citizen's body, constantly attached via a piece of string. The *Manchester Guardian* encouraged parents to hang earplugs around their children's necks to ensure instant access if needed. It was even proposed that women could wear their earplugs as earrings so as to have them ready to insert at any moment (Figure 4.3). The *Daily Mirror* reported, "For the first time those earrings of yours, ladies, can be useful as well as decorative."[124] The official announcement of the plugs' distribution explained, "When worn the plugs do not seriously interfere with the hearing of ordinary speech &c., but they reduce the crash and concussion of explosives. Their object is not so much to obviate physical damage to the ear as to prevent the shattering effect of noise on the nerves."[125] This final reference to nerves suggests that the MRC was aware that the popular association between noise and nervousness promoted by the Noise Abatement League could be put to persuasive use in public information. While the MRC's internal reports rejected the language of nerves in favor of the psychology of neuroses, its public announcement about earplugs plumped for a more easily accessible rhetoric of nervousness in order to build public support for the use of earplugs.

For the first time those earrings of yours
ladies, can be useful as well as decorative.
Because the new ear-plugs are on the small
side, and likely to get mislaid by women-
folk, who have no handy waistcoat pockets
in which to keep them, Major S. W. Humphrey, Mayor of Lowestoft, invented the idea
of making them into earrings. And very
nice they look, don't they ?

FIGURE 4.3 "Plug-in Earrings," *Daily Mirror* (October 23, 1940): 6.
Mirrorpix.

Given the state resources that had been invested in the distribution of
earplugs by the end of 1940, officials were keen to determine the extent and
effectiveness of their use. M-O was able provide this information. Asked by
M-O in October 1940 whether they would use the free earplugs or not, 30
percent of people said that they would, but a majority of 70 percent said that
they would not. "They had made up their minds not to try them beforehand,"
concluded M-O. To support this conclusion, M-O pointed out that prior to
the free issue of earplugs in October 1940 only 13 percent of the Londoners
who took part in their survey had thought to buy earplugs for themselves,
despite their cheap and easy availability in shops. Of that 13 percent, only half
had actually used the plugs. Among those who were most ardently opposed
to them were the working class and women, according to M-O. "Keyed on
the expectation of possible death, they did not want to be taken unawares
or to be cut off from 'what was going on.'" In other words, concluded M-O,
working-class people and women, in particular, "want to listen to possible
death."[126] One respondent said, "No, I wouldn't want to wear earplugs. I want

to hear." Intense and active listening were evidently common features of the air-raid experience, at least for some people.

Working-class householders were the keenest listeners, according to M-O, because their homes were most at risk from air raids. Unlike many of their middle- and upper-class counterparts, they still lived close to the center of towns and cities. Women were keen listeners, according to M-O, because in addition to wanting to hear the sounds of raids, they needed to listen for the welfare of their children. Despite being in the majority of those who said that they would prefer not to use earplugs at night, M-O implicitly constructed these working-class and female listeners as the fearful fault line of home defense. The ill health caused by their self-inflicted sleeplessness was implicitly cast as unpatriotic. M-O's framing of some people's need to hear was characteristic of a wider politics of fear during the Second World War. Fear was attached to specific social groups—to particular races, for example, or to women rather than to men. Fear was a marker of social difference. Overcoming fear, on the other hand, was to transcend this difference and to qualify as a national subject.

Despite the irrefutable evidence of resistance to earplugs among the majority of the population, M-O argued in its reports that their distribution should continue. Although the majority of people M-O surveyed actively wanted to listen for the sounds of enemy air raids, it was concluded that it would be in the interests of these people if they were helped to stop listening. M-O encouraged more effective publicity about the benefits of earplug use, including the idea of issuing a photograph of Winston Churchill sleeping with earplugs in.[127] Not hearing, in this context, came to be constructed and promoted as a positive virtue of the patriotic citizen. M-O insisted, "Many people are longing to be able not to listen."[128] It drew attention, in support of this claim, to a solution developed in working-class households and blocks of flats in which "listening rotas" had been drawn up. One volunteer would listen while others slept with earplugs in. "In some big blocks of flats and in some areas of London," wrote M-O, "a considerable informal organisation has been set up for listening and has brought much relief."[129] In contrast to those who refused to wear earplugs and who insisted on listening, the use of listening schedules, it was suggested, indicated the growth of a people's war spirit. While the working class was reluctant to use earplugs and insisted on listening, *Britons* understood the need to get a good night's sleep.

Eventually, though, it became evident that even if they weren't using earplugs, civilians were responding to the conditions of the blitz by adapting to the new noises rather than succumbing to a nervous breakdown. M-O argued that earplugs could be most profitably used in towns and cities outside of

London that were less used to bombing. The point at which people felt the most intense anxiety, according to M-O, were the earliest days of bombing, but after that anxiety lessened. By late 1940, Londoners were already beginning to adjust to the sounds of the blitz. A survey showed that during the raids of September 19, 1940, 24 percent of people got no sleep and 77 percent got less than four hours sleep, but by the raids of November 10th those figures had fallen to 0 percent and 7 percent respectively. As civilian resilience to the blitz became more widely recognized, psychiatrists reversed their analysis of war neurosis and began to wonder if anxious combatants might not be encouraged to act a little more like London civilians. In one military hospital, it was decided to rehabilitate convalescing soldiers by exposing them to gramophone recordings of air-raid sounds produced by the BBC. This was because, as the *British Medical Journal* explained, "Experience showed that treatment along orthodox psychotherapeutic lines, which included physical training, occupational therapy, route marches, games, etc., was impeded in these cases by too quiet an environment in hospital. While other symptoms had been resolved there remained a certain hypersensitiveness to air-raid noises."[130]

The idea was that if neurotic soldiers could be returned to a normal mental state under noisy conditions, then they would be better equipped to cope once returned to the aural stress of the front line.[131] Civilians' resilience in the face of terrifying air-raid noise was emphasized to those soldiers who were rehabilitated through this method. They were told that "men, women, and children in our badly bombed cities have developed a new lease of life. They are in better mental trim than those in safe areas. They have faced the raids, have found them not so bad as anticipated, and have got over them. They carry on with their jobs and take a pride in being fit for fire-fighting and other duties. You can do the same, and this treatment will help you to get accustomed to raid noises."[132] Ability to adapt to the noises of total warfare thus became a sign of patriotic stoicism in official accounts such as this. To overcome one's natural inclination to fear was to transcend one's self-interest in the interests of the nation.

Propaganda films also played a role in presenting an image of Britons stoically acclimatizing on the home front not only to air-raid noises, but also to the noises of essential wartime industries. Jennings and McAllister's *Listen to Britain*, for example, included lengthy scenes of the war's new women factory workers singing patriotically and productively along to a BBC "Listen While You Work" broadcast. The Crown Film Unit's films are now considered to have been essential to the creation of the people's war spirit.[133] The Unit was well-placed to use sound for the purposes of inspiring the war effort on the home front. Whereas in the 1930s GPO filmmakers had sought an authentic sound record of British working life, during the war they turned their attention to recording and presenting sounds that contributed to a unifying ideal of Britishness. In part due to their preexisting interest in everyday soundscapes, but also because of the prevalence of bomb noises in discussions of civilian morale, Crown Film Unit filmmakers tended to present national unity—the people's war—through sonic means. *Listen to Britain*, like *London Can Take It!* before it, used the familiar sound of Big Ben to signify the nation, but cut immediately to scenes of radio broadcast towers and snippets of BBC broadcasts reaching across the Empire in order to point to the synchronized unity of people working for the war effort across the imperial nation. *Listen to Britain* was in one sense an instruction to its audience, an important segment of which was in North America (British wartime propaganda films were usually intended both to improve morale on the home front and to maintain a favorable impression of Britain around the world): the film tells the heroic story of the war effort in Britain through everyday sound. But the title *Listen to Britain* is also intended to indicate the attitude adopted by those working Britons represented on screen.

Women factory workers, air-raid protection workers, and ambulance crews, among others, are all shown working in the noisiest of conditions, but are listening not for the enemy invader, nor to the sonic impositions of war life, but to the sounds of the national community pulling together at a time of shared crisis: the sounds of BBC radio broadcasts, home defense efforts, and munitions factories. A reminder of what was being fought for was represented in the film by rural scenes of corn fields and trees in which the camera lingers at ground level to indicate the enemy threat from the skies. These scenes are accompanied toward the middle and end of the film by periods of quiet and birdsong on the sound track. They make for a distinct contrast to the noisy sounds of airplanes, factories, and mines elsewhere in the film. The natural soundscape represents the timeless homeland for which the national community is fighting.

In keeping with his earlier film on everyday working life, *Spare Time* (1939), Jennings carefully separated noise and music on the sound track of *Listen to Britain*. However, unlike *Spare Time*'s gentle critique of industrial capitalism, *Listen to Britain* uses the contrast between music and noise to indicate the stoical heroism of the British people united through war. Noisy war work undoubtedly takes its toll, *Listen to Britain* implies, but through the collective power of music Britons overcome this hardship. Jennings wrote, in relation to *Listen to Britain*, that "more than ever when men are flying through the night and women are away from their homes and their children, their hearts have need of music. All kinds of music—classical music, popular music, homemade music, the nostalgic music of a particular region and just plain martial music to march and work to. For music in Britain today is far from being just another escape: it probes into the emotions of the war itself—love of country, love of liberty, love of living, and the exhilaration of fighting for them. Listen . . ."[134] Two key scenes establish the restorative power of music. The first of these is at a music hall where two male singers entrance their audience with popular tunes. The audience whistles along with the music while a meal of fried cod and chips or grilled sausages with greens is served. The second is an orchestral recital at the National Portrait Gallery, which fades dramatically into the noise of a factory at work. The contrast between popular and classical music serves to underline national unity across class divides. Both scenes contain montage shots of trees blowing gently in the wind. The point is to link music making to the earlier birdsong on the sound track. Music and the natural soundscape are shown, in this way, as twin sources of inspiration, restoration, and unification in the face of the noisy war. Community music making represents the spirit of national community in *Listen to Britain*. It is a vital counterbalance, for Jennings, to the noise of bombing. Across self-help writing, expert medical research, and documentary filmmaking, therefore, the three case studies that have been examined in this section—acts of hearing, or not hearing—were incorporated as ideals of wartime citizenship, marking out the contours of the sonic nation.

Conclusion

Since the evocative sounds of air-raid sirens and fighter planes have remained ever-present in the popular memory of the Second World War, and in the British national imagination at large, it is all the more surprising that historians of Britain have devoted so little attention to the Second World War soundscape. This chapter makes a case for incorporating everyday noises into the critical reevaluation of the people's war. At no other time during the early twentieth century, this chapter argues, was the relationship between sound and selfhood under more urgent scrutiny in Britain than during the Second World War. For those with a professional interest in sound—members of the Noise Abatement League, for example, or the technicians and directors of the Crown Film Unit—the war brought with it an extraordinary challenge, which they could never have anticipated. It galvanized them in their work as custodians of the British soundscape and led them to emphasize the national importance of their work. Following the model set out in Chapter 3, this chapter details the ways in which expert claims about sound relied upon the projection of sonic norms on the "social body." It has set out not to recover the auditory experience of war on the home front, but rather to show how expert discourses constructed this experience in their attempt to know and manage everyday sound, as well as to incorporate these sounds into the promotion of national over sectional interests.

What of modernity in the Second World War context? In contrast to the state's interwar fantasies about an ideal planned future, discussed in Chapter 3, in which Britain's social modernism became a staple of official discourse, wartime rhetoric and propaganda tended to elevate a timeless sense of nationhood, often located in the countryside rather than the city, above the imperative to be modern. Following Mandler, this chapter stops short of arguing that rural nostalgia, in plentiful evidence during the war, epitomized early-twentieth-century British culture.[135] Rural ideals were certainly present in debates about church bell ringing, in the organization of the Noise Abatement League's Country Residency Scheme, and in Crown Film Unit films such as *Listen to Britain*. However, the rural fantasies that played such an important part in structuring the response to the wartime soundscape are more usefully explained with reference to Alison Light's notion of "conservative modernity."[136] The term conservatism, in this context, does not refer to party political persuasion, but rather to a cultural attachment to the past, which, Light argues, entered into hybridity with British cultures of modernity in the interwar period. The work of the GPO/Crown Film Unit is in fact a good example of what she means. Films such as *A Midsummer Day's Work* (1939), which follows GPO workers as they lay underground telephone cables from Amersham to Aylesbury in the Chilterns, deliberately juxtaposed the modernity of GPO systems with the timeless traditions of the British countryside. This was a way of indicating the specifically British character of the modernity being enacted by the GPO. Jennings used a similar hybridity of modernity and tradition to narrate British national identity in *Listen to Britain*. The prominence of pastoral fantasies during the Second World War did not indicate a nation turning its back on modernity. It indicated instead the intensification of a trend that already existed in some interpretations of modernity in early-twentieth-century Britain for locating modernity within the specificity of the nation. Whereas in the interwar period the need to be modern was often presented in relation to the value of keeping in rhythm with trade and industry, during the Second World War it made itself felt through ideal listening practices that tied the individual self to the collective nation.

Conclusion

The Second World War marked the apex of the age of noise in Britain. Blitz noise did not, in the end, bring about a crisis of nervousness on the home front; stoical adaptation instead became the order of the day and the age-of-noise narrative faded as a consequence. The problem of noise did not, of course, fade with it. The end of the war may have brought a renewed quiet to the streets of Britain, but the campaign against unwanted sound continued among those who remained committed to tackling it. Horder's Noise Abatement League was disbanded after the war, but its mantle was taken up by a new Noise Abatement Society in 1959, which still operates—aiming to "improve the aural landscape for all"—to this day.[1] Lawmakers continued to take an interest in noise as part of broader attempts to reshape the urban environment after the war: a government committee published a landmark report on the issue in 1963.[2] Although local authorities subsequently gained greater powers to intervene in sonic environments, the problem of noise has remained relatively high on the public agenda, though not with the urgency of the age-of-noise narrative. At the time of writing, a fierce debate is currently raging, for example, about the expansion of London's Heathrow Airport, much of which hinges on the issue of the noise caused by aircraft. Indeed, with the rise of the new sound studies, scholars have often had cause to ask why we appear no closer to finding a solution to the problem of noise.[3] Karin Bijsterveld concludes that twentieth-century noise abatement failed, and left a legacy of continuing failure, because it dealt with unwanted sound as a fundamentally techno-scientific problem rather than as a fundamentally human-social one, wrapping some kinds of noise, such as that made by airplanes, "in formulas beyond citizens' reach" while defining others, such as that made by one's neighbors, as the responsibility of the individual, rather than the state.[4] While it has not been the primary aim of this book to evaluate the relative success or failure of Britain's early-twentieth-century antinoise campaign, reflection on this question can point the way to some wider conclusions.

There is evidence for Bijsterveld's diagnosis of overconfidence in science-as-solution in British state agencies' handling of home and workplace noise in the 1930s, but what the chapters of this book suggest more emphatically than that is the failure of the early-twentieth-century noise abatement campaign to embrace the irresistible rise of the psychological self.[5] The antinoise movement led by Lord Horder lost traction in the formative years of investigation into psychosocial well-being primarily because it embraced an out-of-date theory and narrative of the hearing self. Horder's League and its backers in the general medical profession laid primary emphasis on the pathogenic nature of certain kinds of modern sounds—those caused by motor traffic and other kinds of new technology, in particular. It argued that the British public should be educated about sound etiquette, but, more importantly, that spaces of quiet retreat should be preserved, especially for those engaged in intellectual endeavor and leadership. In its insistence on the need to protect hearers from noise, the Anti-Noise League set itself apart from the trend toward *adaptability* as the dominant culture of twentieth-century selfhood. In this respect, the enchanted occultists discussed in Chapter 2 and the rationalizing technicians introduced in Chapter 3 shared more than they might have liked to admit: both were concerned, in their different ways, with psychologizing the hearing self, placing primary emphasis on self-management rather than on environmental management as the solution to noise. Proponents of esoteric psychologies such as Maud MacCarthy believed that hearers could tune themselves out of damaging sound by harnessing vibrational connection with higher dimensions of resonance. Industrial psychologists such as Millais Culpin, whose advice shaped the official state response to noise, insisted that well-adjusted people could adapt themselves to noise so long as it did not interfere with the normal rhythms of daily life. One way or another, then, the idea that hearers could, and indeed *should*, adapt themselves to the noises of modernity emerged as the dominant scientific and moral paradigm of sonic subjectivity in early-twentieth-century Britain, part of a wider shift toward the self as a "reflexive project," as Anthony Giddens describes it.[6] In the Second World War, as Chapter 4 argued, adaptation to the sound of bomb noise became a credo of national belonging, applied even to those soldiers badly affected by the sounds of the battlefield.

The antinoise agenda of Horder's League emerged from a nineteenth-century language of nerves and nervousness and often from a very specific

medical theory of neurasthenia in the writings of neurologist George M.
Beard. By the 1930s these had become the target both of the new professional psychology, which rejected the scientific credibility of neurasthenia
as a diagnostic category, and of new esoteric cultures of the self, such as that
promoted by Theosophy, which promised nervous regeneration through spiritual self-management. Professional psychology went on to play an increasingly important role in the science of hearing through the emergence of
psychoacoustics, the psychological study of sound perception, which Jonathan
Sterne has shown to have figured prominently in the industrial-scientific
claiming of the hearing self in telecommunications and music technology
research.[7] The esotericism of Theosophy and related movements fed into the
New Age's self-help culture, which has remained a strong current long after
its mid-twentieth-century heyday. The antinoise agenda of Horder's League
was thus left behind by a culture that may not always have liked urban and
industrial noise all that much, but which was altogether more interested in
managing the hearing of noise than it was in managing the creation of it.
R. Murray Schafer's call for sonic ecology in the 1970s was an argument for
the reversal of this trend, an insistence on environmental rather than psychological interventions in the sound cultures of industrialized societies.[8]

In many ways, then, Horder's noise abatement campaign was the least
modern of all the ways of hearing that I have outlined in this book. However,
that is not to say we should downplay the importance of noise abatement as
a conscious engagement with the politics of early-twentieth-century modernity. I have argued exactly the opposite in Chapter 1. Those such as H. G.
Wells and Aldous Huxley, who lent their support to the noise abatement
campaign or who bemoaned what they heard as an ever-rising tide of noise,
contributed to one very important way of encountering and imagining the
modern in early-twentieth-century culture, that is, as a crisis. Noise abatement was part of what I have termed a negative politics of sonic modernity
because it thought of modern noise as an unwelcome departure from a quieter
past. Noise was the preeminent auditory signal of an unnatural and unhealthy
"modern civilization" for those who chose to hear it that way. Rather than
describe this as an antimodern attitude, I have insisted instead that this negative construction of the modern was *constitutive of*, rather than *in opposition
to*, the imaginative project of sonic modernity in early-twentieth-century
Britain. However, I have argued, centrally, that this negative construction
was not the only way to hear modernity in early-twentieth-century Britain.
I have shown throughout the chapters of this book that the modernity of
modern sound lies not intrinsically in any particular kind of sound or sonic
environment, but rather in *hearing attitudes*, or *ways of hearing*, as I have

described them, through which ideologies of sonic modernity were constructed. I have, in other words, promoted a "politics of hearing" rather than a "soundscape" approach in this book. While noise abatement supporters chose to hear the noise of modernity as an indication of the decline of Western civilization, rationalizing industrial welfare investigators, home planners, and state documentary filmmakers, discussed in Chapter 3, chose to hear "bad" noise as the product of an unplanned, and thus unmodern, society, but "good," rhythmical noise as part of the proper working of a modern, regulated social body. Hearing modernity, for them, meant sonic dreams of rhythmic harmony, rather than nightmares of noisy chaos. Nervous susceptibility to noise was, according to the occultists discussed in Chapter 2, a matter of the hearers' poor knowledge of their inner spiritual self, a problem solved by mind-training through the means of experimental music or other self-help techniques. Noise was not "modern" for figures such as MacCarthy. It was, instead, unspiritual. She and others influenced by Theosophy evolved a brand of artistic, social, and psychotherapeutic modernism that strove to deliver a spiritualized future. During the Second World War, discussed in Chapter 4, these various competing ways of hearing modernity were put to work for the national war effort. Ultimately, in the conclusions of the Medical Research Council and other wartime state agencies, hearing modernity was a matter of having the right mental attitude to sound rather than about the inherent modernity of any specific kind of sound. Patriotic hearers were those who knew how to align their hearing acts with the values of the nation as it took increasingly concretized ideological shape during the war.

In presenting a number of different ways of hearing modernity, I have argued that we should, as historians, avoid imposing rigid models of modernity on the sonic past and that we should instead embrace modernity as it imaginatively functioned in the periods we study. I have shown that modernity was contested and fragmentary in the age of noise. Through claims to modernity, a variety of historical actors attempted to assert their claim to expert agency and authority with regard to noise. As Martin Daunton and Bernard Rieger put it in relation to modernity in early-twentieth-century Britain, "the language of the modern provided a highly flexible tool to describe the temporal status of the present as problematic."[9] The occultists discussed in Chapter 2 and the rationalizers discussed in Chapter 3 were both, in contrast to the sonic nostalgia of the noise abatement campaign discussed in Chapter 1, straining to hear the sounds of a modern future but had very different conceptualizations of how to arrive there. I have, nevertheless, deliberately situated both of these as modern ways of hearing in contrast to approaches that would see one as modern and the other as pre- or antimodern. I have argued that a tension remained unresolved in early-twentieth-century Britain between enchantment and disenchantment and that we should view this unresolved tension as a key characteristic of the experience of modernity at this time. In doing so, I have followed Michael Saler in arguing against Max Weber's claim that modern scientific rationality brought about the absolute disenchantment of the world. Saler rightly claims that pre-Enlightenment cultures of enchantment persisted into the imaginational landscape of the twentieth century.[10] Pointing to scholars such as Alex Owen, Saler argues that recent interventions in the historiography of modern enchantment have tended toward an "antinomial" definition of modernity in which the modern is defined "less by binaries arranged in an implicit hierarchy, or by the dialectical transformation of one term into its opposite, than by unresolved contradictions and oppositions, or antinomies: modernity," he concludes, "is Janus-faced."[11] Building on Saler's definition, Chapters 2, 3, and 4 argued that rationalizing attempts to scientifically quiet the modern soundscape existed side by side with, and sometimes even in close contact with, enchanted explanations of sound's magical effects. I argued in the Introduction that while this historicized approach to analyzing modernity has become relatively well established in mainstream historiography, it has not yet had as much impact as a method in historical sound studies. The chapters of this book have therefore been intended as a contribution to the ongoing debate about how we should analyze and interpret the sounds of the past with respect, in particular, to how we deal with the modernity of modern sound. I have argued that rather than view some sounds as inherently modern, we should instead think of modernity as an imaginational imposition on sound worlds and as a matter of ideological contestation relating to how we hear. In early-twentieth-century Britain, sound became an especial target of competing claims to modernity as a consequence of the age-of-noise narrative, a site for testing the authority and authenticity of different kinds of expertise, and a resource for making truth claims stick in the social reality of sensory experience.

My second contribution to the ongoing development of historical sound studies concerns our understanding of the relationship between sound and selfhood. Since Steven Connor's groundbreaking essay, "The Modern Auditory I," challenged scholars to rethink the self as a sonic membrane rather than a fixed visualizable point and to rethink modern subjectivities as the product of new technological experiences of sound in the nineteenth and twentieth centuries, a number of scholars have investigated the sonic constitution of the self in various historical and cultural contexts.[12] Most notably, Tom Rice has made the concept of the "soundself" central to his anthropological research on hearing (in his case, in hospital environments).[13] Rice argues that the sounds of the hospital structure the way in which patients conceive of themselves as patients. The constant repetitive electronic noise of medical equipment serves "as a constant reminder to patients of their own illness and that of others around them," as do the sounds of medical staff coming and going.[14] Patients are rendered knowable through the listening acts performed by doctors and nurses (for example, through stethoscopy) and become the "object of an ear/eye of power" as a result.[15] Mimicking Foucault's concept of the Panoptican, Rice describes the hospital as a "Panaudican," in which the sounds of medical intervention, and of observational routine, serve not only to establish the power relationship between medical professional and patient but, more importantly, to constitute the very nature of the patient's sense of self.[16] Rice argues that one knows that one is ill, is in a hospital, and is subject to the power of medical intervention, primarily by hearing the hospital. Susan Cusick has done similar work on the role of sound in the constitution of prisoner selfhoods. Writing on detainees in the post-9/11 "War on Terror," she claims that isolation from the sounds of external daily life serve to constitute the prisoner's degraded sense of self. She argues that solitary confinement and musical torture are both conscious attempts to act upon and reorder prisoner selfhood.[17] Accounts such as Cusick's and Rice's point the way forward for historical research on sound and selfhood. What Rice calls the "acoustemology of the self" (*acoustemology* being the study of aural sensibilities that locate individuals in particular times and in particular places) can surely open up new possibilities for historical research on selves, subjectivities, and identities.[18]

My contribution toward this trajectory has been centered not so much on following Rice's approach by establishing how the sounds of modern Britain constituted modern British selfhoods, though Chapter 4 showed what might be possible in this regard. Rather, it has been centered on demonstrating that during the period in question the very concept of selfhood was in flux and in the process of coming into being in its twentieth-century sense. I have shown that theorization of sound and hearing played a significant role in the development of new medical, psychological, religious, and cultural understandings of the self in early-twentieth-century Britain, particularly with regard to the question of the relationship between the self and the senses. Rice takes the self to be a more-or-less stable and unproblematic category, and this is entirely reasonable given the current level of scholarly consensus about the term in the humanities. However, I have argued throughout the chapters of this book that, in the late nineteenth and early twentieth centuries, agreement had not yet been reached about how to know and describe the inner worlds of mind, psyche, and soul. Nikolas Rose has described the rise of a new psychological culture in the early twentieth century, which sought to govern populations through the gathering of intimate knowledge about citizens' thoughts and feelings. He argues that this knowledge was collated and codified as psychological data, a process he describes as the visualization of the self.[19] In my account, notions of what constituted selfhood were altogether more contested than Rose allows and hinge on differing theorizations of the relationship between the self and its interactions with sound. The supporters of noise abatement discussed in Chapter 1 drew on a nineteenth-century notion of selfhood, tied to Beard's theory of neurasthenia and to a wider medicalized culture of "nerves," which tended to think of the inner self as ineluctably bound to the sensations passed to it from the external environment. For proponents of this theory, a quiet world would produce a quiet mind, but too much noise, passed on through irregular vibration of the nervous system, would lead to a troubled mind. This was the argument of those such as Dan McKenzie, author of *City of Din: A Tirade against Noise* (1916), who argued against the psychological approach to noise and insisted instead on the need to control sonic environments.[20] Whereas supporters of noise abatement thought that true selfhood could be obtained only in peace and quiet, the Theosophists who formed the case study of Chapter 2 thought that the self-harming properties of urban and industrial noise pointed not toward the need for quiet but rather toward the need to counteract these sounds with magical alternatives. They thought of the true spiritual self as a latent vibrational force, which could be stirred into being only through contact with the right kinds of sonic vibrations. The industrial psychologists examined in Chapter 3 based their theory of the working self on an alternative, ultimately more mainstream, theory of the psychological self, which insisted that noise sensitivity was a symptom rather than the cause of deeper neuroses. They developed a theory of the hearing self in direct contradistinction to Horder's neurasthenic model as well as Edwin Ash's enchanted self-help model. In the Second World War, discussed in Chapter 4, the culture of the malleable self cohered into an ideology of sonic belonging for the national community at war.

It is also my hope that this book points the way toward greater cross-fertilization between the fields of historical sound studies and modern British history. The essence of my contribution, in this respect, is that if historians of modern Britain are to "listen to Britain," to borrow the title of Humphrey Jennings's Second World War film, then they must be sensitive not only to *what* people heard in the past, but also to *how* they heard. Everyday sounds, as the chapters of this book demonstrate in their various ways, do not carry innate meanings but are actively constructed as meaningful in the context of wider processes of cultural and social formation. Moreover, as I have suggested in Chapter 4 in particular, sound and hearing may be considered as atmospheric and sensory dimensions of ideology, forces that may be mobilized to bolster authority and to unite and divide communities and classes. Carolyn Birdsall's conclusion that sounds are not "immediate and intimate" but rather "social and collective" sums up the situation well: historians must pay attention to sound and hearing in the past precisely because it is a fundamental dimension of the social with the affective power to make ideas and ideologies resonate.[21] My approach, vis-à-vis Birdsall's argument, has been to show the ways in which agents of sonic power attempted to intervene in and reshape the "immediate and intimate" as a way of reaching the "social and collective."

Engagements with the age of noise had their part to play in all manner of trends that already interest historians of twentieth-century Britain, including the rise of a psychologized conceptualization of the self, the ebb and flow between sacred and secular, the drive to rationalize everyday social life, and the need to mobilize civilian populations for total war. Familiar questions in modern British history, I have shown, can be given new life by paying attention to sound. The social distinctions of class are only one example but have been central to my discussion of the expert hearer. Bijsterveld's assertion that "between the 16th and the 19th centuries, the elite became increasingly obsessed with its own sound," an argument borne out in James Johnson and William Weber's observations about the rise of bourgeois concert culture in the nineteenth century, holds good for twentieth-century Britain.[22] Johnson and Weber show that the rise of attentive concert hall listening and its associated social conventions was deeply entwined with the evolution of middle-class collective identity formation in nineteenth-century Europe. I have shown here, following John M. Picker's work on Victorian soundscapes, that the desire to control noise was just as powerful a part of middle-class self-identification as concert listening was, especially in the age of motor traffic, gramophones, and wireless loudspeakers, and other sound-emitting machines.[23] However, rather than depict middle-class listening cultures as unitary and singular, I have, instead, shown them to be fragmented and contested. I have presented this contestation as a struggle for professional authority and objectivity among middle-class hearers, a contestation for the right to speak on behalf of society as a whole about noise. Where other sound historians have argued that noise abatement was a mechanism for the powerful to impose their aural proclivities on the powerless by defining the sounds of lower-class people as noise, I have emphasized, instead, the lack of coherence in elite understandings of noise as a result of the need to compete for the right to act as expert hearer.[24] There remains much work to be done, however, in fully unraveling class-bound experiences of sound in this period. Research on the everyday sonic experiences of nonelite groups—for example, those working-class hearers targeted by "Listen While You Work" factory broadcasts or those identified by Mass-Observation as "unskilled working-class" who did not welcome the return of church bell ringing during the Second World War—would greatly enrich the field of historical sound studies but would require different approaches and source materials from those employed here.

In 1908, London Underground issued a poster advertising the Tube suburb of Golders Green. The poster was an advert not just for the Tube, but also for the ideal of suburban life, "A Place of Delightful Prospects." A large family house, with an ample garden, nestles among trees, bushes, and flowerbeds, a blissfully quiet scene. The poster included a poem, written on a scroll laid over the house's lawn. The poem was *Sanctuary*, by the eighteenth-century poet William Cowper:

> 'Tis pleasant, through the loopholes of retreat,
> To peep at such a world; to see the stir
> Of the great Babel, and not feel the crowd;
> To hear the roar she sends through all her gates
> At a safe distance, where the dying sound
> Falls a soft murmur on th' uninjured ear.[25]

As historians, we can do little better than to hear the sounds of the past through Cowper's "loopholes of retreat," but by doing so, as I have shown in this book, we may nonetheless open our ears to new ways of thinking about the past. We must "hear the roar" if we are to make sense of modern selves and modern societies.

Notes

Introduction

1. "The Age of Noise: A Problem of Air Travel," *Manchester Guardian* (January 20, 1928): 19.

2. Marshall Berman, *All That Is Solid Melts into Air: The Experience of Modernity* (London: Verso, 1983), 15.

3. Adam Gowans Whyte, "Reflections on the Age of Noise," *Fortnightly Review* 132 (1932): 72–82, quote at 72.

4. Ibid., 72.

5. W. G. Pennyman, "The Age of Noise," *Times* (May 29, 1933): 15.

6. "The Age of Noise: A Problem of Air Travel," 19.

7. "Modern Noise: Its Effect on Manners and Leisure," *Manchester Guardian* (September 10, 1930): 6.

8. "Anti-Noise Week," *Times* (October 1, 1927): 11.

9. "How to Remain Sane: Doctor's List of Don'ts," *Manchester Guardian* (July 18, 1929): 13.

10. "Noise and Bustle of London: Retired Butler's Suicide," *Manchester Guardian* (September 2, 1933): 12.

11. "'Noise Has Killed Me': Clergyman's Suicide," *Manchester Guardian* (May 15, 1929): 17.

12. "An Anti-Noise Vitamin," *Manchester Guardian* (March 19, 1941): 3.

13. On modernity, shock, and nervousness see, for example, Andreas Killen, *Berlin Electropolis: Shock, Nerves and German Modernity* (Berkeley: University of California Press, 2006).

14. Georg Simmel, "The Metropolis and Mental Life," in *Blackwell City Reader*, ed. Gary Bridge and Sophie Watson (Oxford: Blackwell, 2002), 11–19.

15. "The Curse of Noise," *Times* (March 3, 1922): 13.

16. A. H. Davis, *Noise* (London: Watts, 1937), 1.

17. See John M. Picker, *Victorian Soundscapes* (Oxford: Oxford University Press, 2003) and Emily Cockayne, *Hubbub: Filth, Noise and Stench in England, 1600–1770* (New Haven: Yale University Press, 2007).

18. See Karin Bijsterveld, *Mechanical Sounds: Technology, Culture and Public Problems of Noise in the Twentieth Century* (Cambridge, Mass.: MIT Press, 2008).

19. http://nonoise.selfridges.com/ (accessed May 13, 2013).

20. Karin Bijsterveld and Peter Payer, among others, have traced the growth of an age-of-noise narrative across Europe and North America. See Karin Bijsterveld, "The Diabolical Symphony of the Mechanical Age: Technology and Symbolism of Sound in European and North American Noise Abatement Campaigns, 1900–40," *Social Studies of Science* 31 (2001): 37–70, and Peter Payer, "The Age of Noise: Early Reactions in Vienna: 1870–1914," *Journal of Urban History* 33 (2007): 773–793.

21. Aldous Huxley, Preface, in M. Alderton Pink, *A Realist Looks at Democracy* (London: Ernst Benn, 1930), viii.

22. Peter Bailey, "Breaking the Sound Barrier: A Historian Listens to Noise," in *Hearing History: A Reader*, ed. Mark M. Smith (Athens: University of Georgia Press, 2004), 34.

23. Ibid., 27; Bijsterveld, *Mechanical Sounds*; Alain Corbin, *Village Bells: Sound and Meaning in the Nineteenth-Century French Countryside*, trans. Martin Thom (New York: Columbia University Press, 1998); Picker, *Victorian Soundscapes*; Emily Thompson, *The Soundscape of Modernity: Architectural Acoustics and the Culture of Listening in America, 1900–33* (Cambridge, Mass.: MIT Press, 2004).

24. Douglas Kahn, *Noise, Water, Meat: A History of Sound in the Arts* (Cambridge, Mass.: MIT Press, 1999); Mark M. Smith, *Listening to Nineteenth-Century America* (Chapel Hill: University of North Carolina Press, 2001); Jonathan Sterne, *The Audible Past: Cultural Origins of Sound Reproduction* (Durham: Duke University Press, 2003).

25. Carolyn Birdsall, *Nazi Soundscapes: Sound, Technology and Urban Space in Germany, 1933–1945* (Amsterdam: Amsterdam University Press, 2012); Daniel Morat, ed., *Sounds of Modern History: Auditory Cultures in 19th and 20th Century Europe* (Oxford: Berghahn, 2014); Shelley Trower, *Senses of Vibration: A History of the Pleasure and Pain of Sound* (New York: Continuum, 2012). See also Veit Erlman, ed., *Hearing Cultures: Essays on Sound, Listening, and Modernity* (Oxford: Berg, 2004).

26. Karin Bijsterveld and Trevor Pinch, eds., *The Oxford Handbook of Sound Studies* (Oxford: Oxford University Press, 2013); Michael Bull and Les Back, eds., *The Auditory Culture Reader* (Oxford: Berg, 2003); Jonathan Sterne, ed., *The Sound Studies Reader* (London: Routledge, 2012). See also Michael Bull, ed., *Sound Studies: Critical Concepts in Media and Cultural Studies* (London: Routledge, 2013). Georgina Born, ed., *Music, Sound and Space: Transformations of Public and Private Experience* (Cambridge: Cambridge University Press, 2013) also marks a coming together of previously disparate disciplinary perspectives in the interest of a newly unified sound studies.

27. Sam Halliday, *Sonic Modernity: Representing Sound in Literature, Culture and the Arts* (Edinburgh: Edinburgh University Press, 2013), 6.

28. Work in a wider field of sensory history has accompanied new sound histories. For an overview, see Mark M. Smith, *Sensory History* (Oxford: Berg, 2007).

29. Alexandra Hui, *The Psychophysical Ear: Musical Experiments, Experimental Sounds, 1840–1910* (Cambridge, Mass.: MIT Press, 2013). See also Alexandra Hui, Julia Kursell, and Myles W. Jackson, eds., *Music, Sound, and the Laboratory from 1750–1980* (Chicago: University of Chicago Press, 2013).

30. "Historians and the Question of 'Modernity': Introduction," *American Historical Review* 116 (2011): 631–637, quote at 631.

31. Lynn M. Thomas, "Modernity's Failings, Political Claims, and Intermediate Concepts," *American Historical Review* 116 (2011): 727–740, quote at 737.

32. Sterne, *Audible Past*, 2.

33. Ibid.

34. Thompson, *Soundscape of Modernity*, 1–2.

35. Ibid., 3.

36. Ibid.

37. Halliday, *Sonic Modernity*, 5.

38. Ibid., 13–15. The texts to which Halliday refers are Pierre Schaeffer, "Acousmatics," trans. Daniel W. Smith, in *Audio Culture: Readings in Modern Music*, ed. Christoph Cox and Daniel Warner (New York: Continuum, 2006), 76–81; James Lastra, *Sound Technology and the American Cinema: Perception, Representation, Modernity* (New York: Columbia University Press, 2000); and Kahn, *Noise, Water, Meat*.

39. As representative of this kind of media theory, see Walter Ong, *Orality and Literacy: The Technologization of the Word* (New York: Routledge, 1983) and Marshall McLuhan, *The Gutenberg Galaxy: The Making of Typographic Man* (Toronto: University of Toronto Press, 1962). An example of the scholarship that locates modern forms of power in visual techniques of governance is Jonathan Crary, *Techniques of the Observer: On Vision and Modernity in the Nineteenth Century* (Cambridge, Mass.: MIT Press, 1990).

40. Sterne, *Audible Past*, 3.

41. R. Murray Schafer, *The Soundscape: Our Sonic Environment and the Tuning of the World* (Rochester, Vt.: Destiny Books, 1994).

42. Thompson, *Soundscape of Modernity*, 1.

43. Dipesh Chakrabarty, "The Muddle of Modernity," *American Historical Review* 116 (2011): 663–675, quotes at 674.

44. Thomas, "Modernity's Failings," 734.

45. Ibid.

46. "Historians and the Question of 'Modernity,'" 634. This is a paraphrasing of Zvi Ben-Dor Benite's argument in "Modernity: The Sphinx and the Historian," *American Historical Review* 116 (2011): 638–652.

47. Simon Gunn and James Vernon, "Introduction: What Was Liberal Modernity and Why Was It Peculiar in Imperial Britain?" in *The Peculiarities of Liberal Modernity in Imperial Britain*, ed. Simon Gunn and James Vernon (Berkeley: University of California Press, 2011), 6.

48. Thomas, "Modernity's Failings," 737.

49. Chakrabarty, "Muddle of Modernity," 663.

50. Judith Butler, *Gender Trouble: Feminism and the Subversion of Identity* (New York: Routledge, 1990).

51. Bijsterveld, *Mechanical Sounds*; Sterne, *Audible Past*; Thompson, *Soundscape of Modernity*.

52. Harold Perkin, *The Rise of Professional Society: England since 1880* (London: Routledge, 1989).

53. Perkin, *Rise of Professional Society*, 288.

54. Nikolas Rose, "Government, Authority and Expertise in Advanced Liberalism," *Economy and Society* 22 (1993): 283–299.

55. Michel Foucault, *Power/Knowledge: Selected Interviews and Other Writings 1972–77*, ed. Colin Gordon, trans. Colin Gordon, Leo Marshall, John Mepham, and Kate Soper (Brighton: Harvester, 1980).

56. Picker, *Victorian Soundscapes*, 42.

57. Ibid., 43.

58. Ibid.

59. Ibid., 80.

60. Perkin, *Rise of Professional Society*, 9.

61. Pierre Bourdieu, *Distinction: A Social Critique of the Judgment of Taste*, trans. Richard Nice (London: Routledge, 2010).

62. Following Foucault, Rose uses the term *conduct of conduct* to describe the work of expert professionals in constructing liberal "governmentality." See Rose, "Government, Authority and Expertise," 284.

63. Roy Porter, Introduction, in *Rewriting the Self: Histories from the Renaissance to the Present*, ed. Roy Porter (London: Routledge, 1997), 1–16.

64. Richard Harvey Brown, "Narration and Postmodern Mediations of Western Selfhood," in *The Politics of Selfhood: Bodies and Identities in Global Capitalism*, ed. Richard Harvey Brown (Minneapolis: University of Minnesota Press, 2003), 189.

65. James Kennaway, "Musical Hypnosis: Sound and Selfhood from Mesmerism to Brainwashing," *Social History of Medicine* 25 (2011): 271–289, quote at 271. See also Trower's discussion of vibratory selfhoods in *Senses of Vibration*, 1–12.

66. Greg Goodale, *Sonic Persuasion: Reading Sound in the Recorded Age* (Urbana: University of Illinois Press, 2011), 55.

67. Gustave le Bon, *The Crowd: A Study in the Popular Mind* (London: T. Fisher Unwin, 1896).

68. George Burman Foster, "Noise," *Little Review* (November 1914): 32–39, quotes at 34–35.

69. Ibid., 39.

70. Ibid., 34.

71. "The Present Age: Escaping to the Past," *Manchester Guardian* (December 10, 1936): 8.

72. Nikolas Rose, *Governing the Soul: The Shaping of the Private Self* (London: Routledge, 1989), 7. See also Nikolas Rose, "Assembling the Modern Self," in *Rewriting the*

Self: Histories from the Renaissance to the Present, ed. Roy Porter (London: Routledge, 1997), 224–248.

73. Ibid., 7.

74. Steven Connor, "The Modern Auditory I," in *Rewriting the Self*, 203–223, quote at 206.

75. Ibid., 215.

76. Ibid.

77. Both Bijsterveld and Thompson, for example, include such composers in their discussion of noise. See Bijsterveld, *Mechanical Sound*, 137–158; Thompson, *Soundscape of Modernity*, 130–143.

78. Goodale, *Sonic Persuasion*, 57–58.

79. Ibid., 64–65.

80. Ibid., 69.

81. President of the Anti-Noise League Thomas Horder described his supporters as "the intelligent section" of society in Anti-Noise League, *Silencing a Noisy World* (London: Anti-Noise League, 1935), 42. The second quote is from "The Ring of Bells," *Manchester Guardian* (October 16, 1937): 8.

82. This has also been proposed by Mathew Thomson in *Psychological Subjects: Identity, Culture, and Health in Twentieth-Century Britain* (Oxford: Oxford University Press, 2006), 184.

83. On Luigi Russolo and the occult, see Luciano Chessa, *Luigi Russolo, Futurist: Noise, Visual Arts, and the Occult* (Berkeley: University of California Press, 2012). On the harmony of the spheres, see Joscelyn Godwin, ed., *The Harmony of the Spheres: A Sourcebook of the Pythagorean Tradition in Music* (Rochester, Vt.: Inner Traditions International, 1993).

84. Richard Cullen Rath, *How Early America Sounded* (Ithaca: Cornell University Press, 2003), 180.

85. Alex Owen, *The Place of Enchantment: British Occultism and the Culture of the Modern* (Chicago: University of Chicago Press, 2004); Wouter J. Hanegraaff, "How Magic Survived the Disenchantment of the World," *Religion* 33 (2003): 357–380; Michael Saler, "Modernity and Enchantment: A Historiographic Review," *American Historical Review* 111 (2006): 692–716. See also the essays collected in Joshua Landy and Michael Saler, eds., *The Re-enchantment of the World: Secular Magic in a Rational Age* (Stanford: Stanford University Press, 2009) and Michael Saler, *As If: Modern Enchantment and the Literary Prehistory of Virtual Reality* (Oxford: Oxford University Press, 2012).

86. Gowans Whyte, "Reflections on the Age of Noise," 73.

87. Birdsall, *Nazi Soundscapes*, 103–140.

Chapter 1. Modernity as Crisis

1. On critiques of modernity in early-twentieth-century Britain, see Martin Daunton and Bernhard Rieger, Introduction, in *Meanings of Modernity: Britain from the Late-Victorian Era to World War II*, ed. Martin Daunton and Bernhard Rieger (Oxford: Berg, 2001), 1–24. For a wide ranging discussion of the relationship between

modernity and the body, see Christopher E. Forth, *Masculinity in the Modern West: Gender, Civilization and the Body* (London: Palgrave Macmillan, 2008).

2. "Modern civilization" was increasingly identified as a cause of ill health in the late nineteenth century. This terminology was used, for example, in Max Nordau's influential work *Degeneration* (London: Heinemann, 1895).

3. On nerves and the First World War, see Ben Shephard, *A War of Nerves: Soldiers and Psychiatrists, 1914–1994* (London: Jonathan Cape, 2000).

4. This argument is also put forward, for the German context, by Andreas Killen in *Berlin Electropolis: Shock, Nerves and German Modernity* (Berkeley: University of California Press, 2006), 1.

5. Georg Simmel, "The Metropolis and Mental Life," in *Blackwell City Reader*, ed. Gary Bridge and Sophie Watson (Oxford: Blackwell, 2002), 11–19.

6. On the role of vision and visuality in twentieth-century thought, see Martin Jay, *Downcast Eyes: The Denigration of Vision in Twentieth-Century French Thought* (Berkeley: University of California Press, 1993).

7. Dan McKenzie, "The Crusade against Noise," *English Review* (December 1928): 691–696, quote at 692.

8. Emily Cockayne, *Hubbub: Filth, Noise and Stench in England, 1600–1770* (New Haven: Yale University Press, 2007).

9. John M. Picker, *Victorian Soundscapes* (Oxford: Oxford University Press, 2003). On nineteenth-century urban noise see also Brenda Assael, "Noise, Performers and the Contest over the Streets of the Mid-Nineteenth-Century Metropolis," in *The Streets of London: From the Great Fire to the Great Stink*, ed. Tim Hitchcock and Heather Shore (London: Rivers Oram Press, 2003), 183–197.

10. "Noise and Egotism," *Isis* (May 18, 1907): 323–324.

11. On the development of early-twentieth-century noise abatement campaigns, see, in particular, Lawrence Baron, "Noise and Degeneration: Theodor Lessing's Crusade for Quiet," *Journal of Contemporary History* 17 (1982): 165–178.

12. On the international campaign against noise in the twentieth century, see Karin Bijsterveld, *Mechanical Sound: Technology, Culture and Public Problems of Noise in the Twentieth Century* (Cambridge, Mass.: MIT Press, 2008).

13. Bijsterveld, *Mechanical Sound*; Emily Thompson, *The Soundscape of Modernity: Architectural Acoustics and the Culture of Listening in America, 1900–33* (Cambridge, Mass.: MIT Press, 2004).

14. Ibid., 3.

15. McKenzie, "Crusade against Noise," 693–694.

16. Marijke Gijswijt-Hofstra, "Introduction: Cultures of Neurasthenia from Beard to the First World War," in *Cultures of Neurasthenia from Beard to the First World War*, ed. Marijke Gijswijt-Hofstra and Roy Porter (Amsterdam: Rodopi, 2001), 1.

17. Robert S. Carroll, *The Mastery of Nervousness: Based upon Self Reeducation* (New York: Macmillan, 1918), 5.

18. Amelia Jones, *Irrational Modernism: A Neurasthenic History of New York Dada* (Cambridge, Mass.: MIT Press, 2004).

19. Lord Horder, "Health and Noise," in *Silencing a Noisy World: Being a Brief Report of the Conference on the Abatement of Noise* (London: Anti-Noise League, 1935), 42.

20. Picker, *Victorian Soundscapes*.

21. Henry Richards, "Education and the Problem of Noise," in *Silencing a Noisy World: Being a Brief Report of the Conference on the Abatement of Noise* (London: Anti-Noise League, 1935), 37.

22. George M. Beard, *A Practical Treatise on Nervous Exhaustion (Neurasthenia)* (New York: W. Wood, 1880); George M. Beard, *American Nervousness: Its Causes and Consequences* (New York: G. P. Putnam, 1881); George M. Beard, *Sexual Neurasthenia [Nervous Exhaustion]: Its Hygiene, Causes, Symptoms, and Treatment, with a Chapter on Diet for the Nervous*, ed. A. D. Rockwell (New York: E. B. Treat, 1884). Beard's earliest use of the term *neurasthenia* was in his article "Neurasthenia, or Nervous Exhaustion," *Boston Medical and Surgical Journal* 3 (1869): 217–221.

23. On neurasthenia in British medicine, see Mathew Thomson, "Neurasthenia in Britain: An Overview," in *Cultures of Neurasthenia from Beard to the First World War*, ed. Marijke Gijswijt-Hofstra and Roy Porter (Amsterdam: Rodopi, 2001), 77–96.

24. On electrotherapy, see Iwan Rhys Morus, "Bodily Disciplines and Disciplined Bodies: Instruments, Skills and Victorian Electrotherapeutics," *Social History of Medicine* 19 (2006): 241–259.

25. Beard, *American Nervousness*, 98.

26. Beard, *Sexual Neurasthenia*.

27. Tom Lutz, *American Nervousness, 1903: An Anecdotal History* (Ithaca: Cornell University Press, 1991), 4.

28. Beard, *American Nervousness*, 7.

29. On the literary popularization of neurasthenia, see, in particular, Lutz, *American Nervousness, 1903*.

30. Edwin Ash, *Nerves and the Nervous* (London: Mills and Boon, 1911), 7. These visible signs of neurasthenia, including especially tapered and restless fingers, were captured in "nervous portraits," such as Max Oppenheimer's 1910 portrait of Heinrich Mann, which wealthy sufferers commissioned in order to document the progress of their condition. For discussion of neurasthenia in late-nineteenth- and early-twentieth-century portraiture, see Gemma Blackshaw and Leslie Topp, eds., *Madness and Modernity: Mental Illness and the Visual Arts in Vienna 1900* (Burlington, Vt.: Lund Humphries, 2009).

31. Beard, *American Nervousness*, 96.

32. Beard, *Sexual Neurasthenia*, 15.

33. Edwin Ash, *The Problem of Nervous Breakdown* (London: Mills and Boon, 1919), 5.

34. J. S. Jewell, "Influence of Our Present Civilization in the Production of Nervous and Mental Diseases," *Journal of Nervous and Mental Disease* 8 (1881): 3–4.

35. Beard, *American Nervousness*, vi.

36. For discussion of nerves and nervousness prior to the popularization of neurasthenia, see Janet Oppenheim, *Shattered Nerves: Doctors, Patients and Depression in Victorian England* (Oxford: Oxford University Press, 1991).

37. Barbara Sicherman, "The Uses of Diagnosis: Doctors, Patients and Neurasthenia," *Journal of the History of Medicine* 32 (1977): 33–54, quote at 39.

38. Edwin L. Ash, *Nerve in Wartime* (London: Mills and Boon, 1914), 25.

39. See, for example, Wilfred Northfield, *Frayed Nerves: Simple Ways of Restoring their Tone* (London: The Psychologist, 1940).

40. Beard, *American Nervousness*, 106.

41. Ibid.

42. Ibid.

43. Ibid.

44. Ibid.

45. Ibid., 107.

46. For contemporary discussion of shell shock and neurasthenia, see H. C. Marr, *Psychoses of the War, Including Neurasthenia and Shell Shock* (London: Hodder and Stoughton, 1919). For a contextualized analysis, see Tracey Loughran, "Hysteria and Neurasthenia in Pre-war Medical Discourse and in Histories of Shell Shock," *History of Psychiatry* 19 (2008): 25–46.

47. Ash, *Problem of Nervous Breakdown*, 269–270.

48. Ash, *Nerve in Wartime*, 22.

49. Ibid., 9.

50. Dan McKenzie, *City of Din: A Tirade against Noise* (London: Adlard and Son, 1916), 25.

51. Ibid., 52.

52. Ibid., 28–32 and 51.

53. Ibid., 67.

54. An example of this tradition is the collection of essays in Dorothy M. Schullian and Max Schoen, eds., *Music and Medicine* (New York: Schuman, 1948). For perspectives on music as a healing art, see Peregrine Horder, *Music as Medicine: The History of Music Therapy since Antiquity* (Aldershot: Ashgate, 2000).

55. Jon Agar, "Bodies, Machines and Noise," in *Bodies/Machines*, ed. Iwan Rhys Morus (Oxford: Berg, 2002), 197–220, quote at 198–199.

56. Dan McKenzie, "Noise and Health," *British Medical Journal* (October 6, 1934): 636–637, quote at 636.

57. McKenzie, "Crusade against Noise," 692.

58. Henry Wood, "Noise as Applied to Music," *Quiet* 2 (1940): 17.

59. James Kennaway, *Bad Vibrations: The History of the Idea of Music as a Cause of Disease* (Farnham: Ashgate, 2012).

60. Jewell, "Influence of Our Present Civilization," 5.

61. For discussion of the gendering of neurasthenia, see Christopher E. Forth, "Neurasthenia and Manhood in *fin-de-siècle* France," in *Cultures of Neurasthenia from Beard to the First World War*, 329–361. On hysteria as a specifically female counterpart

to neurasthenia, see Elaine Showalter, *The Female Malady: Women, Madness and English Culture, 1830–1980* (New York: Pantheon Books, 1985) and Elaine Showalter, *Hystories: Hysterical Epidemics and Modern Culture* (London: Picador, 1998).

62. Ash, *Problem of Nervous Breakdown*, 15.

63. Sicherman, "Uses of Diagnosis," 36.

64. Letter from T. Bowden Green, Hon. Sec. of the Betterment of London Association to the Rt. Hon. A., National Archives, A48/242/22.

65. Memorandum of Evidence on Noise and Public Health, British Medical Association Papers, Wellcome Library, SA/BMA/F.81.

66. A copy of the memorandum is also lodged at National Archives, HLG109/7.

67. Memorandum of Evidence on Noise and Public Health, National Archives, HLG109/7.

68. Joint Memorandum of Evidence on Noise presented by British Medical Association and People's League of Health, National Archives, HLG109/7.

69. Ibid.

70. Ibid.

71. "Harmful Effects of Noise: Sapping of Energy," *Manchester Guardian* (December 5, 1936): 20.

72. Ibid.

73. For discussion of Ash's adoption of psychotherapy, see Mathew Thomson, *Psychological Subjects: Identity, Culture and Health in Twentieth-Century Britain* (Oxford: Oxford University Press, 2006), 179–182.

74. Edwin Ash, *Mind and Health: The Mental Factor and Suggestion in Treatment with Special Reference to Neurasthenia and other Common Nervous Disorders* (London: Glaisher, 1910).

75. Ash, *Problem of Nervous Breakdown*, 105.

76. Ibid., 18.

77. H. Ernest Hunt, *Self-Training: The Lines of Mental Progress* (London: William Rider, 1918), 21.

78. Ibid., 81.

79. Ibid., 81.

80. Hunt explicitly discussed the need to train the mind to resist noise in H. Ernest Hunt, *How to Win the War of Nerves* (London: Rider and Co., 1940).

81. Carroll, *Mastery of Nervousness*, 16.

82. Edwin Hopewell-Ash, *On Keeping Our Nerves in Order* (London: Mills and Boon, 1928), 38.

83. Thomson, *Psychological Subjects*, 177–184.

84. Ibid., 184.

85. Petteri Pietikainen, *Neurosis and Modernity: The Age of Nervousness in Sweden* (Leiden: Brill, 2007), 100–101.

86. Carroll, *Mastery of Nervousness*, 23.

87. Memorandum, British Medical Association Papers, Wellcome Library, SA/BMA/F.81.

88. Ibid.

89. Literary studies have proved to be a fertile ground for the historical study of noise. See, for example, Melba Cuddy-Keane, "Modernist Soundscapes and the Intelligent Ear: An Approach to Narrative through Auditory Perception," in James Phelan and Peter J. Rabinowitz, eds., *A Companion to Narrative Theory* (Oxford: Blackwell, 2005), 382–398. A systematized approach to literary acoustics has also been proposed by Philip Schweighauser, *The Noises of American Literature, 1890–1985: Toward a History of Literary Acoustics* (Gainesville: University of Florida Press, 2006).

90. This was pointed out in a special issue of *Les cahiers médicaux français* on noise published in 1946, volume 7.

91. *Les cahiers médicaux français* carried articles on Proust's cork-lined room on the Boulevard Haussmann alongside an article on the soundproofing of hospitals, an article on noise in the work of the Goncourt Brothers alongside a medical text entitled "Les bruits de Paris," as well as articles on the bell-ringing torture in Octave Mirbeau's *Torture Garden* and on Huysmans's hypersensitive lifestyle.

92. For a full discussion of decadent literature's role in interwar French noise abatement campaigns, see James G. Mansell, "Neurasthenia, Civilization, and the Sounds of Modern Life: Narratives of Nervous Illness in the Interwar Campaign Against Noise," in Daniel Morat, ed., *Sounds of Modern History: Auditory Cultures in Nineteenth and Twentieth Century Europe* (Oxford: Berghahn, 2014), 278–302.

93. John M. Picker has demonstrated, in addition, that Wells extended late-nineteenth-century anxieties about disembodied phonographic voices into the radio age. See John M. Picker, "Aural Anxieties and the Advent of Modernity," in Martin Hewitt, ed., *The Victorian World* (London: Routledge, 2012), 603–618.

94. John S. Partington, ed., *H. G. Wells's Fin de Siècle* (New York: Peter Lang, 2007).

95. On *The Time Machine* and degeneration, see Daniel Pick, *Faces of Degeneration: A European Disorder, c. 1848–c. 1918* (Cambridge: Cambridge University Press, 1989), 158–159.

96. H. G. Wells, *The Shape of Things to Come: The Ultimate Revolution* (London: Hutchinson and Co., 1933), 116.

97. Ibid.

98. Ibid., 120.

99. Ibid.

100. H. G. Wells, *The Secret Places of the Heart* (London: Cassell and Co., 1922), 6.

101. Aldous Huxley, *Brave New World* (London: Chatto and Windus, 1932), 22.

102. Ibid., 23.

103. Ibid., 24.

104. Huxley's intervention into the noise abatement debate was significant enough to warrant the attention of the *Manchester Guardian*, which published a report of the opinions expressed in the preface to *A Realist Looks at Democracy*. See "The Age of Noise: Aldous Huxley on Its Spectacular Progress," *Manchester Guardian* (January 2, 1931): 12.

105. M. Alderton Pink, *A Realist Looks at Democracy* (London: Ernst Benn, 1930), 52–53.

106. Aldous Huxley, Preface, in Pink, *Realist Looks at Democracy*, viii.

107. "The Age of Noise," *British Medical Journal* (November 10, 1928): 855–856, quote at 855.

108. Huxley, "Preface," ix.

109. Ibid., x.

110. Ibid.

111. Ministry of Health minute sheet, National Archives, HLG 109/7.

112. Ibid.

113. Adam Gowans Whyte, "Reflections on the Age of Noise," *Fortnightly Review* 132 (1932): 77.

114. "Noise," *British Medical Journal* (August 10, 1929): 267–268.

115. Letter from the Secretary, Campaign for the Protection of Rural England, to Sir A. T. Wilson, October 14, 1930, Council for the Protection of Rural England Papers, Museum of English Rural Life, SR CPRE C/1/55/1.

116. Ainslie Derby and C. C. Hamilton, *England, Ugliness and Noise* (London: P. S. King, 1930), 5.

117. "Noise Abatement," *Times* (November 12, 1932): 9.

118. Anti-Noise League flyer, Council for the Preservation of Rural England Papers, Museum of English Rural Life, SR CPRE C/1/55/1.

119. Anti-Noise League flyer, Council for the Preservation of Rural England Papers, Museum of English Rural Life, SR CPRE C/1/55/1.

120. Printed draft of radio address published by Anti-Noise League, Council for the Preservation of Rural England Papers, Museum of English Rural Life, SR CPRE C/1/55/1.

121. Printed draft of radio address, Council for the Preservation of Rural England Papers, Museum of English Rural Life, SR CPRE C/1/55/1.

122. Draft of speech given to the Marriage Guidance Council on the effects of the war on families, Lord Horder Papers, Wellcome Library, GP/31/B2/23.

123. Unpublished manuscript, "On the Anti-Noise League," Lord Horder Papers, Wellcome Library, GP/31/B.4/4.

124. Draft of a chapter of a book on the necessity of the redistribution of the profits of capitalism, Lord Horder Papers, Wellcome Library, GP/31/B4/6.

125. Richards, "Education and the Problem of Noise," 36–37.

126. Unpublished manuscript, "On the Anti-Noise League."

127. Thomas Jeeves Horder, *Health and a Day: Addresses by Lord Horder* (London: J. M. Dent and Sons, 1937), 4.

128. Ibid., 5.

129. Unpublished manuscript, "On the Anti-Noise League."

130. Ibid.

131. Horder, "Health and Noise," 42.

132. Ibid., 46, emphasis original.

133. Exhibition organizing committee minute sheet, National Archives, HLG/52/1210.

134. Letter from R. F. Millard to the Ministry of Health, December 5, 1934, National Archives, HLG/52/1210.

135. Exhibition organizing committee minute sheet, National Archives, HLG/52/1210.

136. Horder, "Health and Noise," 46.

137. Horder first encountered Wells when undertaking a correspondence course in biology at a tutorial college in Red Lion Square, London. Wells corrected Horder's papers on this correspondence course. Wells later became a patient of Horder once the latter had become a practicing physician. For further details, see the *Oxford Dictionary of National Biography* entry for Thomas Jeeves Horder.

138. Ibid., 42.

139. Ibid.

140. Ibid.

141. Ibid.

142. On noise and the environmental history of the modern city, see Michael Toyka-Seid, "Noise Abatement and the Search for Quiet Space in the Modern City," in *Resources of the City: Contributions to an Environmental History of Modern Europe*, ed. Dieter Schott, Bill Luckin, and Genviève Massard-Guilbaud (Aldershot: Ashgate, 2005), 216–228.

143. Internal memo on noise, BBC Written Archives Centre, R41/101.

144. *Quiet* (July 1937): 23.

145. Richards, "Education and the Problem of Noise," 37.

146. Henry Richards, "The Problem of Noise," *Journal of the Royal Society of Arts* 83 (1935): 629.

147. Richards, "Problem of Noise," 629.

148. Letter from the Commissioner of Police of the Metropolis to the Home Office, October 22, 1935, National Archives, HO45/496339/28.

149. Cosmo Cantvar, "From His Grace the Archbishop of Canterbury," *Quiet* 1 (1937): 5.

150. Internal memos and correspondence with Anti-Noise League, Council for the Preservation of Rural England Papers, Museum of English Rural Life, SR CPRE C/1/55/1. See Darby and Hamilton, *England, Ugliness and Noise*.

151. Internal memo, Council for the Preservation of Rural England Papers, Museum of English Rural Life, SR CPRE C/1/55/1.

152. Letter from E. M. Bullock to the Secretary of the Council for the Protection of Rural England, August 14, 1935, Council for the Preservation of Rural England Papers, Museum of English Rural Life, SR CPRE C/1/55/1.

153. Draft bylaw, National Archives, HO45/196339/47.

154. Ibid.

155. Ministry of Health internal memo, National Archives, HLG/52/1210.

156. Eugène Minkowski, "Bergson's Conceptions as Applied to Psychopathology," *Journal of Nervous and Mental Disease* 63 (1926): 553–568, quote at 563. On Minkowski,

see Stephen Kern, "Time and Medicine," *Annals of Internal Medicine* 132 (2000): 3–9, and Annick Urfer, "Phenomenology and Psychopathology of Schizophrenia: The Views of Eugène Minkowski," *Philosophy, Psychiatry and Psychology* 8 (2001): 279–289.

157. Eugène Minkowski, *Lived Time: Phenomenological and Psychopathological Studies*, trans. Nancy Metzel (Evanston: Northwestern University Press, 1970 [Paris : J. L. L. d'Artrey, 1933]), 3.

158. Thomas Horder, "Cities without Noise," *Journal of the Royal Society of Arts* 99 (1951): 208–209.

159. Bijsterveld, *Mechanical Sound*, 134.

Chapter 2. Re-Enchanting Modernity

1. Alex Owen, *The Place of Enchantment: British Occultism and the Culture of the Modern* (Chicago: University of Chicago Press, 2004).

2. Richard Cullen Rath, *How Early America Sounded* (Ithaca: Cornell University Press, 2003); Leigh Eric Schmidt, *Hearing Things: Religion, Illusion and the American Enlightenment* (Cambridge: Harvard University Press, 2000).

3. Rath, *How Early America Sounded*, 180.

4. Schmidt, *Hearing Things*, 5–7.

5. Rath, *How Early America Sounded*, 180; Max Weber, "Science as a Vocation," in *From Max Weber: Essays in Sociology*, ed. and trans. H. H. Gerth and C. Wright Mills (London: Kegan Paul, Trench, Trubner, and Co., 1947), 139.

6. The epigraph is from Luigi Russolo, *The Art of Noises*, trans. Barclay Brown (New York: Pendragon Press, 1986), 86.

7. Emily Thompson, *The Soundscape of Modernity: Architectural Acoustics and the Culture of Listening in America, 1900–33* (Cambridge, Mass.: MIT Press, 2004), 134–135.

8. Karin Bijsterveld, *Mechanical Sound: Technology, Culture, and Public Problems of Noise in the Twentieth Century* (Cambridge, Mass.: MIT Press, 2008), 140.

9. Luciano Chessa, *Luigi Russolo, Futurist: Noise, Visual Arts, and the Occult* (Berkeley: University of California Press, 2012), 139.

10. Ibid., 132–133.

11. Ibid., 228.

12. Ibid., 226.

13. Anthony Enns, "Voices of the Dead: Transmission/Translation/Transgression," *Culture, Theory and Critique* 46 (2005): 11–27. See also Steven Connor, "The Machine in the Ghost: Spiritualism, Technology and the 'Direct Voice,'" in *Ghosts: Deconstruction, Psychoanalysis, History*, ed. Peter Buse and Andrew Stott (Basingstoke: Macmillan, 1999), 203–225, and Jeffrey Sconce, *Haunted Media: Electronic Presence from Telegraphy to Television* (Durham: Duke University Press, 2000).

14. Thomas Edison quoted in Enns, "Voices of the Dead": 18.

15. Anthony Enns, "Psychic Radio: Sound Technologies, Ether Bodies and Spiritual Vibrations," *Senses and Society* 3 (2008): 137–152.

16. Jonathan Sterne, *The Audible Past: Cultural Origins of Sound Reproduction* (Durham: Duke University Press, 2003), 289.

17. Shelley Trower, *Senses of Vibration: A History of the Pleasure and Pain of Sound* (New York: Continuum, 2012).

18. Owen, *Place of Enchantment*, 4.

19. On spiritualism and occult movements, see Janet Oppenheim, *The Other World: Spiritualism and Psychical Research in England, 1850–1914* (Cambridge: Cambridge University Press, 2002).

20. Owen, *Place of Enchantment*, 4.

21. Alex Owen, *The Darkened Room: Women, Power and Spiritualism in Late Nineteenth-Century England* (London: Virago, 1989); Joy Dixon, *Divine Feminine: Theosophy and Feminism in England* (Baltimore: Johns Hopkins University Press, 2001).

22. For discussion of these issues, see Thomas W. Laqueur, "Why the Margins Matter: Occultism and the Making of Modernity," *Modern Intellectual History* 3 (2006): 111–135, and Corinna Treitel, "What the Occult Reveals," *Modern Intellectual History* 6 (2009): 611–625.

23. Gordon Graham, *The Re-Enchantment of the World: Art versus Religion* (Oxford: Oxford University Press, 2007), 55.

24. Wouter J. Hanegraaff, *New Age Religion and Western Culture: Esotericism in the Mirror of Secular Thought* (Leiden: Brill, 1996).

25. Wouter J. Hanegraaff, "How Magic Survived the Disenchantment of the World," *Religion* 33 (2003): 357–380, quote at 358.

26. Alex Owen, "Occultism and the 'Modern' Self in Fin-de-Siècle Britain," in *Meanings of Modernity: Britain from the Late-Victorian Era to World War II*, ed. Martin Daunton and Bernhard Rieger (Oxford: Berg, 2001), 73.

27. Corinna Treitel, *A Science for the Soul: Occultism and the Genesis of the German Modern* (Baltimore: Johns Hopkins University Press, 2004).

28. Lynda Dalrymple Henderson, *The Fourth Dimension and Non-Euclidean Geometry in Modern Art* (Cambridge, Mass.: MIT Press, 2013).

29. Chessa, *Luigi Russolo, Futurist*, 83.

30. Owen, *Place of Enchantment*, 114–116.

31. Ibid., 184.

32. Treitel, *Science for the Soul*.

33. Rhodri Hayward, *Resisting History: Religious Transcendence and the Invention of the Unconscious* (Manchester: Manchester University Press, 2007), 18.

34. Mathew Thomson, *Psychological Subjects: Identity, Culture and Health in Twentieth-Century Britain* (Oxford: Oxford University Press, 2006), 18.

35. Cyril Scott cited in *Music, Mysticism and Magic: A Sourcebook*, ed. Joscelyn Godwin (London: Arkana, 1986), 285.

36. Letter from Maud Mann to Baillie-Weaver, May 2, 1916, Borthwick Institute for Archives, University of York, MCF 5/3/1/3 (3).

37. Henry Olcott Steel, *Theosophy: Religion and Occult Science* (London: George Redway, 1885), 31.

38. Ibid., 32.

39. Annie Besant, *The Ancient Wisdom: An Outline of Theosophical Teachings* (Adyar: Theosophical Publishing House, 1897).

40. Ibid., 25.

41. C. W. Leadbeater, *A Textbook of Theosophy* (Los Angeles: Theosophical Press, 1918), 28.

42. Ibid., 41.

43. Ibid., 44.

44. Besant, *Ancient Wisdom*, 50.

45. Annie Besant and C. W. Leadbeater, *Thought-Forms* (London: Theosophical Publishing Society, 1905).

46. Besant, *Ancient Wisdom*, 111.

47. Leadbeater, *Textbook of Theosophy*, 2.

48. Besant, *Ancient Wisdom*, 129–130.

49. Ibid., 132–133.

50. Ibid., 133.

51. Leadbeater, *Textbook of Theosophy*, 24.

52. Besant, *Ancient Wisdom*, 52.

53. Joscelyn Godwin, *The Harmony of the Spheres: A Sourcebook of the Pythagorean Tradition in Music* (Rochester, Vt.: Inner Traditions, 1993); Joscelyn Godwin, *Harmonies of Heaven and Earth: The Spiritual Dimensions of Music from Antiquity to the Avant-Garde* (Rochester, Vt.: Inner Traditions, 1987).

54. Besant, *Ancient Wisdom*, 51.

55. Annie Besant, *Religion and Music: A Lecture Delivered to the Shri Parthasarathi Svami Sabha Triplicane on March 7th 1908* (Adyar: Theosophical Publishing House, 1921), 20.

56. C. W. Leadbeater, *The Hidden Side of Things*, Vol. 1 (Adyar: Theosophical Publishing House, 1913), 280–285.

57. Ibid., 284–285.

58. Ibid., 286.

59. I am grateful to Ruth Pasquine for drawing my attention to this image. On Bisttram's relationship to Theosophy, see Ruth Pasquine, *The Politics of Redemption: Dynamic Symmetry, Theosophy, and Swedenborgianism in the Art of Emil Bisttram (1895–1976)*, PhD Dissertation, City University New York, 2000, and Ruth Pasquine, *Emil Bisttram (1895–1976), American Painter: Dynamic Symmetry, Theosophy, Swedenborgianism* (Saarbrücken: Lambert Academic Publishing, 2010).

60. Besant, *Religion and Music*, 15.

61. Ibid.

62. Cyril Scott, *The Influence of Music on History and Morals: A Vindication of Plato* (London: Theosophical Publishing House, 1928), 111.

63. Besant and Leadbeater, *Thought-Forms*, 75–84.

64. Leadbeater, *Hidden Side of Things*, 267.

65. Warren Anderson and Thomas J. Mathiesen, "Plato," in Grove Music Online. Oxford Music Online, http://www.oxfordmusiconline.com/subscriber/article/grove/music/21922 (accessed May 5, 2011).

66. Scott, *Influence of Music*, 3.

67. Untitled, *Transactions of the Theosophical Society* 1 (1907).

68. Besant, *Religion and Music*, 20.

69. Daniel Fleming, "A Vision of the Universal Form," *Theosophical Review* 40 (1907): 497.

70. On the relationship between theosophy and modernism in the arts, see Tim Armstrong, *Modernism: A Cultural History* (Cambridge: Polity, 2005); Tessel M. Bauduin, "Science, Occultism, and the Art of the Avant-Garde in the Early Twentieth Century," *Journal of Religion in Europe* 5 (2012): 23–55; Lynda Dalrymple Henderson, "Mysticism and Occultism in Modern Art," *Art Journal* 46 (1987): 5–8; Sixten Ringbom, "Art in 'the Epoch of the Great Spiritual': Occult Elements in the Early Theory of Abstract Painting," *Journal of the Warburg and Courtauld Institutes* 29 (1966): 386–418; and Christopher Scheer, Sarah Victoria Turner, and James G. Mansell, eds., *Enchanted Modernities: Theosophy, the Arts, and the American West* (London: Fulgur, 2016).

71. Ricciotto Canudo, "The Birth of a Sixth Art," trans. Ben Gibson, Don Ranvaud, Sergio Sokota, and Deborah Young in *French Film Theory and Criticism: A History/ Anthology, 1907–1939*, ed. Richard Abel (Princeton: Princeton University Press, 1988), 58–65; Ricciotto Canudo, *Music as a Religion of the Future*, trans. Barnett D. Conlan (London: T. N. Foulis, 1913). For a discussion of Canudo's influence and involvement with the Theosophical Society, see Claire Euzet, *Le musicalisme: une tendance de l'abstraction* (Lille: ANRT, 2000).

72. Canudo, *Music as a Religion*, 19.

73. On Fischinger, see Cindy Keefer and Jaap Guldemond, eds., *Oskar Fischinger 1900–1967: Experiments in Cinematic Abstraction* (Amsterdam: EYE Filmmuseum and Center for Visual Music, 2012).

74. Recognition of MacCarthy's historical significance has grown in recent years. See Nalini Ghuman, *Resonances of the Raj: India in the English Musical Imagination, 1897–1947* (Oxford: Oxford University Press, 2014), 11–52, and Bob van der Linden, *Music and Empire in Britain and India: Identity, Internationalism, and Cross-Cultural Communication* (Basingstoke: Palgrave Macmillan, 2013), 81–106. MacCarthy was also the subject of an exhibition held at the Borthwick Institute for Archives at the University of York in 2014, which is available to view online at: http://hoaportal .york.ac.uk/hoaportal/pioneering-spirit.jsp (accessed April 20, 2016).

75. Maud Mann, "Reconstruction and Real Values," *Vahan* (November 1914): 67. Maud MacCarthy published under several names during her lifetime, including her first married name, Maud Mann; the pen name, Tandra Devi; and the name she assumed in later life while living in India, Swami Omananda Puri.

76. Swami Omananda Puri, *The Boy and the Brothers* (London: Neville Spearman, 1968), 18–20.

77. Maud MacCarthy, "The Basis of National Power" (lecture given to Sons of India: Panchama Lodge, April 24, 1909), Borthwick Institute for Archives, University of York, MCF 5/3/1/9 (5).

78. Maud MacCarthy, "International Arts," *Orpheus (The Transactions of the Theosophical Art-Circle)* 4 (1908): 21.

79. Maud MacCarthy, "The Place of Art in Evolution: An Address Delivered before the Vrashi Tattra Sabha TS Benares," October 14, 1908, Borthwick Institute for Archives, University of York, MCF 5/3/1/9 (3).

80. Ibid.

81. Besant, *Religion and Music*, 17.

82. Ibid., 5.

83. Ibid., 17.

84. Chessa, *Luigi Russolo, Futurist*, 141–150.

85. This was published as Maud Mann, "Some Indian Conceptions of Music," *Proceedings of the Musical Association* (1911–1912): 41–65.

86. Tandra Devi, *The Ten Plagues of Modern Civilization* (Srinagar: Tandra Devi Publications, 1938).

87. Ibid., 17.

88. Tandra Devi, "Holy Hands! Uncontrolled Machines Kill Personality: Handicrafts Bring Out Man's Real Self," *Bombay Chronicle* (February 21, 1937).

89. Devi, "Holy Hands!"

90. Maud MacCarthy, "The Use of Sensitiveness," *Theosophist* (June 1909): 297.

91. Ibid., 298.

92. Manuscript, "The Theosophical School of Music," published in *Vahan*, Borthwick Institute for Archives, University of York, MCF 5/3/1/9 (11).

93. Ibid.

94. For an overview of Foulds's music, see Malcolm MacDonald, *John Foulds and His Music: An Introduction* (White Plains: Pro/Am Music Resources, 1989).

95. For further discussion of Foulds's music as it developed under MacCarthy's influence, see James G. Mansell, "Music and the Borders of Rationality: Discourses of Place in the Work of John Foulds," in *Internationalism and the Arts in Britain and Europe at the Fin de Siècle*, ed. Grace Brockington (Oxford: Peter Lang, 2009), 49–78.

96. Letter from Maud Mann to Mr Baillie-Weaver, May 2, 1916, Borthwick Institute for Archives, University of York, MCF 5/3/1/3 (3).

97. Maud MacCarthy, "Just Intonation—Clairaudience—Intuition," *Vahan* (February 1918), 185.

98. Ibid.

99. Ibid.

100. Ibid.

101. Manuscript, "The Theosophical School of Music."

102. Publicity brochure for phonotherapy clinic, Borthwick Institute for Archives, University of York, MCF 5/2/3/1 (6).

103. "Illness Cured by Melody," *Daily Mail* (February 10, 1933): 9.

104. Ibid., 9.

105. Publicity brochure for phonotherapy clinic, Borthwick Institute for Archives, University of York, MCF 5/2/3/1 (6).

106. Maud MacCathy, *The Temple of Labour: Four Lectures on the Plan Beautiful in Relation to Modern Industrialism* (London: Theosophical Publishing House, 1926), 13.

107. Ibid., 26.

108. Ibid., 9.

109. Letter from Maud MacCarthy to Mrs Pethwick Lawrence, no date, Borthwick Institute for Archives, University of York, MCF 5/1/1/25 (2).

110. Handwritten manuscript, "The Place of Art in Evolution: An Address Delivered before the Vrashi Tattra Sabha TS Benares, October 14, 1908," Borthwick Institute for Archives, University of York, MCF 5/3/1/9 (3).

111. The score is held by the British Library, additional manuscript 56478.

112. Foulds outlined his music theory in *Music To-day: Its Heritage from the Past, and Legacy to the Future* (London: Nicholson and Watson, 1934).

113. Handwritten note, Borthwick Institute for Archives, University of York, MCF 3/2/3/3.

114. Letter from London Cenotaph Choir to Earl Haig, May 16, 1925, Borthwick Institute for Archives, University of York, MCF 3/2/3/3 (2).

115. Publicity brochure for *A World Requiem*, BBC Written Archive Centre, John Foulds papers.

116. Jay Winter, *Sites of Memory, Sites of Mourning: The Great War in European Cultural History* (Cambridge: Cambridge University Press, 1995).

117. "Music of the Week: The 'World Requiem,'" *Observer* (November 16, 1924): 10.

118. A full discussion of the circumstances surrounding *World Requiem*'s axing in 1927 can be found in James G. Mansell, "Musical Modernity and Contested Commemoration at the Festival of Remembrance, 1923–1927," *Historical Journal* 52 (2009): 433–454. For further discussion of *World Requiem*, see Rachel Cowgill, "Canonizing Remembrance: Music for Armistice Day at the BBC, 1922–7," *First World War Studies* 2 (2011): 75–107.

119. "Queer Temple of Healing," *John Bull* (March 11, 1933): 19.

120. Owen, "Occultism and the 'Modern' Self," 73.

121. Wilfred Northfield, *Frayed Nerves: Simple Ways of Restoring Their Tone* (London: The Psychologist, 1940).

122. W. Charles Loosmore, *Nerves and the Man: A Popular Psychological and Constructive Study of Nervous Breakdown* (London: John Murray, 1920), 195.

123. H. Ernest Hunt, *Nerve Control: The Cure of Nervousness and Stage-Fright* (London: William Rider, 1915); H. Ernest Hunt, *The Spirit of Music* (London: Rider and Co., 1932).

124. Hunt, *Spirit of Music*, 131.

125. Joseph McAleer, "Scenes from Love and Marriage: Mills and Boon and the Popular Publishing Industry in Britain, 1908–1950," *Twentieth Century British History* 1 (1990): 264–288; Edwin Ash, *Nerves and the Nervous* (London: Mills and Boon, 1911).

126. In addition to *Nerves and the Man*, Loosmore published *The Gain of Personality: A Popular Psychological Statement of the Practical Values of Personality* (London: J. Murray, 1921); *The Art of Talking, or, Self-Expression in Speech and Conversation* (London: J. Murray, 1923); *The Lure of Happiness, or, the Response of the Mind to the*

Challenge of Contentment (London: J. Murray, 1925); *Ourselves and Our Emotions: A Practical Study of the Behaviour of the Primitive Element of the Mind* (London: J. Murray, 1928).

127. Other than *Nerve Control* and *Spirit of Music*, Hunt's publications included *A Book of Auto-Suggestions* (London: W. Rider and Son, 1919); *The Hidden Self and Its Mental Processes* (London: William Rider, 1921); *The Gateway of Intuition* (London: Wright and Brown, 1934); *Do We Survive Death?* (London: Rich and Cowan, 1936); and *Constructive Thinking: A Guide to the Art of Clear Thinking* (London: Foulsham's, 1938).

128. Ruth Harris, "The 'Unconscious' and Catholicism in France," *Historical Journal* 47 (2004): 331–354, quote at 332.

129. Graham Richards, "Psychology and the Churches in Britain, 1919–39," *History of the Human Sciences* 13 (2000): 57–84, quote at 58.

130. Ibid., 61.

131. William James, *The Varieties of Religious Experience: A Study in Human Nature* (New York: Longmans, Green and Co., 1902).

132. Petteri Pietikainen, *Neurosis and Modernity: The Age of Nervousness in Sweden* (Lieden: Brill, 2007), 206–215.

133. Rhodri Hayward and Mathew Thomson point to this relationship. See Hayward, *Resisting History*, and Thomson, *Psychological Subjects*.

134. Hanegraaff, *New Age Religion*, 490.

135. Ibid., 45.

136. Ibid., 482.

137. Alfred Taylor Schofield's most important publications from this point of view are *Another World: or, the Fourth Dimension* (London: Swan Sonnenschein, 1890); *The Force of Mind: or, The Mental Factor in Medicine* (London: Churchill, 1902); *Functional Nervous Diseases* (London: Methuen, 1908); *The Borderlands of Science* (London: Cassell, 1917); *Modern Spiritism: Its Science and Religion* (London: Churchill, 1920); *Nerves in Disorder: A Plea for Rational Treatment* (London: Hodder and Stoughton, 1927).

138. Edwin Ash, *The Problem of Nervous Breakdown* (London: Mills and Boon, 1919), 186.

139. Ibid., 186.

140. Edwin L. Ash, *Mental Self-Help: A Practical Handbook* (London: Mills and Boon, 1912), 87.

141. H. Ernest Hunt, *Self-Training: The Lines of Mental Progress* (London: William Rider, 1918), 224.

142. Ibid.

143. Ibid.

144. Hunt, *Gateway of Intuition*, 97.

145. Hunt, *Self-Training*, 230.

146. Ibid., 236.

147. Ibid., 236.

148. Ash, *Nerves and the Nervous*, 125.

149. Edwin Hopewell-Ash, *On Keeping Our Nerves in Order* (London: Mills and Boon, 1928), 70.

150. Ibid., 70–71.

151. Ibid., 71.

152. Ibid.

153. Ibid., 70–71.

154. Ibid., 72.

155. Ibid., 72–73.

156. Ibid., 73.

157. Ash, *Mental Self-Help*, 108.

158. Ibid.

159. Ash, *Problem of Nervous Breakdown*, 186.

160. Hunt, *Gateway of Intuition*, 97.

161. Ibid.

162. Hunt, *Spirit of Music*, 29.

163. Ibid., 29.

164. Ibid., 134.

165. Arthur Eaglefield Hull, *Cyril Scott: Composer, Poet, Philosopher* (London: K. Paul, Trench, Trubner and Co., 1918).

166. Loosmore, *Nerves and the Man*, 196.

167. Ibid., 48.

168. Ibid.

169. Ibid., 198.

170. Ibid., 197.

171. Ibid., 198–200.

172. Ibid., 201.

173. Ibid., 202.

174. Ibid., 207.

175. Ibid.

176. Ibid.

177. Ibid., 208.

178. Ibid., 209.

179. Ibid., 207.

180. Hunt, *Gateway of Intuition*, 26.

181. Ibid.

182. Hunt, *Nerve Control*, 109.

183. Ralph Waldo Trine, *In Tune with the Infinite or, Fullness of Peace, Power and Plenty* (New York: Thomas Y. Crowell Publishers, 1897), 16.

184. Hanegraaff, *New Age Religion*, 489–490.

185. Trine, *In Tune with the Infinite*, 23.

186. Ibid., 10. On harmonial religion, see Hanegraaff, *New Age Religion*, 494–495.

187. Hunt, *Nerve Control*, 112–113.

188. Ibid., 109.

189. Hunt, *Spirit of Music*, 33.

190. Loosmore, *Nerves and the Man*, 209.

191. Edwin Ash, *Nerve in Wartime* (London: Mills and Boon, 1914), 27.

192. Ibid., 9.

193. Hunt, *Self-Training*, 81.

194. Hunt, *Gateway of Intuition*, 49.

195. Ibid.

196. Treitel, "What the Occult Reveals," 612.

197. Owen, *Place of Enchantment*, 6.

198. On the role of spiritualism and theosophy in the commemoration of the First World War, see Winter, *Sites of Memory*. See also Jenny Hazelgrove, *Spiritualism and British Society between the Wars* (Manchester: Manchester University Press, 2000).

Chapter 3. Creating the Sonically Rational

1. The epigraph is from Hope Bagenal, *Practical Acoustics and Planning against Noise* (London: Methuen, 1942), frontispiece.

2. Charlotte Wildman argues that anti-Victorianism was at the heart of attempts to rebrand cities such as Liverpool and Manchester as fit for the twentieth century. See Charlotte Wildman, "Urban Transformation in Liverpool and Manchester, 1918–1939," *Historical Journal* 55 (2012): 119–143, and Charlotte Wildman, "*A City Speaks*: The Projection of Civic Identity in Manchester," *Twentieth Century British History* 23 (2012): 80–99.

3. Denis Linehan, "A New England: Landscape, Exhibition and Remaking Industrial Space in the 1930s," in *Geographies of British Modernity*, ed. David Gilbert, David Matless, and Brian Short (Oxford: Blackwell, 2003), 132–150, quote at 140.

4. On the political context of this new technocratic ethos in British government, see Daniel Ritschel, *The Politics of Planning: The Debate on Economic Planning in Britain in the 1930s* (Oxford: Clarendon Press, 1997).

5. Anson Rabinbach, *The Human Motor: Energy, Fatigue and the Origins of Modernity* (Berkeley: University of California Press, 1990), 271–272.

6. Ben Highmore, *Everyday Life and Cultural Theory: An Introduction* (London: Routledge, 2002), 75–112.

7. Letter from Industrial Health Research Board to R. F. Millard, May 20, 1937, National Archives, FD1/4048.

8. Lord Horder, "Health and Noise," in *Silencing a Noisy World: Being a Brief Report of the Conference on the Abatement of Noise* (London: Anti-Noise League, 1935), 42.

9. Mary Poovey, *Making a Social Body: British Cultural Formation, 1830–1864* (Chicago: University of Chicago Press, 1995), 8.

10. Nikolas Rose, "Government, Authority and Expertise in Advanced Liberalism," *Economy and Society* 22 (1993): 283–299, quote at 284.

11. Patrick Joyce, *The Rule of Freedom: Liberalism and the Modern City* (London: Verso, 2003).

12. Rose, "Government, Authority and Expertise," 285.

13. Ibid.

14. Hope Bagenal, "Noise and the New Planning," *Architects' Journal* (March 20, 1947): 236.

15. Ibid.

16. Henri Lefebvre, *Rhythmanalysis*, trans. Stuart Eldon (New York: Continuum, 2004), 68.

17. Tim Edensor, "Introduction: Thinking about Rhythm and Space," in *Geographies of Rhythm: Nature, Place, Mobilities and Bodies* (Aldershot: Ashgate, 2010), 8.

18. For a discussion of pre–First World War work science, see Rabinbach, *Human Motor*, 5.

19. Quoted in May Smith, *An Introduction to Industrial Psychology* (London: Cassell, 1943), 23.

20. Rabinbach, *Human Motor*, 275.

21. Quoted in Smith, *Introduction to Industrial Psychology*, 23.

22. R. S. F. Schilling, "Industrial Health Research: The Work of the Industrial Health Research Board, 1918–44," *British Journal of Industrial Medicine* 1 (1944): 145.

23. On the gendered aspects of industrial psychology, see A. J. McIvor, "Manual Work, Technology, and Industrial Health, 1918–39," *Medical History* 31 (1987): 160–189, and Vicky Long, "Industrial Homes, Domestic Factories: The Convergence of Public and Private Space in Interwar Britain," *Journal of British Studies* 50 (2011): 434–464.

24. Millais Culpin, "A Study of the Incidence of the Minor Psychoses—Their Clinical and Industrial Importance," *Proceedings of the Royal Society of Medicine* (December 13, 1927): 419–430.

25. "Psychoneuroses as a Cause of Incapacity among Injured Persons," *British Medical Journal Supplement* (March 9, 1935): 85–88. For discussion of this study, see Mathew Thomson, *Psychological Subjects: Identity, Culture and Health in Twentieth-Century Britain* (Oxford: Oxford University Press, 2006), 167, and Rhodri Hayward, "Enduring Emotions: James L. Halliday and the Invention of the Psychosocial," *Isis* 100 (2009): 827–838.

26. Thomson, *Psychological Subjects*, 162.

27. Ibid., 199.

28. The rise of psychological experts in Britain is discussed in Nikolas Rose, *Governing the Soul: The Shaping of the Private Self* (London: Free Association, 1999).

29. Millais Culpin, *The Nervous Patient* (London: H. K. Lewis, 1924), 3.

30. Millais Culpin, "Some Cases of 'Traumatic Neurasthenia,'" *Lancet* (August 1, 1931): 233–237, quotes at 233 and 237.

31. E. Farquhar Buzzard, "The Dumping Ground of Neurasthenia," *Lancet* (January 4, 1930): 1–4.

32. Ibid., 3.

33. Culpin, "Some Cases of 'Traumatic Neurasthenia,'" 234.

34. Ibid., 237.

35. The National Institute of Industrial Psychology was founded in 1920 by C. S. Myers. See McIvor, "Manual Work, Technology, and Industrial Health," 173–174. C. S. Myers's *Mind and Work* (London: University of London Press, 1920) was a foundational text for the discipline of industrial psychology.

36. Millais Culpin, *Recent Advances in the Study of the Psychoneuroses* (Philadelphia: P. Blakiston's Son and Co., 1931), 8.

37. Ibid.

38. Ibid., 1.

39. Ibid., 1, 116.

40. Culpin, "Study of the Incidence of the Minor Psychoses."

41. Ibid., 422.

42. Ibid., 420.

43. Ibid., 425.

44. Ibid., 420.

45. McIvor, "Manual Work, Technology, and Industrial Health," 170.

46. Ibid., 175.

47. Millais Culpin, "Nervous Disease in Industry," *Industrial Welfare* (September 1928): 283–286, quote at 284.

48. Ibid., 283.

49. Ibid.

50. Ibid., 286.

51. "Noise and Neurasthenia," *British Medical Journal Supplement* (September 29, 1928): 146–147.

52. Ibid., 147.

53. Culpin quoted in Smith, *Introduction to Industrial Psychology*, 57.

54. F. C. Bartlett, *The Problem of Noise* (Cambridge: Cambridge University Press, 1934), 29.

55. Ibid., 50–52.

56. Culpin, "Study of the Minor Psychoses," 423.

57. Millais Culpin and May Smith, *The Nervous Temperament; Industrial Health Research Board Report No. 61* (London: His Majesty's Stationery Office, 1930).

58. Ibid., 28.

59. Ibid.

60. Ibid., 28–29.

61. Ibid., 30.

62. Smith, *Introduction to Industrial Psychology*, 60.

63. K. Pollock and F. C. Bartlett, "Psychological Experiments on the Effects of Noise," in *Two Studies in the Psychological Effects of Noise; Industrial Health Research Board Report No. 65* (London: His Majesty's Stationery Office, 1932), 8.

64. Ibid., 6.

65. H. C. Weston and S. Adams, "The Effects of Noise on the Performance of Weavers," in *Two Studies in the Psychological Effects of Noise; Industrial Health Research Board Report No. 65* (London: His Majesty's Stationery Office, 1932), 58.

66. Pollock and Bartlett, "Psychological Experiments," 34.

67. Smith, *Introduction to Industrial Psychology*, 157.

68. Pollock and Bartlett, "Psychological Experiments," 30.

69. Ibid., 33.

70. Smith, *Introduction to Industrial Psychology*, 56.

71. McIvor points out that IHRB scientists were disappointed about the slow uptake of their principles by employers. See McIvor, "Manual Work, Technology and Industrial Health," 182–185.

72. Dan McKenzie, "Noise and the Medical Research Council," *Journal of Laryngology and Otology* 48 (1933): 110–113, quotes at 112.

73. Ibid., 112.

74. Culpin and Smith, *Nervous Temperament*, 30.

75. Smith, *Introduction to Industrial Psychology*, 59–60.

76. Pollock and Bartlett, "Psychological Experiments," 17–21.

77. Horder, "Health and Noise," 42.

78. Smith, for example, used the term *brain-working* to identify those occupied in intellectual work in *Introduction to Industrial Psychology*, 56.

79. Smith discusses the findings of industrial psychologists with regard to typists and noiseless typewriters and points out that reduction of noise in this context did not produce a significant improvement of working performance. Smith, *Introduction to Industrial Psychology*, 61–62.

80. Pollock and Bartlett, "Psychological Experiments," 29.

81. This was shown by S. Wyatt and J. N. Langdon in *Fatigue and Boredom in Repetitive Work; Industrial Health Research Board Report No. 77* (London: His Majesty's Stationery Office, 1937). For further discussion, see Keith Jones, "Music in Factories: A Twentieth-Century Technique for Control of the Productive Self," *Social and Cultural Geography* 6 (2005): 723–744, and Emma Robertson, Marek Korczynski, and Michael Pickering, "Harmonious Relations? Music at Work in the Rowntree and Cadbury Factories," *Business History* 49 (2007): 211–234.

82. Jones, "Music in Factories," 723. On the role of music while you work during the Second World War, see Marek Korczynski, Emma Robertson, Michael Pickering, and Keith Jones, "'We Sang Ourselves through That War': Women, Music and Factory Work in World War Two," *Labour History Review* 70 (2005): 185–214.

83. It did this through the Rent and Mortgage Restriction Act 1915. See Marian Bowley, *Housing and the State, 1919–1944* (London: George Allen and Unwin, 1945), 3.

84. Mark Swenarton, *Homes Fit for Heroes: The Politics and Architecture of Early State Housing in Britain* (London: Heineman, 1981).

85. A. H. Davis, *Noise* (London: Watts and Co., 1937), 107.

86. Bartlett, *Problem of Noise*, 60.

87. Ibid., 52.

88. File Report, "Some Psychological Factors in Home-Building," March 1943, Mass-Observation Archive, FR 1616.

89. Dennis Chapman, *People and Their Homes* (London: Bureau of Current Affairs, 1950), 6.

90. Mass-Observation, *An Inquiry into People's Homes, A Report Prepared by Mass-Observation for the Advertising Service Guild, the Fourth of the "Change" Wartime Surveys* (London: John Murray, 1943), 171.

91. File Report, "Some Psychological Factors in Home-Building," March 1943, Mass-Observation Archive, FR 1616.

92. Ibid.

93. Letter from Elizabeth Wilton to Minister of Health, May 6, 1943, National Archives, FD1/4042.

94. On health and the home in the twentieth century, see Mark Jackson, "Home Sweet Home: Historical Perspectives on Health and the Home," in *Health and the Modern Home*, ed. Mark Jackson (New York: Routledge, 2007), 1–18.

95. Hope Bagenal and Alex Wood, *Planning for Good Acoustics* (London: Methuen, 1931), v.

96. Ibid., 200.

97. Bartlett, *Problem of Noise*, 76.

98. Bagenal and Wood, *Planning for Good Acoustics*, 200.

99. Hope Bagenal and P. W. Barnett, *The Reduction of Noise in Buildings: Recommendations to Architects*, Building Research Bulletin No. *14* (London: His Majesty's Stationery Office, 1933), 1.

100. Dennis Chapman, *The Location of Dwellings in Scottish Towns: An Inquiry into Some of the Factors Relevant to the Planning of New Urban Communities Made for the Department of Health for Scotland* (London: Wartime Social Survey, 1943), 69.

101. League of Nations Health Organisation, *Bulletin, Vol. 6* (London: George Allen and Unwin, 1937), 541.

102. Hope Bagenal and P. W. Barnett, *The Reduction of Noise in Buildings: Sound Insulation and Acoustics, Post-War Building Studies No. 14* (London: His Majesty's Stationery Office, 1944).

103. *Design of Dwellings: Report of the Design of Dwellings Sub-Committee of the Central Housing Advisory Committee Appointed by the Minister of Health and Report of a Study Group of the Ministry of Town and Country Planning on Site Planning and Layout in Relation to Housing* (London: His Majesty's Stationery Office, 1944), 9.

104. *Housing Standards and Statistics: The Second Report of the Council for Research on Housing Construction* (London: P. S. King, 1935). E. D. Simon pointed out, in the case of Manchester, that the majority of the new homes built after 1919 provided alternative accommodation for "the clerk and the artisan" rather than the slum-dwelling poor. See *How to Abolish the Slums* (London: Longmans, Green and Co., 1929), 1.

105. Ministry of Health, *Construction of Flats for the Working Classes, Final Report of the Departmental Committee* (London: HMSO, 1937).

106. Bagenal went on to find fame as the acoustic designer for several important public buildings, including the Royal Festival Hall. See the Oxford Dictionary of National Biography entry for (Philip) Hope Edward Bagenal.

107. "Interim Recommendations on Planning against Noise," *Journal of the Royal Institute of British Architects* (June 1935): 2–8, image on 7.

108. Hope Bagenal, "Migration of Noise in Buildings," in *Noise Abatement Exhibition: Science Museum, South Kensington, 31st May–30th June 1935* (London: Anti-Noise League, 1935), 35.

109. "Interim Recommendations on Planning against Noise," 7.

110. See memo discussion in National Archives, FD1/4042.

111. Bagenal, "Noise and the New Planning," 236.

112. This was undertaken at the NPL. See G. W. C. Kaye, "The Measurement of Noise," *Reports on Progress in Physics* 3 (1936): 130–142.

113. A. H. Davis and C. J. Morreau, *The Reduction of Noise in Buildings, Building Research Special Report No. 26* (London: His Majesty's Stationery Office, 1939), iii.

114. Ibid., 29.

115. Ibid., 5.

116. Ibid., 4–5.

117. R. Fitzmaurice and William Allen, *Sound Transmission in Buildings: Practical Notes for Architects and Builders* (London: His Majesty's Stationery Office, 1939), 9.

118. Mass-Observation, *Inquiry into People's Homes*, 46.

119. Ibid., 174.

120. Ibid.

121. Dennis Chapman, *A Survey of Noise in British Homes, National Building Studies Technical Paper No. 2* (London: His Majesty's Stationery Office, 1948), 2.

122. Ibid.

123. Ibid., 3, 11.

124. Ibid., 11–12.

125. Ibid., 21.

126. Ibid., 15–17.

127. W. A. Allen, "A Study of Domestic Noise," in *Noise and Sound Transmission: Report of the 1948 Summer Symposium of the Acoustics Group* (London: The Physical Society, 1949), 81.

128. Chapman, *Survey of Noise in British Homes*, 2.

129. Dennis Chapman, *The Home and Social Status* (London: Routledge and Kegan Paul, 1955), 8.

130. *Design of Dwellings*, 55.

131. Mass-Observation, *Inquiry into People's Homes*, 49.

132. Ibid., 48.

133. Letter from Dennis Chapman to G. Allen, November 29, 1943, National Archives DSIR4/2183.

134. For an extended discussion of *Night Mail*, see Scott Anthony, *Night Mail* (London: British Film Institute, 2007).

135. Patrick Joyce argues that "in Britain, until well into the twentieth century, the Post Office was the state for most people, the most ever-present and largest state institution in the country." See Patrick Joyce, "Postal Communication and the Making of the British Technostate," *CRESC Working Paper Series* 54 (2008): 16.

136. On postal communications and the power of the liberal state, see Andrew Barry, "Lines of Communication and Spaces of Rule," in *Foucault and Political Reason: Liberalism, Neo-Liberalism and Rationalities of Government*, ed. Andrew Barry, Thomas Osborne and Nikolas Rose (London: Routledge, 1996), 123–142.

137. Yasuko Suga, "GPO Films and Modern Design," in *The Projection of Britain: A History of the GPO Film Unit*, ed. Scott Anthony and James G. Mansell (London: Palgrave Macmillan, 2011), 18–27. On GPO films as advertising, see Amy Sargeant, "GPO Films: American and European Models of Advertising in the Projection of Nation," *Twentieth Century British History* 23 (2012): 38–56.

138. Ian Aitken, *Film and Reform: John Grierson and the Documentary Film Movement* (London: Routledge, 1990).

139. On Tallents, see Scott Anthony, *Public Relations and the Making of Modern Britain: Stephen Tallents and the Birth of a Progressive Media Profession* (Manchester: Manchester University Press, 2012).

140. On the promotion of telecommunications by the GPO Film Unit, see David Hay, "The GPO Film Unit and Telecommunications Culture," in *Projection of Britain*, 206–232.

141. Benedict Anderson argues that synchronicity—the ability of a spatially disparate community to imagine common daily rhythms and customs—was an important component of modern nationhood. See Benedict Anderson, *Imagined Communities: Reflections on the Origin and Spread of Nationalism* (New York: Verso, 2006).

142. On music in *Night Mail*, see E. Anna Claydon, "National Identity, the GPO Film Unit and Their Music," in *Projection of Britain*, 179–187.

143. Alberto Cavalcanti, "L'étude du cinéma en tant que moyen d'expression," in *Alberto Cavalcanti*, ed. Lorenzo Pellizzari and Claudio Valentinetti, trans. Roland Cosandey, Monique Farhi, and Claudine Reymond (Locarno: Éditions du festival international du film de Locarno, 1988), 232.

144. John Grierson, "Creative Use of Sound," in *Grierson on Documentary*, ed. Forsyth Hardy (London: Collins, 1946), 91.

145. Ken Cameron, "All Squeak and No Bubble," in *Projection of Britain*, 119–132, quote at 123.

146. Ken Cameron, *Sound in Films: A Speech Delivered at the British Film Institute's Summer School at Bangor, August 1944* (London: British Film Institute, 1944), 4.

147. Before joining the GPO Film Unit, Cavalcanti had worked as an experimental filmmaker in Paris. See Ian Aitken, *Alberto Cavalcanti: Realism, Surrealism and National Cinemas* (Trowbridge: Flicks Books, 2000).

148. Alberto Cavalcanti, "Sound in Films," in *Film Sound: Theory and Practice*, ed. Elisabeth Weis and John Bolton (New York: Columbia University Press, 1985), 109.

149. Ken Cameron, *Sound and the Documentary Film* (London: Sir Isaac Pitman and Sons, 1947), 5.

150. Andrew Buchanan, "The Sound Film," *Quiet* 2 (April 1939), 25.

151. Ibid.

152. Ibid., emphasis original.

153. On railway spine and noise, see Shelley Trower, *Senses of Vibration: A History of the Pleasure and Pain of Sound* (New York: Continuum, 2012), 94–125.

154. *Lancet*, January 11, 1862, 52.

155. Ibid., 51.

156. "Sound and Fury—Signifying Something," *All the Year Round* 9 (1873): 559.

157. Dan McKenzie, *The City of Din: A Tirade against Noise* (London: Adlard and Son, 1916), 77–78.

158. Ibid., 78.

159. On rhythm in GPO films, see James G. Mansell, "Rhythm, Modernity and the Politics of Sound," in *Projection of Britain*, 161–167.

160. Paul Rotha, *Documentary Diary: An Informal History of the British Documentary Film, 1928–1939* (London: Secker and Warburg, 1973), 132. Musique concrète is a technique of musical composition, associated primarily with French composer Pierre Schaeffer, which used recordings of nonmusical sounds in place of traditional musical instruments.

161. On Jennings, see Anthony W. Hodgkinson and Rodney E. Sheratsky, *Humphrey Jennings: More than a Maker of Films* (Hanover, N.H.: University Press of New England, 1982) and Kevin Jackson, *Humphrey Jennings* (London: Picador, 2004). On Jennings's film work, see Philip C. Logan, *Humphrey Jennings and the British Documentary Film: A Re-assessment* (Farnham: Ashgate, 2011).

162. *Monthly Film Bulletin* 6 (1939): 153.

163. Humphrey Jennings, *Pandæmonium, 1660–1886: The Coming of the Machine as Seen by Contemporary Observers*, ed. Mary-Lou Jennings and Charles Madge (London: Deutsch, 1985).

164. Ibid., 232.

165. Edensor, "Introduction," 11.

Chapter 4. National Acoustics

1. *London Can Take It!* was intended for North American audiences. The film was retitled for domestic release as *Britain Can Take It!*

2. Clare Corbould, "Streets, Sounds and Identity in Inter-war Harlem," *Journal of Social History* 40 (2007): 859–894; Mark M. Smith, *Listening to Nineteenth-Century America* (Chapel Hill: University of North Carolina Press, 2001).

3. Work on Nazi Germany is suggestive of the power of sound in war. See Carolyn Birdsall, *Nazi Soundscapes: Sound, Technology and Urban Space in Germany, 1933–1945* (Amsterdam: Amsterdam University Press, 2012) and Brian Currid, *A National Acoustics: Music and Mass Publicity in Weimar and Nazi Germany* (Minneapolis: University of Minnesota Press, 2006).

4. For histories of the English Musical Renaissance, see Robert Stradling and Meirion Hughes, *The English Musical Renaissance 1860–1940: Constructing a National Music* (Manchester: Manchester University Press, 2001) and Andrew Blake, *The Land without Music: Music, Culture and Society in Twentieth-Century Britain* (Manchester: Manchester University Press, 1997). On the English folk music revival, see Georgina Boyes, *The Imagined Village: Culture, Ideology and the English Folk Revival*

(Manchester: Manchester University Press, 1993) and Vic Gammon, "Folk Song Collecting in Sussex and Surrey, 1843–1914," *History Workshop Journal* 10 (1980): 61–89.

5. George Revill, "Music and the Politics of Sound: Nationalism, Citizenship and Auditory Space," *Environment and Planning D: Society and Space* 18 (2000): 597–613, quote at 610. For further discussion of the role of music in the construction of spatial identity, see Andrew Leyshon, David Matless, and George Revill, ed., *The Place of Music* (New York: Guilford Press, 1998). For another perspective on how the nation has been encapsulated in music, see Michael J. Shapiro, "Sounds of Nationhood," *Millennium: Journal of International Studies* 30 (2001): 583–601.

6. Revill, "Music and the Politics of Sound," 602.

7. Richard L. Hernandez, "Sacred Sound and Sacred Substances: Church Bells and the Auditory Culture of Russian Villages during the Bolshevik Velikii Rerelom," *American Historical Review* 109 (2004): 1475–1504, citation at 1495.

8. Sonya O. Rose, *Which People's War? National Identity and Citizenship in Wartime Britain, 1939–1945* (Oxford: Oxford University Press, 2004), 13.

9. Angus Calder, *The People's War: 1939–45* (London: Jonathan Cape, 1969).

10. Rose, *Which People's War?* 13.

11. Benedict Anderson, *Imagined Communities: Reflections on the Origin and Spread of Nationalism* (London: Verso, 1983).

12. Rose, *Which People's War?* 1.

13. Draft of speech given by Lord Horder to the Marriage Guidance Council, Wellcome Library, GP/31/B/2/23.

14. See, for example, Stephen Daniels, *Fields of Vision: Landscape Imagery and National Identity in England and the United States* (Cambridge: Polity, 1997) and Jan Marsh, *Back to the Land: The Pastoral Ideal in England, from 1880 to 1914* (London: Quartet, 1982).

15. Peter Mandler, "Against 'Englishness': English Culture and the Limits to Rural Nostalgia, 1850–1940," *Transactions of the Royal Historical Society* 7 (1997): 155–175.

16. Ibid., 171.

17. Rose, *Which People's War?* 198.

18. By "total war," historians mean that all citizens, not just military personnel, had a role to play in fighting the war and that everyday life on the home front was transformed in the name of the war effort. See Peter Calvocoressi and Guy Wint, *Total War: Causes and Courses of the Second World War* (London: Allen Lane, 1972) and Arthur Marwick, ed., *Total War and Social Change* (Basingstoke: Macmillan, 1988).

19. "Social Services in War-Time," *Lancet* (February 10, 1940): 285.

20. This chapter does not discuss radio listening at any length. On this topic, see John Hartley, "Radiocracy: Sound and Citizenship," *International Journal of Cultural Studies* 3 (2000): 153–159.

21. Tom Rice, "Soundselves: An Acoustemology of Sound and Self in the Edinburgh Royal Infirmary," *Anthropology Today* 19 (2003): 4–9.

22. On total war in Britain, see Jay Winter, *The Great War and the British People* (London: Macmillan, 1986).

23. This list was included in the drafting of the Control of Noise Order, National Archives, HO322/5.

24. Ibid.

25. Various draft reports and letters between government and industry confirm this logic in, for example, National Archives, HO186/2074.

26. Draft of the Control of Noise Order, National Archives, HO322/5. Such exemptions were made only in the second version of the Control of Noise Order passed into law in November 1939.

27. Numerous examples of such letters are held at National Archives, HO186/2070.

28. Letter from Welsh Civil Defence Region to Home Office, October 1944, National Archives, HO186/2074.

29. Letter from Welsh Regional Controller of Ministry of Fuel and Power to Home Office, October 1944, National Archives, HO186/2074.

30. On the regulation of time and the interests of capitalist production, see E. P. Thompson, "Time, Work-Discipline and Industrial Capitalism," *Past and Present* 38 (1967): 56–97.

31. Home Office internal memo, National Archives, HO186/2074.

32. Home Office internal memo, National Archives, HO322/5.

33. Letter from the Home Secretary to the Archbishop of Canterbury, March 12, 1959, Church of England Record Centre, GSEC/JGS/CORR/1/8 1969/39.

34. "Sounding the Tocsin," *Church Times* (June 21, 1940): 445.

35. "Church Bells Cause Alarm," *Manchester Guardian* (September 9, 1940): 5.

36. Alain Corbin, *Village Bells: Sound and Meaning in the Nineteenth-Century French Countryside*, trans. Martin Thom (New York: Columbia University Press, 1998). Hernandez's article on the Bolshevik campaign to dismantle church bells in early Soviet Russia is a second outstanding example. See Hernandez, "Sacred Sound and Sacred Substances." For a brief nonhistorical perspective on the auditory culture of church bells, see Isaac Weiner, "Sound," *Material Religion* 7 (2011): 108–115.

37. Corbin, *Village Bells*.

38. "Sounding the Tocsin," 445.

39. Hernandez, "Sacred Sound and Sacred Substance," 1482.

40. Ibid.

41. Pamphlet on "Care of Church Buildings in Wartime," Church of England Record Centre, CARE/WAR2/1.

42. This clipping, entitled "The Care of Church Bells in War-Time," is contained in a file about care of churches during the Second World War in the Church of England Record Centre, CARE/WAR2/1.

43. "Sounding the Tocsin," 445.

44. "Sir,—Why Should Our Church Bells Be Silenced?" *Times* (June 22, 1940): 7.

45. "Church Bells," *Times* (June 22, 1940): 7.

46. Newspaper clippings relating to the ringing of church bells, National Archives, HO186/2070.

47. "Rang His Church Bell: Vicar Goes to Gaol," *Manchester Guardian* (July 16, 1940): 5; "Bell-Ringing Rector: Conviction Quashed after Imprisonment," *Manchester Guardian* (October 5, 1940): 4.

48. Matthew Grimley, "The Religion of Englishness: Puritanism, Providentialism, and 'National Character,' 1918–1945," *Journal of British Studies* 46 (2007): 884–906, quote at 885. On religion and British national identity, see also John Wolffe, *God and Greater Britain: Religion and National Life in Britain and Ireland, 1843–1945* (London: Routledge, 1994).

49. "Sir,—Why Should Our Church Bells Be Silenced?" 7.

50. Peter Donnelly, ed., *Mrs Milburn's Diaries: An Englishwoman's Day-to-Day Reflections 1939–45* (London: Fontana/Collins, 1980), 196.

51. J. L. Hodson, *Home Front* (London: Victor Gollancz, 1944), quoted in Rose, *Which People's War?* 201.

52. Newspaper clippings relating to the ringing of church bells, National Archives, HO186/2070.

53. "Youth at the Rope: Ringing the Bells of Britain," *Manchester Guardian* (November 15, 1940): 7.

54. The Archbishop of York's interjection was also reported by newspapers. See, for example, "The Silent Bells: Archbishop of York's Strong Criticism," *Manchester Guardian* (April 1, 1943): 2.

55. Letter from Archbishop of Canterbury to Prime Minister, March 31, 1943, Lambeth Palace Library, W. Temple Papers, Vol. 58.

56. "The Bells Return," *Manchester Guardian* (April 21, 1941): 4.

57. "Public Opinion on Bells," *Manchester Guardian* (May 22, 1943): 4.

58. Jeffrey Cox, *The English Churches in a Secular Society: Lambeth 1870–1930* (Oxford: Oxford University Press, 1982); Adrian Hastings, *A History of English Christianity, 1920–2000* (London: SCM Press, 2001).

59. Sarah Williams, *Religious Belief and Popular Culture in Southwark, c. 1880–1939* (Oxford: Oxford University Press, 1999).

60. "Public Opinion on Bells," 4.

61. Ibid.

62. James Purves-Stewart and Arthur Evans, *Nerve Injuries and Their Treatment* (Oxford: Oxford University Press, 1919). See also James Purves-Stewart, *The Diagnosis of Nervous Diseases* (London: Arnold, 1906). Purves-Stewart's memoir contains an explanation for his involvement in the noise abatement campaign. See *Sands of Time: Recollections of a Physician in Peace and War* (London: Hutchinson, 1939).

63. James Purves-Stewart, "Noise and Nerves in Wartime," *Quiet* 2 (1941): 7–9, quote at 7.

64. Lord Horder, "To our Readers," *Quiet* 2 (1940): 3.

65. Ibid., 4.

66. Ibid., 5.

67. Ibid., 4.

68. Ibid.

69. Joan Woollcombe, "Noise in Wartime, from the Woman's Point of View," *Quiet* 2 (1940): 19.

70. Purves-Stewart, "Noise and Nerves in Wartime," 7.

71. Joan Woollcombe, "It Needed a War," *Quiet* 2 (1941): 15.

72. Ibid.

73. Lord Horder, "Sleep for A.R.P. Workers: Nights away from London: A Recent Experiment," *Times* (October 15, 1940): 5.

74. Ibid.

75. Ibid.

76. Ainslie Darby and C. C. Hamilton, *England, Ugliness and Noise* (London: P. S. King and Son, 1930).

77. Joan Woollcombe, "Rest for A.R.P. Workers," *Times* (October 25, 1940): 5.

78. Woollcombe, "It Needed a War," 15.

79. Joint War Organization Committee Files, British Red Cross Archive, JWO1/1/2.

80. "Convalescent Home for A.R.P. Workers: A Centre for Rest and Solace," *Times* (May 16, 1941): 7.

81. Joint War Organization Committee Files, British Red Cross Archive, JWO1/1/2.

82. Letter from Sir Arthur MacNalty to Lord Horder, August 17, 1943, National Archives, HO1871476.

83. Letter from A. A. Davies to Home Office, National Archives, HO1871476.

84. A copy of such a certificate is held in the National Archives, HO1871476.

85. Joint War Organization Committee Files, British Red Cross Archive, JWO1/1/2.

86. Joan Woollcombe, "Peace and 'Quiet,'" *Quiet* 2 (1943): 15.

87. Ibid., 16.

88. Ibid., 17.

89. Lord Horder, "Health and Noise," in *Silencing a Noisy World: Being a Brief Report of the Conference on the Abatement of Noise* (London: Anti-Noise League, 1935), 42.

90. Woollcombe, "Peace and 'Quiet,'" 17.

91. Lord Horder, "Rest Houses: A Civil Defence Example: Health of Industrial Workers," *Times* (March 1, 1943): 5.

92. "Resthouses for Workers: Lord Horder on Aid to Civil Defence," *Times* (October 21, 1943): 2.

93. Horder, "Rest Houses," 5.

94. Woollcombe, "Peace and 'Quiet,'" 17.

95. Joan Woollcombe, "Beating a Peaceful Retreat," *Times* (August 9, 1968): 11.

96. The extent of psychiatric illness in the civilian population during the Second World War nonetheless remained a matter of debate among medical experts and has since divided historians. For an overview of these debates, see Edgar Jones, Robin Woolven, Bill Durodié, and Simon Wessely, "Civilian Morale during the Second World War: Responses to Air Raids Re-examined," *Social History of Medicine* 17 (2004): 463–479.

97. Purves-Stewart, "Noise and Nerves in Wartime," 9.

98. Joanna Bourke, "Fear and Anxiety: Writing about Emotion in Modern History," *History Workshop Journal* 55 (2003): 111–133, quote at 124.

99. John Langdon-Davies, *Nerves versus Nazis* (London: George Routledge, 1940), 7.

100. Several Second World War self-help books described the conflict as a "war of nerves." See, for example, H. Ernest Hunt, *How to Win the War of Nerves* (London: Rider and Co., 1940). Others offered practical advice about how to train the nerves in order to meet the conditions of the war. See Milton Powell, *How to Train Your Nerves: A Manual of Nerve Training* (London: Athletic Publications, 1943) and Wilfred Northfield, *Frayed Nerves: Simple Ways of Restoring Their Tone* (London: The Psychologist, 1940).

101. Langdon-Davies, *Nerves versus Nazis*, 29.

102. Ibid., 30.

103. Ibid., 32.

104. Hunt, *How to Win the War of Nerves*, 19.

105. Ibid., 120.

106. Ibid.

107. Amy Bell, "Landscapes of Fear: Wartime London, 1939–1945," *Journal of British Studies* 48 (2009): 153–175.

108. Letter from J. L. Taylor to Department of Scientific and Industrial Research, May 23, 1940, National Archives, FD1/6258.

109. John D. Sutherland, "A Survey of One Hundred Cases of War Neuroses," *British Medical Journal* (September 13, 1941): 367.

110. F. L. McLaughlin and W. M. Millar, "Employment of Air Raid Noises in Psychotherapy," *British Medical Journal* (August 2, 1941): 158.

111. Amy Bell argues that narrative and psychiatric constructions of fear were an essential part of the discourse on morale during the Second World War. See Bell, "Landscapes of Fear."

112. Medical Research Council report on "Air Raid Noise," National Archives, FD1/6258.

113. Ibid.

114. Daily Morale Report for September 18, 1940, Mass-Observation Archive, FR 409.

115. Draft of an article for the *Lancet* on nonphysical earplug problems, November 1940, Mass-Observation Archive, FR 489.

116. Donnelly, *Mrs Milburn's Diaries*, 63.

117. Hunt, *How to Win the War of Nerves*, 122.

118. Ibid., 124.

119. Ibid.

120. Ibid., 124–125.

121. Ibid., 124.

122. Medical Research Council report on "Air Raid Noise," National Archives, FD1/6258.

123. "Ear Plugs for Manchester," *Manchester Guardian* (November 23, 1940): 5.

124. "Ear Plugs," *Manchester Guardian* (January 21, 1941): 3l; "Plug-in Earrings," *Daily Mirror* (October 23, 1940): 6.

125. "Ear Plugs," *Lancet* (October 12, 1940): 459.

126. File Report on Ear Plugs, October 21, 1940, Mass-Observation Archive, FR 464.

127. Ibid.

128. Ibid.

129. Ibid.

130. McLaughlin and Millar, "Employment of Air Raid Noises," 158.

131. A similar logic had led to "neurosis centres" for civilians being set up within cities, rather than in the countryside, because recovering from neurosis within earshot of bombing noises was thought to produce more stable recovery. See Jones et al., "Civilian Morale during the Second World War," 468.

132. McLaughlin and Millar, "Employment of Air Raid Noises," 158–159.

133. On the British documentary film movement and the "people's war," see Wendy Webster, "*The Silent Village*: The GPO Film Unit Goes to War," in *The Projection of Britain: A History of the GPO Film Unit*, ed. Scott Anthony and James G. Mansell (London: Palgrave Macmillan, 2011), 263–271.

134. Humphrey Jennings, "The Music of War," from a handwritten file entitled "The Music of War Treatment, Crown Film Unit" relating to *Listen to Britain*, British Film Institute National Library, Humphrey Jennings Collection Item 7.

135. Mandler, "Against 'Englishness.'"

136. Alison Light, *Forever England: Femininity, Literature and Conservatism between the Wars* (London: Routledge, 1991).

Conclusion

1. http://noiseabatementsociety.com/about-us/what-we-do/ (accessed May 21, 2015).

2. Alan Wilson, *Noise* (London: HM Stationery Office, 1963).

3. For a recent attempt to chart this history, see Mike Goldsmith, *Discord: The Story of Noise* (Oxford: Oxford University Press, 2012).

4. Karin Bijsterveld, *Mechanical Sound: Technology, Culture and Problems of Noise in the Twentieth Century* (Cambridge, Mass.: MIT Press, 2008), 3.

5. On this trend I have drawn particularly on Mathew Thomson, *Psychological Subjects: Identity, Culture, and Health in Twentieth-Century Britain* (Oxford: Oxford University Press, 2006).

6. Anthony Giddens, *Modernity and Self-Identity: Self and Society in the Late Modern Age* (Stanford: Stanford University Press, 1991), 32.

7. Jonathan Sterne, *MP3: The Meaning of a Format* (Durham: Duke University Press, 2012).

8. R. Murray Schafer, *The Soundscape: Our Sonic Environment and the Tuning of the World* (Rochester, Vt.: Destiny Books, 1994).

9. Martin Daunton and Bernard Rieger, Introduction, in *Meanings of Modernity: Britain from the Late Victorian Era to World War II*, ed. Martin Daunton and Bernard Rieger (Oxford: Berg, 2001), 5.

10. Michael Saler, "Modernity and Enchantment: A Historiographic Review," *American Historical Review* 111 (2006): 692–716.

11. Saler, "Modernity and Enchantment," 700. See Alex Owen, *The Place of Enchantment: British Occultism and the Culture of the Modern* (Chicago: University of Chicago Press, 2004).

12. Steven Connor, "The Modern Auditory I," in *Rewriting the Self: Histories from the Renaissance to the Present*, ed. Roy Porter (London: Routledge, 1997), 224–248.

13. See Tom Rice, "Soundselves: An Acoustemology of Sound and Self in the Edinburgh Royal Infirmary," *Anthropology Today* 19 (2003): 4–9, and Tom Rice, *Hearing and the Hospital: Sound, Listening, Knowledge and Experience* (Canon Pyon: Sean Kingston Publishing, 2013), 21–37.

14. Rice, "Soundselves," 8.

15. Rice, *Hearing and the Hospital*, 33.

16. Rice, "Soundselves," 8.

17. Susan Cusick, "An Acoustemology of Detention in the 'Global War on Terror,'" in *Music, Sound and the Reconfiguration of Public and Private Space*, ed. Georgina Born (Cambridge: Cambridge University Press, 2013), 275–291.

18. Rice, "Soundselves," 4.

19. Nikolas Rose, *Governing the Soul: The Shaping of the Private Self* (London: Routledge, 1989).

20. Dan McKenzie, *City of Din: A Tirade against Noise* (London: Adlard and Son, 1916).

21. Carolyn Birdsall, *Nazi Soundscapes: Sound, Technology and Urban Space in Germany, 1933–1945* (Amsterdam: Amsterdam University Press, 2012), 174.

22. Karin Bijsterveld, "The Diabolical Symphony of the Mechanical Age: Technology and Symbolism of Sound in European and North American Noise Abatement Campaigns, 1900–40," *Social Studies of Science* 31 (2001): 37–70, quote at 44; James Johnson, *Listening in Paris: A Cultural History* (Berkeley: University of California Press, 1995); William Weber, *Music and the Middle Class: The Social Structure of Concert Life in London, Paris and Vienna* (New York: Holmes and Meier, 1975).

23. John M. Picker, *Victorian Soundscapes* (Oxford: Oxford University Press, 2003).

24. Bijsterveld makes useful observations about the class politics of noise abatement in this way in "Diabolical Symphony."

25. *Poster Art 150: London Underground's Greatest Designs* (London: London Transport Museum, 2013), 112.

Index

acclimatization, to bombing, 170–71
acousmatic sounds, 9
acoustemology of the self, 187
acoustics in homes. *See* homes
Adams, S., 111
adaptability 183
Agar, Jon, 35
The Age of Noise (*Times*), 2
The Age of Noise (Tucker), 1
AHR (American Historical Review), 7–8, 12
aircraft noise, 182
air raids. *See* bombing
Allen, William, 128–30, 132
all sound concept, 9
American Nervousness, 33; and modernity, sound, 7–14
Anderson, Benedict, 148
Antheil, George, 19
antimodernist view, 60–61
antinoise campaigns, 12–15, 60, 164, 183
Anti-Noise League, 20–21, 24, 26, 29, 37, 43–44, 48–59, 62, 67, 72, 98, 100, 109, 110, 112, 114, 117, 122, 138, 140, 142, 183
anxiety neurosis, 51
Anzieu, Didier, 19–20, 21
architectural acousticians, 9
Armistice Day silence, 2
Armstrong-Jones, Robert, 38
arrhythmic sounds, 56, 87
art of noises, 22, 63
Ash, Edwin, 31, 32–34, 40–41, 86, 88, 89–92, 96, 97, 106, 122, 188

astral bodies, and noise, 72
astral matter, 69
Auden, W. H., 134–35
The Audible Past, 8
auditory culture, and disenchantment, 22
auditory experts, 14–17
auditory habitus, 16
auditory histories, 6
auditory respite, 2
aviation noise, 4

bad noise, 185
Bagenal, Hope, 120–23
Bailey, Peter, 6
Bartlett, F. C., 109–14, 118
Beard, George M., 30–34, 35, 36, 37, 42, 43, 45, 50, 51, 87, 184, 188
Bell, Amy, 172–73
Berman, Marshall, 1
Besant, Annie, 68–72, 74, 76, 77, 86
Bijsterveld, Karin, 14, 27, 60, 63, 182–83, 189
Birdsall, Carolyn, 23–24, 189
Bisttram, Emil, 72–73, 75
Blavatsky, Helena Petrovna, 68
Blitz. *See* bombing
BMA (British Medical Association), 37, 38, 41, 42, 47–48, 49, 52, 108, 109, 110
bombing, 3, 145, 154, 161, 163–65, 167, 170–78, 182
bourgeois concert culture, 189
Bourke, Joanna, 171
British Medical Journal, 46–47

JAMES G. MANSELL is an assistant professor of cultural studies at the University of Nottingham.

Studies in Sensory History

The University of Illinois Press
is a founding member of the
Association of American University Presses.

———————————————————

Composed in 10.5/13 Adobe Caslon Pro
by Kirsten Dennison
at the University of Illinois Press

University of Illinois Press
1325 South Oak Street
Champaign, IL 61820-6903
www.press.uillinois.edu